EMERALDS IN TINSELTOWN

THE IRISH IN HOLLYWOOD

First published in 2007 by
Appletree Press Ltd
The Old Potato Station
14 Howard Street South
Belfast BT7 1AP

Tel: +44 (0) 28 90 24 30 74
Fax: +44 (0) 28 90 24 67 56
Email: reception@appletree.ie
Web: www.appletree.ie

A catalogue record for this book is available from the British Library.

EMERALDS IN TINSELTOWN — THE IRISH IN HOLLYWOOD

ISBN: 978-1-84758-048-1

Desk & Marketing Editor: Jean Brown
Copy-editor: Jim Black
Design and Cover: Stuart Wilkinson
Production Manager: Paul McAvoy

9 8 7 6 5 4 3 2 1

AP3404

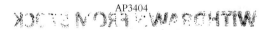

THE IRISH IN HOLLYWOOD

EMERALDS IN TINSELTOWN

STEVE BRENNAN
BERNADETTE O'NEILL

CONTENTS

INTRODUCTION

The street signs of Hollywood: Orange, Citrus, Laurel, Olive, Sierra Bonita and Buena Vista paint a picture of the sunny and sleepy farming community that today's movie metropolis resembled at the end of the nineteenth century. Other street signs tell of the history of Hollywood by naming those who helped found the film town and Los Angeles: Wilcox, Pico and Culver. But the most famous street sign of them all is the one that points to Mulholland Drive, a serpentine road that crests the Hollywood Hills and provides the most spectacular views of the San Fernando Valley to the north – and to the west... Hollywood.

Mulholland Drive has been the setting for countless movies. In fact this world-famous, spectacular thread of concrete has become synonymous with the American movie industry and Hollywood... and it's named after a man from Dublin called William Mulholland. He is the Irishman who planned and created a colossal engineering infrastructure that made possible all that Hollywood and Los Angeles are today.

Irish actors and directors are a hot commodity in Hollywood these days with stars like Colin Farrell, Pierce Brosnan, Liam Neeson, Gabriel Byrne, Fionnula Flanagan, Jonathan Rhys-Myers and Brendan Gleeson – and directors Neil Jordan and Jim Sheridan – leading the march. But, as vouched by the legend of Mulholland, they are merely the vanguard in a parade of gigantic Irish personalities who charmed and battled their way through a century of Hollywood history. In fact, the Irish played a spectacular role in American cinema even before Hollywood entered the picture. Irish immigrants were to be found playing major parts in the first silent movies being produced in the early 1900s out of crude studios in New York and other East Coast cities, before the film business had even heard of Hollywood.

Take for example the first movie star Mary Pickford. Irish-Canadian Pickford was a pioneer in Hollywood with her Irish-born husband the silent screen star and director Owen Moore. Pickford and Moore arrived in Hollywood when the town was a rural back lot a few miles west of Los Angeles. She would later recall gathering poppies at what is now the world-famous intersection of Hollywood and Vine in downtown Hollywood.

Pickford and Moore were among the first Irish pioneers to reach Hollywood when the moving picture business began its migration west from New York. The cramped city studios presented constant challenges in terms of stage lighting and production space. The Los Angeles Chamber of Commerce had been savvy enough to realise that this embryonic movie business could be a potential goldmine for the city. They organised a clever marketing campaign extolling the wonderful California climate, its deserts, the pristine beaches

The screen's first movie star, Canadian-Irish Mary Pickford, recalled having stopped to pick poppies at a dusty cross street in early Hollywood called Hollywood and Vine. The development of the film town was so rapid that by the 1920s the flowers had long gone – and by the 1950s Hollywood and Vine was one of the busiest junctions in California.

and the mountains… one stop shopping for any movie company. The lure worked like a charm. The film industry – along with its myriad Irish participants – was headed to Los Angeles, and, inevitably, Hollywood.

Typical of these early Hollywood studios was one established by movie mogul Samuel Goldwyn in a rented barn. Partitions were set up within the structure to create an office, dressing rooms, a stage, and so on. Orange trees were dug up to create a space for filming. That studio famously hired an out-of-work movie extra in 1912 called Hal Roach. The Irish-American Roach would go on to become a legendary producer of such classic comedy as the Laurel & Hardy films, the films of Harold Lloyd and the *Our Gang* series. It should be noted that Roach's biggest rival in early Hollywood was Mack Sennett who once boasted, 'My people were pure Irish when I arrived weighing twelve pounds and not considered large for my age.' It was Sennett who gave the world those wacky, bumbling policemen *The Keystone Kops*, among other early Hollywood treasures.

It was hardly surprising that the Irish played a pivotal role within the creative adjunct of the early movies considering the massive emigration from Ireland over the preceding years. The proliferation of Irish clubs, Irish neighbourhood cinemas and social networks presented the early moviemakers with a vast audience. The Irish became the subjects of endless short films. One production outfit, the Kalem Film Company, even set up a small studio in County Kerry to make films in Ireland especially for this audience. That expedition was led by famous Irish-Canadian producer Sidney Olcott.

By the early 1920s the Hollywood studios grew out of the barns and the shanties around Hollywood to become much more sophisticated structures, with vast amounts of money invested in them by Wall Street. The movies had become a multi-billion dollar industry with more than twenty million people going to the movies every day in America alone.

Waterford-born Pat Powers was mining a fortune from the film town as one of the original founders of Universal Studios back in 1912 when his Powers Motion Picture Company merged with Carl Laemmle's IMP production house to create Universal. Powers would also play a major role in the career of one of cinema's greatest geniuses – Irish-born Rex Ingram who brought the classic *The Four Horsemen of the Apocalypse* to the silent screen. Soon after sound came to the movies and actors actually spoke and sang on screen Powers produced a movie sound recording system. He would later sell this to Walt Disney so that Disney could make Mickey Mouse talk. Disney too was of Irish extraction.

Joseph P. Kennedy Sr – father of President John F. Kennedy – was part of a group of backers that invested $1.2 million in a movie studio venture headed by Gloria Swanson, based at United Artists, the studio founded partly by Mary Pickford. This was not Kennedy's only foray into Hollywood. Kennedy led a group of investors in purchasing a small Hollywood studio and he moved to the film town in 1926 to run the business. He later went on to acquire a national chain of movie houses in which to exhibit the films he made.

This was the notorious 'Roaring Twenties' in America, and Hollywood would have more than its share of wild parties and murders. Irish-born director, William Desmond Taylor, a leading figure in Hollywood and first president of the Directors Guild, was murdered in his Los Angeles home in 1922. The subsequent police investigation exposed an unsavoury underbelly of Hollywood that would lead to strictly enforced codes of conduct for the movies and movie people.

The 1920s and 1930s and the invention of 'the talkies' were turbulent years for Hollywood in other ways too – and the Irish were to play their own roles in the scenario. Irish-born director Herbert Brenon's once brilliant career in the silent screen days was badly impacted. The man who had towered in Hollywood in its silent days never made another movie after his career stumbled with the coming of sound.

But others thrived. Hollywood looked to celebrate its new stature on the world stage and invented The Academy Awards. MGM creative executive Cedric Gibbons, who boasted of having been born in Dublin, designed Hollywood's most famous icon of all – the Oscar. For more than three decades Gibbons toiled at MGM as head of its design department. Quiet and seemingly unassuming, this genius dreamed up the legendary sets and design for *The Wizard of Oz*. Having designed the Academy Award statuette, he went on to win eleven 'Oscars' for his own Hollywood achievements.

One of Hollywood's hardest-working stars in this era was Galway-born George Brent. He endured the system, thrived in it in fact, to become one of the industry's most lauded stars rivalling even Clark Gable in the star power hierarchy of his day.

Irish-American directors John Ford and Raoul Walsh continued to reign in Hollywood throughout this period. Some critics credit the two directors with having played a profound role in the creation of the Western as an authentic and realistic film genre. The cowboys of the silent screen and the early sound days were usually portrayed by actors in ten-gallon hats – the good guys wore white and the bad guys black. Ford and Walsh were part of a new breed of moviemaker. They knew the ways of the real west and wanted to portray its grit and reality in a new era of Hollywood film. They also took their lead from men like William S. Hart, the first great Western star, and son of an Irish trader. Hart went to school on the range with Native American children and learned to handle a six-shooter by the age of ten. With movies classics such as *Stagecoach*, and *She Wore A Yellow Ribbon*, Ford ripped a swathe through the studio system in his unswerving pursuit of authenticity.

Ford's insistence on authenticity on the screen was also partly responsible for one of the greatest, in some instances the saddest, chapter of Hollywood's Irish history, the Abbey years. After Ford made his screen version of *The Informer* in 1935 with Victor McLaglen supported by a large cast of Abbey Theatre actors, the director continued over the years to look to Abbey actors for their boundless talent and presence. Barry Fitzgerald and his brother Arthur Shields were principal among the many great Abbey actors who made their way to Hollywood – some also to heartbreak – at Ford's invitation.

Irish-American actors such as Pat O'Brien, James Cagney and Spencer Tracy, came into their own as the talkies became more sophisticated. Playing mostly cops, tough guys and priests, they came to represent the Irish as perfectly assimilated into American society. But these were also the days when the 'studio system' was in full flight in Hollywood; actors and directors were constantly at the mercy of bilious contracts that could punish them for any transgression. Actors were regularly suspended for refusing to work in movies that they felt could damage their careers. Actors' social lives were now controlled by studio bosses – actors were even told who they could and could not date. Cagney, Tracy and O'Brien were the three leading lights of an Irish-American Hollywood fraternity fondly referred to as 'The Irish Mafia'. They stood back-to-back when Hollywood turned nasty. Cagney even saved O'Brien's life on a carelessly rigged set. Outraged by how actors were treated, Cagney put everything on the line in a bitter brawl with his studio employers for better pay and better conditions.

Mary Pickford was among the first business-savvy Hollywood denizens to realise the potential of Beverly Hills that lay just a few miles west of Hollywood and she built one of the first great homes there. Eventually Beverly Hills would boast some of the costliest real estate in the world, vast estates that sprawl behind the city's palm trees and pristine streets.

Irish women also fared badly at the hands of the studio chiefs in those days. Greer Garson found herself frustratingly typecast as the prim English housewife after great success in the role of Mrs Miniver. Courageous Geraldine Fitzgerald's battles with movie studio boss Jack Warner over the films and the parts she was being cast in are the stuff of Hollywood legend even today. 'I truly, honestly thought that film studios were trying to make masterpieces, and that when they didn't they were terribly upset,' she would recall. Maureen O'Sullivan did succeed in creating memorable roles in worthy films in the Hollywood of

The hills above Hollywood, where the sign once read 'Hollywoodland'.

the day – but still felt aggrieved sometimes when her body of work was overlooked for her role as Jane in a series of *Tarzan* films. The queen of the Irish movie beauties, Maureen O'Hara, was no pushover in Hollywood either and was very vocal about the roles she accepted, and in particular about refusing to do what she described as "leg art".

Although the so-called Hollywood studio system was infamous for its treatment of even the biggest stars of the day, these were also known as the golden years for the movie capital. After all, these were the years of the great musicals, many of them standing today as masterpieces of cinema. Again the Irish were on hand to play major roles in this chapter of Hollywood history. Singing, dancing actors Gene Kelly, Donald O'Connor and George Murphy were giants in their day. When the mood of America changed in the Cold War period and the McCarthy communist witch-hunt shook Hollywood to its core, Kelly was in outspoken opposition.

The post-war period in Hollywood also saw a diminished demand for the myriad smaller character roles that had so heavily populated the movies just a few years earlier. The shift in film story-telling led in turn to fewer Irish actors taking a chance on Hollywood. The town had ceased to be a ready source of income for any worthwhile character actor with a genuine Irish accent. A new breed of Irish actor had come on the scene, those who had achieved star power back home or in British theatre and films – actors such as Richard Harris, Peter O'Toole, Dan O'Herlihy and Stephen Boyd.

It would not be until the creation of Irish national television, RTÉ, in the 1960s and the building of Ardmore Studios in County Wicklow, and still later the formation of the Irish Film Board, the Broadcast Council of Ireland, and other funding bodies and tax incentives for film investment that Irish actors, directors and producers could carve out

Grauman's Chinese Theatre where stars continue to make their impression on Hollywood Boulevard

screen careers on their home turf before Hollywood beckoned as a lucrative place to visit and work – but not necessarily to set up home in. With these developments the Irish are increasingly in charge of their own destiny in terms of film and television production. Gone are the days when it was necessary to live permanently in Hollywood – even though some such as Fionnula Flanagan do still reside in Los Angeles. Mostly the relationship of Irish artists with Hollywood is not as resident colonists but as visiting dignitaries. Today's generation of Irish stars – Brosnan, Byrne, Gleeson, Farrell and Murphy, and leading directors such as Sheridan and Jordan – are regularly head-hunted by Hollywood for leading participation in major films. Ireland provides fertile ground today for producing home-grown Hollywood stars. In a glorious irony we see today that the leading lights of the Irish film scene such as Sheridan and Brosnan come to mine Hollywood for financing to make important movies back home. The story has come full circle.

CHAPTER 1

WILLIAM MULHOLLAND AND THE WATER OF LIFE

The history of Ireland's formidable role in the annals of Hollywood and American cinema begins long before the first crude flickers were produced, long before the first movie studios were built, long before the term 'movie star' was heard. It begins back in the 1870s when the town of Los Angeles was still but a pueblo, a wild place where outlaws were commonly shot down in gunfights and hanging was almost an every-day occurrence. This was the infancy of Los Angeles. Southern California had only been some three decades under American dominion and the Southern Pacific Railroad had just begun to trundle migrants into town from the East. In the town's hinterland orange groves, fig tree forests and grape vines flourished all the way to the west where the town of Hollywood would one day emerge. The population of Los Angeles was a mere 9,000 souls. Two of the most recent additions to this count in 1877 were Irish immigrant brothers William and Hugh Mulholland. William's education at the time consisted of a few years at O'Connell's Christian Brothers School in North Richmond Street, Dublin, where he had grown up. The young William Mulholland was destined to play the lead role in a saga that has been lauded as one of the greatest feats in the history of America. He would in time be recognised as the most powerful single force in transforming this pueblo of adobe houses into the metropolis that Los Angeles was destined to become. He is justly credited with having made possible the development of Hollywood from a rural, farming back lot of Los Angeles into a business-savvy township, that would one day become the home of the multi-billion dollar movie business and home to the greatest display of wealth and glamour ever seen in America. William Mulholland was the man upon whose dreams the so-called 'dream factory' of the world was built.

The town of Hollywood spreads under a purple night sky and winks up at you with a billion lights like a siren. You are parked on a ribbon of road that curls over the eucalyptus scented crescent of the Hollywood Hills. Below you, beneath the scraggly bluffs and precariously perched houses, an ocean of luminescence shines its way west to a dark horizon where the Pacific tides to shore. Here is Hollywood in her evening finery and you are spying upon her tonight from a high-hilled place called Mulholland Drive. This route affords the most spectacular views of Hollywood, and is named for an Irish immigrant who created all that you can see – William Mulholland.

Mulholland's genius and mercenary political savvy brought life-giving water in the early decades of the twentieth century to a town stunted in its growth by the constant threat of drought. Like some great conquering Alexander, Mulholland rallied an army of more than 5,000 workmen and herds of mules to dig, dynamite and tunnel across hundreds of miles of the scorched Mojave Desert, a river bed of concrete and steel that would channel a bountiful new water supply to Los Angeles in the first decade of the twentieth century. Without the water that Mulholland battled and schemed for years to deliver to Los Angeles, the city's population could not have grown much beyond a half a million and certainly Hollywood as we know it today would simply not exist, City officials concede. 'No other individual has had so much to do with the creation of the modern metropolis of Los Angeles... as William Mulholland,' writes William L. Kahrl in his book about the city's war for water, *Water and Power.*

For many of the Irish who came after Mulholland, Hollywood would come to represent a limbo of unreality to which they had been lured by outrageous payments for their considerable talents. The late Dublin-born actor Keith McConnell confessed to the authors over dinner one evening at his house in the Hollywood Hills, "I feel like Rip Van Winkle. I arrived in Hollywood with the intention of lingering a month or two. This morning I awoke to find that I have been here for the past twenty years. Or perhaps it's thirty. I really don't care to find out." A roll call of Irish names that are legend in the early years of Hollywood and the American film industry laid the foundation blocks upon which the movie capital of the world is built. These included D.W. Griffith, Mary Pickford, Sidney Olcott, Mack Sennett, Rex Ingram, Pat Powers, Herbert Brenon and a multitude of others. But the one who prepared that foundation was Mulholland, a man prepared to risk a veritable civil war in Southern California to build his dream.

"The world was my oyster and I was just opening it... Los Angeles was a place after my own heart," Mulholland would recount. "It was the most attractive town I had ever seen. The people were hospitable. There was plenty to do and a fair compensation offered for whatever you did. The country had the same attraction for me that it had for the Indians who originally chose this spot as a place to live. The Los Angeles River was the greatest attraction. It was a beautiful, limpid little stream with willows on its bank. It was so attractive to me that it at once became something about which my whole scheme of life was woven. I loved it so much."

Mulholland's fateful arrival in Los Angeles was the final stop on an odyssey that had begun when he was just fifteen years old, shipping out aboard the merchant vessel *Clennifer* from Dublin. Mulholland was born in Belfast in 1855, the son of a postal clerk, but the family moved to Dublin when he was still a baby. He was a bright boy and excelled at the Christian Brothers O'Connell School, though he left before completing his full term there to join the British Merchant Navy.

He served for four years at sea on the *Clennifer* before disembarking in New York City in 1874. His first job in America was on a ship that traded the Great Lakes. The young man also tried his hand at lumberjacking. He later teamed up with his brother Hugh, who had also been at sea before setting foot in America. They spent some time with relatives in Pittsburgh before deciding to head west to California. Mulholland had become captivated by the thrilling accounts of California told by Charles Nordhoff. It was land for the undaunted, he thought.

Mulholland's granddaughter Catherine Mulholland still recalls her grandfather's stiff-backed figure and chiseled features. She was twelve when he died. She melded her personal memories

William Mulholland, surveying in the hills around Los Angeles in the early 1900s

and recorded accounts of the era to tell the history of Los Angeles and her grandfather's role in the story in her book *William Mulholland and the Rise of Los Angeles*. She recalls in her book and in conversation with the authors how the brothers stowed away on a ship bound for California by way of the Panama Canal. But the pair were caught 'and dumped on the Isthmus of Panama'. They hiked nearly fifty miles across the isthmus and signed on with a ship headed for Acapulco, Mexico. They crewed another ship north to San Francisco. From there they rode on horseback to Los Angeles. Broke and out of work, Mulholland took stock of his life, thinking and pondering along the quiet places of the Los Angeles River which he came to cherish. So strong was the spell cast by the willowed waters on the dreamer that he went to work as a ditch tender for the Los Angeles Water Company.

'And when he was not pulling weeds or working with hoe and shovel that summer, he spent the long hours of dusk striding the river's banks, learning its peculiarities, and dreaming of the ways he could fashion its uncertain flows to build a great city,' Kahrl tells. But these were much more than idle dreams. After his day's work was finished, he would sit up through the night, straining his eyes by lantern light to teach himself engineering. 'His library at the time of his start in the Water Works was Fanning's *Treatise on Hydraulics*, Trautwine's *Engineer's Pocket Book*, Kent's *Mechanical Engineer's Pocket Book*, a geometry, a trigonometry, and Shakespeare's works,' a friend of Mulholland's remembered. Mulholland's great enthusiasm and energy attracted the attention of the Water Company's bosses and he was moved rapidly up the corporate ladder. But Mulholland would never boast or brag of this incredible tenacity – not even under oath! Once in a court of law, older and now head of the city's Water Authority, Mulholland faced down a lawyer who demanded to know what qualifications the old man held as an engineer. 'Well, I went to school in Ireland when I was a boy, learned the three Rs and the Ten Commandments – or most of them – made a pilgrimage to the Blarney Stone, received my father's blessing, and here I am,' informed a stone-faced Mulholland.

It was a response that typified the dichotomy that was 'Willie' Mulholland, at once a light-hearted dreamer who relished his day at the baseball park, humorous and feisty, and then a visionary who would brook no fool or halt at any hindrance, a man who would proclaim, 'Damn a man who doesn't read. The test of a man is his knowledge of humanity, of the politics of human life, his comprehension of the things that move men.'

This was just the kind of thinking that Los Angeles and its tiny neighbour to the west, Hollywood, was waiting for. The railroads, hammered and dynamited into existence by an army of labourers made up mostly of Irish and Chinese immigrants, had opened a gateway to the West and were delivering new settlers by the thousands. But the water supply situation was getting desperate and the town fathers realised that the town could never flourish without more water. It was a huge dilemma that had ambitious business leaders frustrated. It was in this atmosphere that Mulholland, sober, brilliant, ambitious, studious, began a remarkable rise through the ranks of the Water Company, a private enterprise. A mere eight years after signing on as a labourer, he had come to be regarded as 'the protégé and heir apparent' to the head of the entire operation, a man called Fred Eaton. But the immigrant refused to be tied down with administrative work. His place was out with his men. Once he erected a lean-to in the Elysian Hills above the city and lived there like a hermit for months.

This odd, elusive and very private man did finally take over the reins of the Water Company and he would oversee the purchase of the enterprise by the City of Los Angeles soon after. The people of Los Angeles were in for a shock. After officially taking over the company, following several years of negotiations, the City discovered to its dismay that there were no maps, charts, or documents of any kind to indicate the extent of its newly acquired water system. The location and size of every pipe and valve was securely secreted away in Mulholland's memory. 'The city bought the water works and me with it,' Mulholland declared triumphantly.

Now he was in a position to fulfill the dream that had come to him by the banks of the Los Angeles River when he was a labourer. Now he could build his metropolis. To this end Mulholland had another astonishing revelation to take to the people of Los Angeles. The city's swelling population could no longer be supported by the Los Angeles River alone. 'The time has come when we shall have to supplement its flow from some other source,' he gravely announced.

That source would be the water-rich Owens Valley that lay some 230 miles distant, a lush agricultural community where once the Paiute Indians thrived. 'Nature has been lavish in her stores,' recorded an early explorer to the Valley back in 1859, Captain J.W. Davidson. 'The mountains are filled with timber, the valleys with water and meadows of luxuriant grass.' Mulholland had a fight on his hands if he hoped to snatch such a bountiful treasure trove of nature for his adopted home.

Years of political wrangling, bargaining and bullying lay ahead, but Mulholland would have his way. Mulholland and Eaton quietly bought up huge amounts of lands in the Owens Valley on behalf of the City of Los Angeles. Catherine Mulholland comments 'even though they had been kept in the dark about its beginnings, the citizenry, who had long put up with a water system that at its best was merely adequate, did not boggle at the means by which an improved water supply was secured. Had it been a military operation, it would have earned high marks for adroit stratagems…'

Mulholland's dream of a gushing wealth of water racing through a massive aqueduct across the desert to Los Angeles from the Owens River hundreds of miles away was ultimately realised. He was the visionary who schemed and planned virtually all of the operation that has been likened in scale to the building of the Panama Canal. The life-giving water would serve the people of Los Angeles, business and industry, including the Hollywood movie studios, with water that springs from the icy streams and crystal lakes fed by the snows of the lofty Eastern Sierra.

Mulholland's force of 5,000 men took five years to blast and dig the aqueduct. Then on November 5th 1913 he presented his creation to the people of Los Angeles at a grand civic ceremony that took place at the North end of the San Fernando Valley where the aqueduct terminates. As the waters gushed their way into the city from the Owens Valley, he gestured toward it and said simply, 'There it is, take it.'

A Hollywood trade paper, *Weekly Variety*, detailing the growth of the town's film industry, reported in July 1998: 'The industry boom was intertwined with the growth of L.A. In the Hollywood district alone, the population between 1910 and 1920 skyrocketed from 5,000 to 36,000.'

So angry were the people of Owens Valley that attacks – often with dynamite – on the aqueduct were not uncommon. Mulholland had to employ armed guards to patrol his creation while scorning the protests of the Owens Valley residents. "Dissatisfaction is a sort of condition that prevails there, like Foot and Mouth Disease… there are those in the Valley like Tam O'Shanter's wife, who nursed her wrath to keep it warm," he told the *Los Angeles Times* in an interview published May 28th 1924. But Mulholland could hardly have guessed that the wrath which he had dismissed so casually would rise again more than half a century later. In 1976 the Los Angeles Department of Water and Power announced its plans to double the pumping of subsurface water from the Owens Valley. An arrow with a stick of dynamite and

The memorial fountain dedicated to William Mulholland in 1940. The Irish-born engineer made the growth of Hollywood possible.

two blasting caps attached was shot at a fountain in Glendale, California that had been built to honour the memory of Bill Mulholland. The crude bomb did not explode. Ironically it landed and fizzled out in the fountain, in water from Mulholland's aqueduct.

Even more ironic is the fact that the fountain is set on the site where a one-roomed wooden shack once stood at the intersection of Los Feliz Boulevard and Riverside Drive. This was the shack in which Mulholland lived during those early ditch-tending days. The fountain dedicated to him was completed in 1940. Approximately 3,000 people attended the dedication ceremony on August 1st 1940. A memorial plaque at the foot of the fountain reads, 'To William Mulholland (1855– 1935): A Penniless Irish Immigrant Boy who Rose by the Force of his Industry, Intelligence, Integrity and Intrepidity to be a Sturdy American Citizen, a Self-Educated Engineering Genius, a Whole-Hearted Humanitarian, The Father of this City's Water System, and the Builder of the Los Angeles Aqueduct. This Memorial is Gratefully Dedicated to those who are the Recipients of His Unselfish Bounty and the Beneficiaries of His Prophetic Vision.'

Mulholland died in 1935, having planned and built the vast majority of the dams, waterways and aqueducts that provided the seeds for the growth of Los Angeles and Hollywood into the vast cities that they are today. His life in America was marked by one mighty achievement after another, though, as in every life, there was one great tragedy. In 1928 the St Francis Dam, which Mulholland had planned, burst killing eighty-four people. The catastrophe broke Mulholland's heart and it was said that he was never the same man again, despite the fact that he was ultimately exonerated of all blame. But as the City of Los Angeles proclaims in its dedication to its Irish founding father, 'His work lives on. Every time a faucet is turned the water it releases is a reminder of the man whose life was devoted to the service of the public.'

Mulholland had prepared the way in the West for a new type of American adventurer who would follow the railroads from the East: the moviemakers. Many of these film folk were Irish and among them was a young man from County Meath called Owen Moore, Ireland's first movie star and director.

CHAPTER 2

PARADISE FOUND AND LOST

The moving picture business was a hit with the public from its beginning back in 1888 when inventor Thomas Edison announced, 'I am experimenting upon an instrument which does for the eye what the phonograph does for the ear.' The public was intrigued. When a few years later he began producing what he called the Kinetoscope and installed just twenty-five of the machines in store fronts in New York, Chicago and Atlantic City, the movies had begun. Soon the first one-reel flickers such as *The Great Train Robbery* were packing audiences into cramped spaces with wooden benches to watch with awe and often terror the first moving pictures. Just a few years later the uncomfortable wooden benches were being replaced by stylish cushion seats in cavernous and luxurious cinemas that were being erected around America. One of the earliest of these picture houses was built in 1918 and dubbed 'the million dollar theatre' having cost a million dollars to build.

The public appetite for this exciting new medium was patent and it wasn't long before little studios began springing up in the cities of the eastern seaboard to feed the public demand for movies. But the exciting new medium put a serious crimp in the traditional form of public entertainment, Vaudeville. Audiences were being drawn away in droves from the vaudeville theatres and performers were cast out-of-work and often onto the street. It was a given that they would gravitate toward the moving picture craze that was sweeping the country. Out-of-work actors lined up outside studios with names like Biograph, Essenay, IMP. The pay was good if you could get work in the flickers – as much $5 a day. It was into this cauldron of change that a young Irishman called Owen Moore, a stage actor, was flung. Little could he have known that he would soon be a player in the birth of the American movie business, and in the foundation of the Hollywood entertainment empire.

Owen Moore pulled up the collar of his coat against a New York winter wind and cursed himself again for choosing such a foul night to elope. It was January 1910 and icy damp numbed his face as he waited. Out of the gloom came the petite figure of a young girl. Wisps of blonde hair peeked from beneath the sealskin coat that she draped about her. The girl was Mary Pickford. In time she would be a legend in the annals of Hollywood.

The Americans dubbed it the 'million dollar theatre' and it was one of the first great movie palaces. Albert C. Martin's Churrigueresque exterior was impressive, but the baroque interior by William L. Woolett placed Los Angeles film audiences in an atmosphere of style and luxury never seen before in movie houses, which just a few years earlier offered hard wooden benches in ramshackle halls.

Tonight she was in love. She was seventeen and running away with her handsome Irish actor.

A stinging New York drizzle was their confetti, and a ferry boat was their wedding carriage, as Owen Moore and Mary Pickford steamed up river to New Jersey to keep an appointment with a Justice of the Peace and share marriage vows in solemn secrecy. Later that night the bride would creep silently back into her family home, praying her mother would not awaken. The groom went away to find a bar and drink. They would share their secret with nobody, not family, not friend. They dared not risk the wrath of a woman who disliked Moore intensely. The woman was Mary Pickford's mother Charlotte.

The couple had first met when Moore had wandered late one evening into the plain brownstone building on New York's East 14th Street which housed the fledgling moving picture enterprise, The Biograph Company. A leading actor with the company for the past two years, Moore treated the studio as a second home, often sleeping overnight in one of the dressing rooms after a night on the town.

Moore heard voices raised in loud and heated conversation. One of the voices he recognised as that of director David Wark Griffith, an imposing Southerner of Irish extraction and the creative dynamo of the picture company. The other voice belonged to a girl he did not know. Peeking into the building's ballroom, which served as the main stage, he was spotted by Griffith, who ordered Moore to join them. Moore sauntered over, casually inspecting the young girl with Griffith. She was a newcomer and Griffith had been auditioning her for a love scene that would be central to a one-reel melodrama soon to go into production.

In the absence of an actor Griffith had ordered the would-be film actress who called herself Mary Pickford to embrace a pillar. She had been objecting strenuously to making love to this "cold pillar" when Moore made his entrance. He was delighted to take the pillar's role and the newcomer didn't object either. "I shall never forget that moment when Owen Moore put his arms around me. My heart was pounding so fast from embarrassment that I was sure he could hear it," she would remember in her memoirs, *Sunshine and Shadow*.

Pickford describes Moore as "five feet eleven inches tall, extremely handsome, with a ruddy Irish complexion, perfect teeth, dark blue eyes, and a very musical voice. Moreover he was the Beau Brummel of Biograph, always dressed with immaculate elegance. Like the other actors and actresses in the company there, he was using Biograph for what it was worth until he could find a way to get back into legitimate theatre."

Pickford, who was just seventeen at the time, got the part and a permanent job at Biograph. Within a few days she and Moore, seven years her senior, would be playing lovers in their first film together, *The Violin Maker of Cremona*. They were to be lovers on and off the screen for years to come.

Moore and Pickford's love for each other radiated on the silver screen. Audiences that crowded into crude 'nickelodeon' houses that were sprouting up across America began to recognise the girl with the golden curls and her rakishly good-looking hero. Their paycheques doubled and tripled as fan letters poured into the studio. The first movie stars were being created. Moore had come a long way from Fordstown in County Meath and the farm where he was born in 1886. The Moores emigrated to America when Owen was a boy. They teamed up with relatives in Toledo, Ohio. The Moore patriarch John Moore was not afraid of hard work but his skills lay with the land, and in this new city life he never managed to bring home more than a labourer's wage that provided only the barest essentials for his family. But America had better to offer... as the Moore family was about to find out. An article in the movie fan magazine *Photoplay* would tell of this years later. 'The Moore boys got something of an education, by the grace of God they didn't need much – they were smart and quick... and Irish. They all took different trails out of Toledo with carnivals and one night stands.' The brothers, Owen, Matt and Tom would all eventually make their way to Hollywood where each would find his share of fame in the young film industry. As *Who's Who on the Screen* from 1920 reads, 'Like many other stage and screen stars, Owen Moore is a son of Erin. When eleven years old, Owen arrived in America and a year later found him behind the footlights. He first attended school in Toledo, Ohio. More than ten years ago he sensed the possibilities of the screen and joined the old Biograph Company.'

Like Moore, Pickford's early memories were of poverty and penny pinching. But things were also looking up for her now. She had made a name for herself in New York theatre literally, having changed her given name – Gladys Smith. She had taken it from the first half of her mother's family name of Pickford Hennessy. Mary Pickford was a name that would become synonymous with the birth of Hollywood and the studio system. She would be the industry's first great star and one of its earliest and smartest studio owners. "I took my name by which I have long been known to the public from my Irish grandfather, John Pickford Hennessy, who came out of a comparatively rich family from Tralee, County Kerry in the South of Ireland. My grandmother was also born in Tralee, but she was a miller's daughter and very poor. Had the two of them remained in Ireland they would never have met; they moved in entirely different social worlds," Pickford recalls in her autobiography.

Silent screen star
and director Owen
Moore from County
Meath. Seen here
with Mae West in
*She Done Him
Wrong.*

Pickford was just a child when she took her first acting role with the Cummings stock company in her home town of Toronto, Canada, in order to earn some much-needed money for the household. The family had been thrown into dire straits when her father died tragically young. A natural talent for the stage and a keen survival instinct led to New York and Broadway and star billing in a production of *The Fatal Wedding*. 'Baby Gladys Smith is a wonder,' proclaimed the show's producers in handbills distributed around the theatre district.

But a spell of unemployment followed and family funds were on a worrying retreat. It was then that her mother, a protective and strong presence throughout much of Pickford's life, made what seemed to be a "shocking proposal". She urged her daughter to look for work with the Biograph Studios – the moving picture people!

Dreading the idea but feeling responsible for her siblings and mother, the youngster set out for an audition with the director D.W. Griffith at Biograph. She had some vague idea that moving picture people were a strange breed of vagabonds and hustlers, but a paycheque was a paycheque. That was the audition that would throw Pickford and Moore together and the first moments of a monumental Irish tale in Hollywood were written.

At the time that Moore and Pickford met, fell in love and eloped, Hollywood was just beginning to beckon to the film pioneer companies that were based in the Eastern cities. Hollywood slumbered in the scented air of citrus blossoms and pineapple farms that spread out below the coyote dens and wild scrub on a ribbon of hills above. The 3,000 or so residents of this hinterland a few miles west of Los Angeles were aware but unconcerned at the metamorphosis taking place in the neighbouring Los Angeles, transforming itself from the pueblo it had been just a few decades earlier into a metropolis. The farmers of Hollywood tended their orange groves and avocado orchards.

Owen Moore didn't like what he was hearing about the place out West. If all the reports were true that he'd listened to over beer in his favourite bar, Luchows, it was a hot and dusty place much too far away from Broadway to suit his tastes. Moore understood why his acting buddies had allowed themselves to be shanghaied to such a place. If their bosses in the film companies chose to heed the propaganda campaign being directed at the picture business, then who were mere actors to protest? These flickers were paying even the lowliest players five dollars a day and up – more than 'legitimate' theatre could offer in the early 1900s. The lines of unemployed actors outside these studios – Biograph, Essenay, IMP and others – told their own story. The great thespians of the day may have looked down their noses at this new entertainment business, but for many an out-of-work actor, the moving pictures were heaven sent. The work was gruelling, long days and nights shut up in tiny studios, churning out three or four flickers a week for a slave master called the motion picture camera – but they were glad to have it. Few of these actors would argue when they were dispatched to California where, according to the Los Angeles Chamber of Commerce, movie makers could exploit a 'golden sunlight almost year round, open plains, snowy mountains, deserts and wild seashores.'

Most of the film outfits, frustrated by the shortcomings of artificial lighting in their cramped studios of New York or Chicago were sending out scouting parties to Los Angeles. A few had even set up permanent operations as early as 1908. The citizens of Hollywood were curious about these moving picture makers and costumed actors who would descend into their midst and vanish again, motoring back to headquarters in Los Angeles. But curiosity turned to keen interest when in 1911 a film pioneer called David Horsley came to Hollywood and stayed.

Horsley leased a vacant tavern and set about making his motion pictures. Other film companies followed his lead and Hollywood, motion picture capital of the world, was born. A little more than a decade later Irish-American advertising executive John Roche would lead a posse of workers and mules into the Hollywood Hills and erect a series of fifty-foot high letters made of timber. Seen from the town below they spelt HOLLYWOODLAND. Later, the LAND portion of the sign would be taken down and one of the world's most recognised landmarks made its bow.

D.W. Griffith, impressed by what he had heard about California and its seemingly limitless sunlight and scenery, wangled permission from his bosses to transport a film unit out to Los Angeles. Moore and Pickford were to have been part of that pioneer venture, but Moore demanded a hefty salary increase if he was to move. He was quite determined in this matter. Griffith was equally as determined to refuse and it became a battle of wills. Moore's squabble over the ten-dollar-a-day pay hike continued until the company, including Pickford, was boarding the ferry for New Jersey, the first port of call on the way to Los Angeles via Chicago on the California Limited. Moore's bluff was called and he was left behind on that first Hollywood venture.

The Biograph expedition returned from California three months later and the couple picked up the threads of their interrupted romance. But the redoubtable Mrs Charlotte Pickford was having none of it. She forbade her daughter to see Moore except on the set as work required. She barred the young Irishman from her home. Ironically, this was one

The Hollywood
sign was originally a
marketing ploy
designed by Irish-
American John
Roche. The first
incarnation read
Hollywoodland but
it was later
shortened to just
Hollywood.

of the couple's most productive periods together as an acting team, working together in dozens of one-reeler melodramas including the romantic tales *In Old Kentucky* and *The Peach Basket Hat*.

The frustration of this clandestine love affair got the better of Moore and he decided to take the initiative: he proposed marriage. When Pickford suggested that her mother might turn murderous at the prospect of having Moore as a son-in-law, he threatened to leave Biograph and New York... never to return. Faced with this ultimatum, Pickford accepted his proposal. But she thought it might be wise if mother didn't know. They must elope; the wedding must be their secret. It was a mad plan and destined for doom.

By springtime of the year they were married Pickford and Moore were on their way to becoming the screen's first stars. But Pickford's wayward innocence and the blonde ringlets that flowed down her back were attracting much more notice than her screen partner. She had negotiated her weekly salary up to an unheard of $100 a week while Moore could do no better than $60. Moore was not happy. Angry at Biograph for what he perceived as an insult Moore orchestrated a move to a new studio, the Independent Motion Picture Company (IMP), which was willing to pay the popular screen couple a good deal more than Biograph. It was a disastrous move. This was the time of the film industry's Patents War, a violent and traumatic chapter in the early motion picture industry. Moore's ambitions landed the couple squarely in the middle of this ugly and all too dangerous feud. Biograph, Edison, Essenay and other picture companies had banded together to protect the patented process of film-making. They operated under the umbrella of the Patents Company Trust. Independent film companies that made movies outside the protection of this clique were treated as pirates, and The Trust did not fall short of protecting its hold on the film industry with violence. Gangs of paid thugs would descend on the 'pirate' film companies to smash equipment, threaten crew and actors and even beat them up if they tried to resist. IMP, Moore and Pickford's new employer, was one of those outside the Trust. When IMP decided to move its operations to Cuba to avoid the violence of the Trust's heavies, Moore and Pickford had to go along. Pickford's mother, sister and brother went along on the trip also.

It was on the trip to Cuba that Moore insisted it was time to bring the secret marriage out into the open. Mrs Pickford was taken aside and informed that the man she despised as a drinker was her son-in-law. She went berserk.

Mrs Pickford took to her bed and cried for three days while Moore's new brother- and sister-in-law took on a raging silence, refusing to speak to the couple for the rest of the journey. But the debacle aboard ship was nothing compared to the disaster that Cuba was to prove. It would be an understatement to say that Moore was in a sour mood when the company disembarked in Havana. And nothing about this venture was about to change that. He disliked the company's director Thomas Ince, a man who would find his own place in Hollywood's roll call of legend and have a street named after him today in Culver City. But as far as Moore was concerned Ince was an ill-mannered swine. Pickford too was unhappy at this "amateurish and boorish" IMP team, as she described it. One day on set Moore overheard an assistant of Ince's insulting his wife and he floored him with a punch to the jaw. The local police were called and Moore made himself scarce. He managed to hide out until he and Pickford could smuggle aboard a passenger ship headed back to the USA.

Safely back in America the couple joined up with the Majestic Film Company in Hollywood where Moore began to direct as well as star in the films he made with his wife. He directed Pickford in some memorable melodramas including the romance *Love Heeds Not The Showers*. But despite his newfound success as a director, Moore could not compete with the overwhelming love affair that the patrons of the nickelodeon houses were having with his wife. Sacks of fan letters were pouring into the company every day demanding to know who this girl was. In those days the flickers did not carry actors' credits and the letters read simply, 'Who is that girl with the golden curls?' The star system was being born and Moore and Pickford were among its principal architects. But Moore hated playing second fiddle to his wife, and when newspapers started referring to Pickford as 'America's Sweetheart' he comforted himself with drink.

Moore then did the unthinkable. He broke up the screen partnership and went it alone with the Victor Film Company. Pickford returned to Biograph. For Moore the magic was gone: his screen fame was fading.

Later in that year of 1912 there was a brief professional reunion between Moore and Pickford that spurred a new drive in his ambitions. The couple was contracted to an ambitious new film company, The Famous Players Company. They boasted the slogan 'Famous Players in Famous Plays.' Moore was cast alongside Pickford in the classic love story *Caprice*. He became her prince in *Cinderella* and her kingly Charles II in *A Tale of a*

Mary Pickford married Douglas Fairbanks after her divorce from Owen Moore. The new movie-star couple would become known as the 'king and queen of Hollywood'.

Merry Time 'Twixt Fact and Fancy. But the reunion was to be all too brief – doomed once again by Pickford's ever-increasing star earning power and the jealousy and rage this raised in Moore.

By 1914 Pickford was earning the phenomenal salary of $2,000 a week and she constantly overshadowed Moore's career. But something else was happening which should have worried Moore even more. A young lion had appeared and his name was Douglas Fairbanks.

By now the picture industry's creative adjunct had moved almost entirely to the West Coast. And it was here that Fairbanks, a handsome and athletic stage actor, made his first moving picture under the direction of D.W. Griffith. *The Lamb* brought instant stardom for the jaunty young actor. Moore could have no idea the role that Fairbanks was about to play in his life.

A seemingly innocent cocktail party at the home of an actress friend of Moore and Pickford set the stage. It was there that Pickford, now estranged from Moore, was introduced to Fairbanks who was accompanied by his young wife Beth. Pickford was apparently smitten with the handsome young Fairbanks. Subsequently Pickford's mother chaperoned her daughter to 'teas' at the home of Fairbanks's mother-in-law's New York home. At Fairbanks's own home in Hollywood Pickford became a regular visitor at the invitation of Beth Fairbanks. Pickford and Fairbanks began to meet secretly in Hollywood hideaways, often disguising themselves elaborately to avoid detection. Moore, meanwhile, was drinking more heavily. Life for Moore and Pickford was becoming a sordid melodrama played out from coast to coast. Pickford demanded a divorce in 1919 that would free her to marry

Fairbanks who was also separating from his spouse. Moore responded to the divorce petition by threatening to shoot "that climbing monkey".

But the divorce went ahead regardless. On March 1st 1919 Mrs Owen Moore (Mary Pickford to the world) climbed into a witness box in a Nevada court and told a judge that she had been abused by a drunken Irish husband, concluding, "I was a wife and not a wife." The divorce was granted and she returned to Hollywood to marry Fairbanks.

Moore was on the sidelines now as his former wife and her new husband came to be known as 'the king and queen of Hollywood,' founders with Charles Chaplin of the film company that would become United Artists, supreme stars known and adored across the world. Moore would re-marry and continue to make films until 1937, when in something of an irony he played a movie director in *A Star is Born*. But the place he craved on Hollywood's golden list was denied him. The story of this dreamer, tortured by his own ambitions, would play out its final act amid circumstances that truly belong in the scripts of those dramatic melodramas of the silent screen in which Moore once shone so brightly.

Mary Pickford sat one evening later in her life listening to her Irish maid tell of the predictions she saw in the tea leaves that remained at the bottom of a cup that Pickford had just used. 'I see that someone close to you and not yet close will die,' the maid confided. 'I don't see you crying.' Owen Moore died that night of June 12th 1939, from a massive cerebral haemorrhage. Six months later, to the very day, Douglas Fairbanks died on December 12th. This was the day Owen Moore would have been celebrating his birthday.

CHAPTER 3

THE 'O'KALEMS'

Irish politics and stories have never been far removed from the Hollywood screen. Ireland and its history has been a regular backdrop for the movies, from John Ford's screen version of *The Informer* to *The Devil's Own* or the far-fetched *Blown Away.* Long before romances such as *The Quiet Man* or *Ryan's Daughter* Irish-themed movies were churned out by the hundreds in the early days of the industry for the burgeoning Irish populace of America. One studio, The Kalem Film Company, became so closely associated with Hollywood movies about the Irish that they became known as the 'O'Kalems'. The studio was also overflowing with Irish and Irish-American actors and directors in the silent screen days before the First World War.

It is said that the silent film director Sidney Olcott was called in by his bosses at the New York-based Kalem Film Company, shown a map of the world, and asked to pick a country for his next film. Olcott, whose mother was from Dublin, picked Ireland. It's a good yarn, but the reality is that the silent screen company's decision to send an expedition to Ireland in 1910 to make Irish-themed movies was simply a clever marketing ploy to appeal to the millions of first- and second-generation Irish who had come to America over the previous years. The Kalem Company saw the value of such a potentially enormous audience. An article in *Moving Picture World* thought it a brilliant move and described the Irish film venture as 'the linking of the old and the new worlds.'

The company set up base in Beaufort, County Kerry. Olcott, described by Irish film historian Liam O'Leary as "a great-hearted man, demanding in his pursuit of perfection, hypnotic in his control of actors and tasteful in his film presentations," hoisted an American flag in front of his studio on the main road from Killarney to the Gap of Dunloe and started making movies set against backdrop of Irish politics. So prodigious was the Kalem Company's output of Irish films that they were dubbed 'The O'Kalems'.

Working with his lead screenwriter Gene Gauntier, Olcott first made *The Lad from Old Ireland*, a story of one man's emigration and flight from poverty. Irish audiences in America flocked to see the movie and any other Irish film that the 'O'Kalems' sent their way. Olcott's passion for his mother country soon began to influence his creativity, and his films became increasingly seditious as far as the British Censorship Office was concerned. The tenor of Olcott and Gauntier's films changed as they became more aware of the Irish political situation. Olcott continued to produce movies with such titles as *Ireland the Oppressed, Rory O'More* and *Robert Emmet.* The censorship authorities based in Dublin Castle were becoming seriously

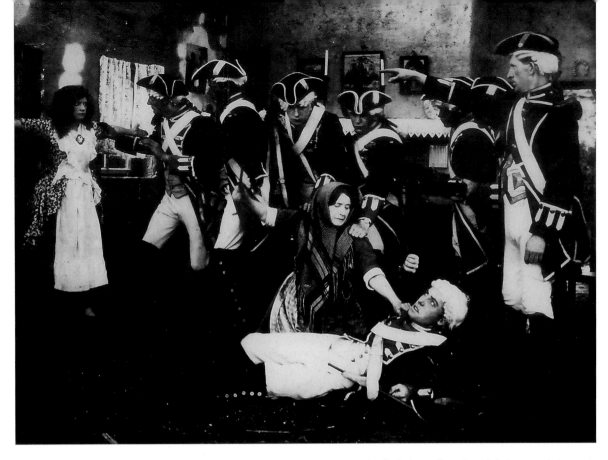

Films with Irish themes were extremely popular with Irish immigrant audiences who flocked into the early nickelodeon movie houses in America. The Kalem Film Company sent its Irish-American director Sidney Olcott to County Kerry in 1910 to set up a small studio and make movies with patriotic and romantic Irish themes and titles such as *Ireland the Oppressed, Rory O'More* (above), *Robert Emmet* and *Do You Remember Ellen* (which features as the chapter icon on page 29).

concerned that Olcott and his movies would 'incite the natives and the Irish throughout the world.' The British government became so agitated with Olcott that a sharply worded letter was dispatched to the Kalem head office back in the U.S. While Olcott eventually agreed to tone down his film plots, he continued to make films in Ireland. But the outbreak of the First World War caused the Kalem Company to withdraw completely from the country and return to the United States.

The Kalem Company seemed a natural lure for many of the Irish who were turning to the new film business for a living back in the 1910s and Olcott was not short of Irish colleagues, counting among his friends and associates actor Tom Moore, brother of Owen Moore, and the gregarious and self-destructive Irish American director Marshal Neilan. Most of them had come to the company broke and hungry for work. Olcott himself had started out as a newspaper seller on the street corners of his native Toronto before setting out for New York with dreams of becoming an actor. He drifted into the film business, signing on with the Kalem Company in 1907, young and brimming with enthusiasm as a fledgling director. But a little experience in this new business might have saved his new employer a bundle of money. One day Olcott spotted a newspaper advertisement announcing a chariot race that would be held in conjunction with a fireworks display on Long Island. "I took a cameraman and a couple of actors down to the track and shot the race… and presto, *Ben Hur*," recalled Olcott. But as quick as he could say 'presto', the publishers of the classic novel hit them with a lawsuit which cost the film company $25,000. It was a landmark court decision establishing for the first time that films could not be made from copyrighted materials without legal permission. But at least the experience left Olcott with the credit of having made the first screen version of *Ben Hur*.

Olcott enjoyed an illustrious career in Hollywood, working in the early days with Mary Pickford, and later Rudolph Valentino in *Monsieur Beaucaire*. Other legendary names who came under his sure direction included Norma Talmadge, Pola Negri, Betty Bronson and Richard Barthelmess. Around 1927, Olcott abandoned Hollywood and went to England to work for British Lion at the new Elstree Studios. This venture ended up in a lawsuit when he declared that a script the company wanted him to direct was nothing more than a cheap glorification of crime and criminals. He won his case and with a $10,000 court award he returned to the U.S. never to make another movie. Apart from his films, the other great contribution made to America by this son of Irish immigrants was the Motion Picture Actors' Welfare League for Prisoners that he founded with his actress wife Valentine Grant. He died of a heart attack at the age of sixty-eight on March 12th 1949. A story in a trade paper about the funeral service at the Hollywood Memorial Cemetery reported, 'About a hundred people turned out, none of them current Hollywood hotshots... Pat O'Brien and Jean Hershot were among the few present-day film folk.'

The Kalem Company was a revolving door for the Irish, but the most permanent Irish fixture for a long time at Kalem was Marshal Neilan, the Irish-American director who did not simply enjoy life... he wallowed in it. He was a buccaneer in Hollywood with a taste for the high life, a tormented genius who became the industry's highest paid director only to crash and burn in one of Hollywood's most spectacular riches to rags scenarios.

One sunny day in March 1921 a young writer from the fan magazine *Photoplay*, Clodagh Saurin, went to interview Neilan on his set. She found him lounging with the Irish-American stars of his movie, Colleen Moore and Pat O'Malley. The three were trading old Irish poems and ballads. "It's the most natural thing in the world that we should be here together," Neilan volunteered when the reporter expressed astonishment at finding an Irish hooly in full jig on the set in mid afternoon. "When you stop to think about it we Irish are the only race in the world that can go anywhere, do anything, belong to other countries and still be ourselves."

The sing-along was fully in character for the fun-loving director. 'Of all the personalities who made Hollywood glitter in the Twenties, none was more irresponsible so expensively as Marshal ('Mickey') Neilan,' wrote Hollywood journalist Jack Spears. 'Handsome, witty, and possessed of instinctive charm, he directed a virtually unbroken string of box-office hits, and squandered the millions he made thereby with an abandon that was often spectacular, sometimes arrogant, and always ruinous. He died in a charity ward – alone.'

Back in 1909 when the eighteen-year-old Neilan applied for work at the Glendale California adjunct of the Kalem Company he was almost destitute, in shabby old jacket and derelict pants. He had moved up to Los Angeles from San Bernadino, California, where he was born in 1891 to Irish-American parents. The death of his civil engineer father when Neilan was a baby forced him to take odd jobs from childhood to help support himself and his mother. So when things started to move for him at Kalem and the dollars came rolling in, 'Mickey' was ready to enjoy life a little. He signed on as a writer, but within a few months had impressed his bosses sufficiently to get a shot at directing.

Sidney Olcott is shown here directing the Kalem cast on location in Kerry while shooting *Rory O'More*. The film is set during the 1798 Rising and was based on a Samuel Lover story.

The Kalem Company was based in Beaufort, County Kerry. Director Sidney Olcott hoisted an American flag in front of his studio on the main road from Killarney to the Gap of Dunloe, shown above.

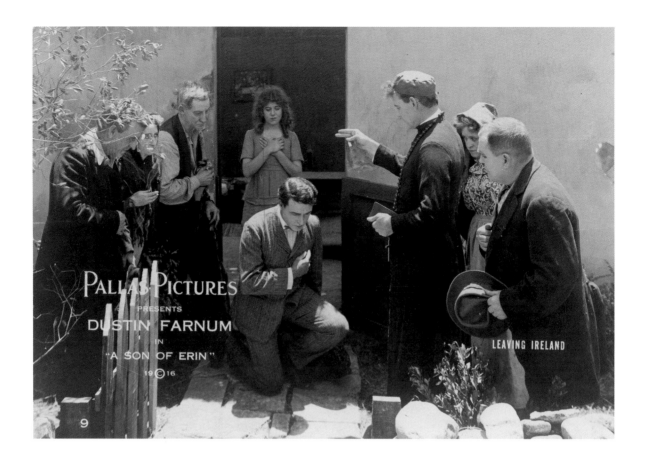

PALLAS PICTURES
PRESENTS
DUSTIN FARNUM
IN
"A SON OF ERIN"
19 ©16

LEAVING IRELAND

Dustin Farnum kneels in a scene from *A Son of Erin* in front of the rest of the cast to receive a priest's blessing before leaving his home country. It is a scene that would have been experienced at first-hand by many Irish-American movie audience members.

Neilan's brilliance was immediately obvious and within a couple of years he was supervising the entire Kalem production operation in Glendale – he was just twenty-two. After Kalem Neilan moved on to the Famous Players Laskey, where he directed Mary Pickford in one of her most enduring classics *Rebecca of Sunnybrook Farm*, for which he was paid a reported $150,000. He directed Pickford in another five of her greatest films including *Stella Maris* and *Poor Little Rich Girl*.

Other star names that demanded the Neilan directorial touch included Charlie Chaplin, George M. Cohan, John Barrymore, Coleen Moore, Jean Harlow, Wallace Beery and Blanche Sweet with whom he shared a short and turbulent marriage. But Neilan's light quickly failed. His wild parties and bacchanalian lifestyle caught up with him – and as his talent suffered so did his reputation.

He and Owen Moore would often hoist glasses together, two roustabout Irish guys sinking in the bog waters of their own individual destructive cravings. They were a feature of the Hollywood bars and clubs that began springing up around the studios that were spreading over the once quiet citrus groves that cradled La Brea Avenue, Melrose Avenue, and a dusty 'bridle path' called Sunset Boulevard.

The beginning of the end for Neilan came when Pickford, unhappy with his work on her latest movie *Secrets*, closed down production and wrote off a loss of $300,000. He found himself unemployed and broke in the late Twenties. "This is a great town," he complained. "One year I made $15,000 a week. The next I couldn't get fifteen

Robert J. Flaherty directs Maggie Dirrane (as 'Man of Aran's wife'), and Michael Dillane (as a 'Man of Aran') in the classic film *Man of Aran* made in 1934.

cents." Within a year or two Neilan was in bankruptcy court, $190,000 in debt. "I had to keep up a front. To get a job in Hollywood, you have to keep up appearances," he told reporters.

Neilan was never to regain the acclaim and talent which had seemingly deserted him. The coming of sound to the movies didn't help either. The new medium didn't suit him and just made his slide to disaster all that more rapid. Minor acting and some low budget directorial work kept him barely solvent until World War II when he took a job as an aircraft riveter. A columnist for trade paper *Variety*, W.A.S. Douglas met the director on Hollywood Boulevard coming home one day from the factory. Neilan, dressed in overalls and a cap, showed Douglas an 'E Pin' which had been awarded him that day at work for 'excellence on the job.' "I feel better than the night of the preview of *Rebecca of Sunnybrook Farm*," declared Neilan. He remained in obscurity for the rest of his life, although there was to be just one more brief appearance in Hollywood. In 1957, Marshal Neilan, the man they once dubbed variously 'the boy millionaire' and 'the boy genius' was an extra in Elia Kazan's *A Face in the Crowd*. He died in Hollywood in 1958 at the Motion Picture Country Home. Mary Pickford headed a contingent of stars who attended his funeral. Almost every newspaper report of the service referred to him as 'the bad boy' of Hollywood.

In some respects the 'O'Kalems' were in Ireland to film the landscapes and the people as they actually existed – not some early Hollywood back lot fantasy meant to represent that reality. Irish-American documentarian Robert J. Flaherty operated in much the same way when making such monumental works as *Man of Aran* (1934). It was filmed in a true-to-life fashion that documented the harsh realities of Irish island life, battling the sea in curraghs, coaxing potato crops from barren land, hunting basking sharks to use their oil for lamps. But Flaherty in fact did use cinematic license to create *Man of Aran* in that he cast the central family of the film from various island families. A film made more than forty years after Flaherty completed his masterpiece claimed that in fact Aran Islanders had not hunted sharks for half a century as O'Flaherty's film depicted. Nonetheless, the film is still considered a masterpiece of story telling and cinematography and was one of many Flaherty reality films that places him on a pedestal in the history of the cinema.

Flaherty was born of Irish-German parents in 1884 in Iron Mountain Michigan. He spent his early years working as a prospector, working for a railroad company as his father before him had done. At the behest of his employer Flaherty began to take a motion picture camera into the wilderness of Hudson Bay to film the wildlife. There he came in contact with the Inuit people and out of that came his first film *Nanook of the North* in 1922. The reality film depicted the Inuit as they lived and hunted in the frozen north. There followed a contract with Paramount which brought him to Samoa to make yet another reality film about indigenous people entitled *Moana*. This was a visual account of events in the daily life of a Polynesian youth and his family.

Robert Flaherty is often hailed as one of the founding fathers of the documentary film, despite his tendency to dramatise reality. His films stand today as masterpieces of story telling and cinematography.

CHAPTER 4

THE IRISHMAN, THE MERMAID AND THE FOX

Showdowns are a way of life in Hollywood. Power struggles, particularly between the creative community and the industry power brokers are daily fodder for the town's trade papers and the golden rule is simple, 'He who owns the gold rules.' But none of this is new. It's been part of Hollywood daily life since the movies began. But one unsung champion of artistic independence and a genius of the screen has remained mysteriously assigned to the bottom drawer of Hollywood history: Dublin-born Herbert Brenon, the unlikeliest buccaneer of them all.

The great William Fox, a czar in early Hollywood, the same William Fox whose name now crests an entertainment and communications empire, was strangely silent and his blood pressure was rising to a dangerous degree. He asked his assistant again, just to be certain he'd heard correctly the first time.

"He's doing what?"

"He's suing you," the assistant repeated.

It seemed incredible. But there it was, duly served, entirely legal and fraught with dangerous implications not just for Fox and his unassailable power, but also for the very power structure of Hollywood.

Herbert Brenon, the director described disarmingly by one film journalist as 'a slight man physically, blessed with the bright blue eyes and pink cheeks of Ireland where, in Dublin, he was born on January 13, 1880,' was tilting at the windmill of Fox's might. The whole thing had seemed such a good idea to Fox just a year before. Here was this brilliant young director come to him with a track record of money-making pictures, films the like of which had never been seen before, with barely disguised nudity and exotic settings. Brenon was a winner; let him have his way, Fox reasoned. Let him go to Jamaica to make this *Daughter of the Gods* picture that he's so keen on. With the star 'bathing beauty' Annette Kellerman as the film's lead what could go wrong?

Brenon really had the mogul sold on the idea of making a spectacular exotic island picture on location in Jamaica. But the director had a lot to bargain with. He had already made a

Born in Kingstown, now Dun Laoghaire, Herbert Brenon graduated from the footlights of Vaudeville in America to the early movie business. He became one of the screen's early major motion picture directors. He is pictured here in August 1916.

'mermaid spectacular' starring Kellerman that had broken box office records. But when Fox gave his wonder director the green light for the expedition, he could not have dreamed in his wildest nightmare what Brenon had in mind. In August 1915 Brenon arrived with his team at the virgin seas and paradise settings of Jamaica and immediately set about transforming the landscape. The story called for a Spanish fort. 'Build it,' Brenon commanded. A Moorish town complete with mosques was built at the director's whim. A splendid ivory tower perched above the ocean would be perfect for Kellerman to execute a dramatic dive from. A great tower arose.

Brenon was pleased with his work. What a picture this would be. What splendour. Back in Hollywood Fox was in shock. Brenon, he worried, was out of control and so was the budget. But the bills kept coming in and Fox kept paying them. He had no choice. The studio was in too deep now to call off the production. Fox swore revenge.

Brenon faced the wrath of movie mogul William Fox when the budget of his epic *A Daugher of the Gods* starring Annette Kellerman spiralled out of control.

When Brenon brought the picture in nine months later, the mogul made his move. He ordered that Brenon's name be struck off the film's credits. It was a devastating blow to the young director who saw *A Daughter of the Gods* as the crowning achievement of his career. He decided to fight back and took the only course open to him. He sued. Nobody in Hollywood, not even Brenon himself, believed he could successfully challenge the power of William Fox. But he was ready to try. It was a costly battle for Brenon and predictably one he did not win. But the case marked a milestone in the film industry, and thereafter all directors insisted on clauses in their contracts that ensured their work could not be attributed to another director that an irate studio might bring in, or credit on the movie as punishment for failing to toe the company line.

A Daughter of the Gods became another box office record with Brenon's trademark island maidens and shimmering tropical vistas. As for the inflated budget that Brenon left behind? In as brazen a stunt that Hollywood had ever witnessed Fox billed Brenon's unaccredited epic in screaming headlines as 'the first million-dollar' moving picture ever made. And Brenon? The battle that might have been the end of a short but illustrious career became just one of many legends in an Irish immigrant's triumphant life in Hollywood.

Brenon was born in Dun Laoghaire (then called Kingstown). When his father, a writer, was appointed theatre critic of a London newspaper, young Brenon was transplanted out of quiet Kingstown into the hurly-burly metropolitan world of London theatre. The boy was agog as he trawled the West End theatre circuit with his father, experiencing the excitement of opening nights, giggling at the antics of his father's theatre friends, hanging on their ribald thespian tales spun amid the heady atmosphere of cocktails and green rooms. The footlights, the boy decided, were his life's beacons.

When his father moved the family to New York a few years later, sixteen-year-old Brenon haunted Broadway. He worked as an office boy in a theatrical agency by day and moonlighted as a stage extra by night. There was nothing he wouldn't or couldn't do to be part of this world of wonder they called Vaudeville. He was a stage manager, a messenger, an actor, a lighting assistant, a director. The boy was becoming a showman. A trip to the sticks of Minneapolis in 1904 to direct a vaudeville circuit show changed his life. A pretty actress, Helen Oberg, was the beauty of the theatre company and Brenon fell for her at first sight. They married and hit the vaudeville circuit as a team, billing themselves Herbert Brenon and Helen Dowling. Their act was a hit.

The vaudeville circuit was their home for the next few years until Brenon began to notice that audiences were beginning to thin out. At the same time, the moving picture nickelodeon houses were booming. The death knell was sounding for vaudeville and Brenon heard it loud and clear. He had just turned thirty, he was a husband and recently a father. He was a top of the bill name on vaudeville when he took a job as a lowly paid story editor with Carl Laemmle's Independent Motion Picture Company and set about making a complete nuisance of himself.

He wasn't shy about showing off his years of training and deep understanding of theatre, and would even suggest camera setups and stage timing of shots, much to the annoyance of the established directors at the company. But Laemmle decided to give this loudmouth story editor a shot at directing his own picture; Brenon delivered a finely honed one-reeler called *All For Her,* a romantic ditty that audiences seemed to like. It was enough to earn Brenon a full-time directing job and for the next year he was a whirlwind of creativity, often directing two or three shorts a week for IMP.

But the unmitigated vaudeville showman in him could not be suppressed and increasingly he began to step from behind the camera to do dangerous stunts that his actors baulked at. This penchant for doubling as stuntman in his own movies became his trademark, even at the height of his fame, and on more than one occasion it nearly killed him. Brenon was filming yet another one of his now-famous 'mermaid movies,' *Neptune's Daughter* with Annette Kellerman on location in Bermuda. Brenon had carefully positioned his cameras around the giant glass tank in which he would film an underwater swimming scene. Every dangerous moment of this spectacular shot had been carefully planned. A villain would attack Kellerman underwater. But she would fight off and strangle him. It was a key scene and Brenon wasn't taking any chances. He made a final check on the cameras, satisfied himself that the lighting was as he wanted it, repeated some instructions to his assistant directors, then climbed up the steps to the top of the giant tank, took a deep breath, and dived in.

Reluctant to entrust the crucial scene to an actor, Brenon had decided to play Kellerman's attacker himself. The cameras were rolling, and Brenon and Kellerman grappled underwater. Kellerman fought and struggled and gripped Brenon around the neck. Then it

Irish-born silent screen director Herbert Brenon was the Steven Spielberg of his day – his name above the title on every movie.

happened. The tank burst with a gunshot explosion. Shattered glass and water cannoned outwards hurtling Brenon and Kellerman with it like flotsam. They were both badly injured in the mishap and Brenon spent a month recovering in a Bermuda hospital before he could return to the set. When it finally hit the nickelodeon circuit, in 1914 *Neptune's Daughter* set a new record of ticket receipts for the industry and made his bosses at IMP very happy. It was also the movie that would prompt William Fox to hire Brenon. Fox was moulding the career of screen siren Theda Bara at the time and Brenon was assigned as her director. He made two very successful pictures with Bara, *The Kreutzer Sonata* and *The Clemency Case*. Fox was pleased with his new director and was happy to entertain the young man's idea of taking a crew to Jamaica to make a great spectacular called *A Daughter of the Gods*.

Following the war with Fox over *A Daughter of the Gods*, Brenon formed his own production company and poured his financial resources into a film called *War Bride* that would depict the hardship of the wives of servicemen who had gone to battle in World War I. Just as Brenon's film was about to go on release, Fox vindictively rushed out a picture with a similar theme and backed it with an enormous publicity campaign. Brenon's independent film was swamped and crashed at the box office.

Bitter and angry, Brenon was finished with Hollywood, or so he said. He was headed to England and to hell with Hollywood. He did move to England for a time, but it was a brief sojourn. Ever since he had steamed out of Kingstown to London as a boy Brenon had been

Annette Kellerman starred in several 'mermaid spectacular' films. This still is from *A Daughter of the Gods*. Another of her films was *Neptune's Daughter*. During filming, both she and Brenon were badly injured when a water tank exploded on set during a stunt. Brenon was famous for doing the most dangerous stunts in his own movies.

an itinerant, but if there was one other place he *could* call home it was Hollywood, centre of the world of the craft he loved – the movies.So it was to Hollywood that Brenon inevitably returned in 1920 declaring, "I found the English fearfully handicapped by undramatic, phleg-matic temperament and a bad photographic climate."

Hollywood, in the form of his friend the Russian-born producer Joseph M. Schenck, welcomed home the prodigal son. Schenck hired him to direct the silent screen star Norma Talmadge in three pictures that would put Brenon's name back in the limelight. He became one of the biggest names in the industry, directing such stars as Clara Bow, Pola Negri, Betty Compson, Ernest Torrence and Betty Bronson. Brenon thrived for decades in Hollywood and was cel-ebrated as one of its most brilliant talents. But by the late 1920s something was happening in the movie industry that was about to change everything for Brenon.

Brenon set up his own independent company to make a film called *Sorrell and Son*. He bor-rowed heavily to buy the rights from Paramount and set up the production on the silent movie that would be remembered as one of his great masterpieces. The director was even nominated for an Oscar for this work on the film. The year was 1927 and Brenon could not have chosen a worse time to set out on his own. The business was about to undergo one of the most traumatic periods in its history: the talkies.

'Eet is a fad,' declared the strongly accented silent screen star Pola Negri of the coming of sound to the movies. But Brenon was more inclined to believe the words of Al Jolson when he declared in the movie that is generally considered to be the first sound picture *The Jazz Singer*, 'Wait a minute, wait a minute, you aint heard nothin' yet.' *Sorrell and Son* would become one of the last great silent movies ever made and it suffered at the box office as a consequence of this unfortunate timing. Brenon was devastated. He was not a young man now and the transition to sound could not have been more traumatic. Many of the great stars of the day were openly laughed at by the public for their strange accents or high-pitched voices. The microphone picked up and made thunderclaps out of clothes rustling or a fork being clanked. It was a nightmare for directors just beginning to figure out how to make talkies. But Brenon was game for the challenge. He began to master this new way of making movies, and things were looking up when the Wall Street Crash and The Great Depression hit him hard. The man that had once been at the pinnacle of the American film industry, an icon, was reduced to working with a second-tier producer, I.E. Chadwick, who released films through Monogram Pictures. A subsidiary of United Artists, Monogram put out the 'second features' which accompanied the major releases. Humiliated and depressed Brenon once again abandoned Hollywood for England announcing in 1935, "I feel it is too exciting a time in England to miss. Only now are the British beginning to increase the quality of their product."

He worked for five years in England and produced two more films, *The Housemaster* (1938) and, two years later, *The Flying Squad* – starring a young Jack Hawkins, who would become one of England's most enduring stars – before once again landing back in Hollywood. But this time he had not come back to do battle, he had come "home" to retire. Brenon died in Los Angeles in 1958 without ever making another Hollywood picture.

CHAPTER 5

HOLLYWOOD GENIUS – REX INGRAM

The embryonic film town of Hollywood was growing up financially in the early 1920s. The Disney Studio and Warner Bros. were founded in 1923. Columbia Pictures and MGM came into being just a year later. Movie audiences in the U.S. were estimated at some forty million people in 1920 alone. As many as twenty studios in Hollywood were now churning out movies. 'Movie makers were drifting gypsy-like to the west coast and the Los Angelenos were discovering that theirs was more than just a drowsy market town,' writes Bosley Crowther in his book *The Lion's Share*. Producer Carl Laemmle pronounced that more money was being spent on production than ever before and Cecil B. DeMille went to work on *The Ten Commandments*, the costliest picture ever made by 1923 with a budget of $1.5 million. Hollywood was a boomtown, a money town, and a hostile place for true artists, as one of the greatest masters of early cinema Rex Ingram would discover.

A howling mob of fifteen hundred revolutionaries beats its way through the narrow Parisian street, cudgels and scythes shaken in anger above a faultless blue sky. Perched on a wooden podium high above these risen people an orchestra plays a rousing Irish tune, 'The Wearing of the Green'. It was 1923 and they were filming *Scaramouche* in Hollywood, the silent screen classic set against the backdrop of the French Revolution. The film's director Rex Ingram had ordered the studio orchestra to belt out his favourite Irish marching and battle songs to set the blood of his extras aboil. Once again eyebrows were raised in Hollywood at the antics of this eccentric Irishman who was known to wear a silk top hat and formal evening wear when working.

But nobody at Metro, the studio where he was working then, was about to complain. For one thing, this young Irishman was the hot new director in town and his movies were box office dreams for the studio brass. And for another, this guy could box – as more than one misguided Hollywood pug found upon mistaking Ingram's eccentricities, refined accent and impeccable manners as weakness.

He was born Reginald Ingram Montgomery Hitchcock in Dublin city on January 15th 1893, the son of clergyman and scholar Francis Ryan Montgomery Hitchcock and his wife Kathleen Ingram, daughter of the Dublin Fire Brigade Chief. They were a financially secure and academic family and Rex would inherit his father's love of the arts – and of boxing. Ingram's was a privileged boyhood in many ways. He attended the best schools,

Rex Ingram

studied the classics, honed his boxing skills to the point where he became school champion, and devoured any articles he could find on the United States. He wasn't quite sure why he wanted to see America; unlike most other Irish who were heading across the Atlantic he certainly had no financial motivation to do so. But there it was — America, and he was going, one way or another.

Ingram would never forget his departure at the age of eighteen from Ireland, soon after his mother's death. He stared at the wake of the White Star liner *Celtic* taking him out of Ireland. 'And that was the last I saw of Ireland… the grey coast of Ireland slipping away… slipping away, slowly — and for how many years!' Ingram would recall in a memoir published in esteemed Irish film historian Liam O'Leary's seminal biography, *Rex Ingram — Master of the*

Silent Cinema. Ingram's writings show that he was having serious doubts about this great American adventure: '… my courage left me, and left me too the spirit of adventure that had got me this far, and I wondered what was going to happen to me… '

He didn't know it then, but he would never see Ireland again.

The young man spent his first year in America working as a railroad company clerk before enrolling in Yale's School of Fine Arts where he became a promising sculptor and artist. Ingram had decided on a career as an artist, a decision strongly influenced by his tutor, noted American artist Lee Laurie, when he took a trip out to Long Island in the spring of 1913 and came across a Nickelodeon that was screening the Vitagraph Company's 1911 production of *A Tale of Two Cities*. He was spellbound on that first trip to a moving picture show. There and then he decided that this was the medium of the future and he wanted to be part of it.

Quitting his studies, he signed on at the Edison picture company in the Bronx. His precise role at the company was somewhat ill-defined. He helped write the scenarios, played bit parts in the films, built sets, even utilised his artistic skill to paint portraits of the company's leading players for billboards. But it was those seemingly inconsequential walk-on roles that would help catapult him into the spotlight of the industry. He was an extremely handsome young man with an intense smouldering look that was *de rigueur* then for leading men of the screen. 'He has the blue-grey eyes of Ireland and the whimsical wit of the Irish,' was how a budding Hollywood columnist named Louella Parsons described the young Ingram.

But acting before the camera was simply a way of honing his skills and expanding his understanding of the medium which he saw as an underdeveloped art form, a moving masquerade of shadow and light, a new landscape between the novel and the play, between the canvas and the clay.

To this end he applied successfully for a directing job. 'The latest recruit to the ranks of the directing staff of the William Fox Film Corporation is Rex Ingram, formerly of the Vitagraph forces,' a small announcement of Ingram's first directing job in *Motion Picture News* declared. 'Mr Ingram will be started immediately. The title selected for this photoplay is *Mother Love*, and the drama itself was conceived and written especially for Miss Nansen (a star actress of the day), by Mr Ingram.' He was twenty-two and Ingram was about to discover that what was a new art form to him was money-making pabulum to his bosses. Trouble was not far off.

The young 'recruit' annoyed and alienated just about everybody at the studio. He was scornful of the 'dabbling' of company executives in the creative arena and brooded when questioned about accounts, sneered when lectured about schedules and positively erupted when queried about script ideas or his decisions as a director. As far as Ingram was concerned, his job was to make great movies, great art and no office monkey was going to stop him. 'The same laws apply to the production of a film play which has artistic merit as to the making of a fine piece of sculpture or a masterly painting,' Ingram avowed. This was a foreign language to his bosses at the studio and inevitably Ingram and the Fox Company parted ways in 1916. The same year he hitched over to Laemmle's New Jersey based Universal Film Manufacturing Company, which was planning its move to Hollywood. Ingram would be going there with them. But oil and water would make a better mix than Ingram and Hollywood. "Hollywood is no place to make pictures," he complained to his employers who had followed the movie makers' trail to the West.

'Ingram associated with those who had a deep reverence for art, young men who were striving to do things in the arts and were willing to suffer for their ideals, and Rex knows more than most producers about paintings and sculpture and the allied arts. That is probably why he prefers to look beneath the surface of screen acting and prefers portraying realities rather than superficial histrionics,' an article in the *New York Morning Telegraph* said of him in 1924.

A few years earlier Ingram had delivered his first big box office hit for Universal, a drama set in pre-Revolutionary France called *Black Orchids*. It was a hit, but Ingram had brought the film in more than two thousand dollars over budget. He was out, fired. And word of his reckless artistic priorities, art above cost, spread quickly through the executive ranks of rival film companies. Nobody wanted to encourage this kind of thinking, not in Hollywood, not in the moving picture business.

But something far more menacing than Hollywood's ire was dominating Ingram's thoughts. The Great War, as some were calling it. He wanted to be part of it. Not being an American citizen, he was turned away from the recruiting office in Los Angeles. But Canada was part of the British Commonwealth, and he enlisted in the Royal Canadian Flying Corps. Hollywood and the movies would be put on hold. But he would never see any dogfights. A training session went wrong one day and the aircraft in which Ingram (acting flying instructor) and a pupil were circling the base spun out of control and crashed. They survived, but his near-fatal injuries forced him out of the service and back to a very unforgiving Hollywood. He found himself unemployed and unemployable.

There were no flags or ribbons for the veteran back in Hollywood where he stalked the studios seeking work. Once when visiting Universal he came across the legendary German-born director Erich von Stroheim at work. Ingram and von Stroheim would later become great friends but at that time, von Stroheim recalled in an interview with O'Leary, Ingram exploded, 'What's that son of a bitch doing here? He's got my job.' That's when Irishman Patrick A. ('Pat') Powers entered the picture and Ingram's fortune would take a turn for the better.

Pat Powers had 'clout' in Hollywood. He was one of the founders of Universal Film Manufacturing Company, the forerunner of the present Universal Studios, along with Carl Laemmle, R.H. Cochrane, Charles Bauman, David Horsley and W.H. Swanson. Powers later sold his share of the company and moved on to organise the Film Booking Offices of America (FBO) which was ultimately absorbed into RKO Studios. He also developed the Powers Cinephone, one of the first sound devices used in the early 'talkies.' It was through these enterprises that Walt Disney's original *Mickey Mouse* and *Silly Symphony* animated cartoons were launched.

Born in Waterford, Ireland in 1869, Powers had come to America as a blacksmith. But he started his business career in the movies in Buffalo as a distributing representative for the Edison Phonograph Co. and Victor. He was credited with bringing worldwide recognition to Victor's trademark 'His Master's Voice'. He was at the height of his power when he heard that a fellow Irishman, Ingram, needed a hand. Powers ordered that Ingram be given two films to direct at Universal, *The Day She Paid*, a story of the world of haute couture, and *Under Crimson Skies* a swashbuckling yarn. 'Only a fragment of these early films exist but contemporary reviews praise Ingram's fine sense of pictorial composition, his feeling for lighting and atmosphere and his use of 'non actors' as well as his skilful direction of players. At times his realism was more than critics could stomach,' recorded O'Leary in his book

Rex Ingram cast Rudolph Valentino as the star of *The Four Horsemen of the Apocalypse*, bringing fame to them both.

about Ingram. *Under Crimson Skies* was a hit with audiences and Ingram was back on top, thanks entirely to the intervention of Powers. Those wretched days of unemployment had left Ingram with a legacy, however, and the name of that legacy was Rudolph Valentino.

Ingram had met Valentino briefly during one of his days of studio wanderings in search of work. The Latin actor, who had not yet become the legend, was working on a film called *Talk of the Town* when Ingram came across him. Ingram immediately recognised that there was something special about Valentino and he made a mental note to work with him one day. That day came when Ingram, now working for the Metro Company, was given the job of adapting for the screen the hugely successful novel, *The Four Horsemen of The Apocalypse*, a devastating tale of war and destruction. The principal role in the drama, that of Julio, a playboy, would require a handsome and versatile young actor. Valentino, Ingram decided, would be Julio. Hollywood history was in the making.

'His name is Rex Ingram. He is the director of *The Four Horsemen of the Apocalypse*. That may have meant very little to you in the past, but it is going to be a tremendous force in the artistic creation of motion pictures in the future,' Louella Parsons wrote when the film premiered in 1921. 'In the few hushed moments of appreciation following the unreeling of Ibanez's story, the name Ingram was on everyone's lips. The imagination, the technique, the splendid conception of the four horsemen, the symbolic Christ figure – is not the work of a mere motion picture director – it is the expression of genius,' exclaimed Parsons who had the power to make or break Hollywood careers through her syndicated column. The kudos didn't end there. In an unprecedented acknowledgement of the contribution of motion pictures to the general advancement of culture, Yale University, Ingram's Alma Mater, awarded him with an honorary Arts Degree for his achievement with *Four Horsemen*. Journalist Harold Harvey wrote of the ceremony. 'If at twenty-eight the art which this grey-eyed young Irishman has put on the screen is worthy of such commendation, it is an assured fact that under his direction pictures will continue to develop in artistry as his craftsmanship matures. Still higher honours await him and still greater beauty is to be expected of his work.'

The Four Horsemen was also the making of Valentino, whose legendary career began with the film. It was also a career milestone for the actress Alice Terry who was about to become a major player in Ingram's life.

Ingram had met Terry in 1917 just before his ill-fated sojourn in the Canadian Flying Corps. And she was one of the few old Hollywood pals who had encouraged and supported him during those troubled days of rejection. But to Ingram the relationship had never seemed more than platonic friendship. A long separation from Terry during a trip to New York made Ingram realise pretty quickly that he was in love with her. He proposed to Terry by phone from New York to Los Angeles and she accepted. The couple talked of returning to Ireland for the wedding but the idea was shelved because of work pressures. They married in a simple ceremony in a cottage in the Hollywood Hills on November 5th, 1921, spent the weekend in town, went to the movies twice, and on Monday morning were back at work in the studio. Terry would star in all but two of Ingram's remaining films.

A string of films followed the triumph of *The Four Horsemen*, including the classic *The Prisoner of Zenda* when Ingram found himself with yet another Latin actor to groom, Ramon Navarro. Ingram's inspired direction of Navarro in the film launched the actor to a brilliant career. These were peak years for Ingram. His mastery of film-making guaranteed success at the box office. Across the country fans awaited each Ingram picture as they might a Spielberg movie today. When his films went on release it was Ingram's name that appeared above the title.

Hollywood was changing. The film town had lost any frontier appeal it may once have had for Ingram and he continued to criticise the ever-increasing degree of executive involvement in his movies. Ingram insisted that absolute control of a production should rest with the director. Nor was he happy with other changes taking place in Hollywood. Narcotics, sex parties, exploitation movies and speakeasies were now commonplace in the boomtown atmosphere of the day.

Ingram complained, "Whether I tell an audience they are on the Marseilles waterfront, inside a German submarine, in Baghdad or in the Sahara Desert, I want them to accept my statement without question. They will never do so when they know that my Sahara was in Bakersfield, my Marseilles waterfront was built at Venice, California, and my bit actors and extras were in a sexual epic the week before." Ingram was growing tired of Tinseltown.

'You cannot believe all you hear,' a gossip columnist gushed when it was rumoured that Ingram was abandoning the movie business. 'It is not true that Rex Ingram plans to leave the film business, but rather it is his intention to return to Europe and make motion pictures. But he is done with romantic dramas and the like… It is now Mr Ingram's avowed intention to make pictures straight from life as it were. He wishes to catch glimpses of life as it is lived today, whether it is in the frozen places of the North, or in burning India, or sunny France. "Hollywood is no place to make pictures," says young Rex.'

Ingram's first venture out of Hollywood was to North Africa where he made *The Arab* with Navarro and Alice Terry in 1924. Later that year Ingram pulled out of Hollywood entirely to establish his own studios in Nice, France, taking over the run down buildings of the French La Victorine film company. His Hollywood employers, the newly formed alliance of Metro-Goldwyn-Mayer paid for some of the refurbishment, but the overall deal cost Ingram $5 million. 'In Nice Ingram was a figure of international importance and the visitors to his studio read like a Who's Who of the Twenties,' writes Liam O'Leary. 'Crowned heads, literary men and the theatrical profession thronged to visit him.' But back in Hollywood, the tide was turning against Ingram. His employer, MGM was worried that Ingram's work was deteriorating, particularly since his latest movie *The Magician* was poorly received at the box-office. The studio brass was beginning to wonder if this Nice set up had been such a good idea after all. When Ingram's next movie *Garden of Allah* crashed at the box-office, the brass was sure it had been a mistake. Ingram was ordered back to Hollywood. But Ingram held on doggedly, refusing to leave his studio. MGM refused to do any further business with him and effectively cut him off. Ingram continued to make independent films in Nice, but within two years he would lose the entire operation in a bitter legal battle with a French partner in the studio, Edouard Corniglion-Molinier.

Ingram and Terry retired to Egypt and North Africa for a few years before returning to Hollywood and settling in the San Fernando Valley in 1936 where he devoted himself to his sculpture and writing. He was considering making a comeback in the movies when he fell ill.

It was July 21st 1950, three days before Terry's birthday. She visited him in hospital where he was undergoing medical tests. Ingram was in a happy mood and insisted that she go out

Frustrated by Hollywood, Rex Ingram travelled to Tunisia in 1924 to make his movie *The Arab*. He became fascinated by Arab culture and was feted as an honoured guest. He and his wife Alice Terry adopted an Arab boy, Abd-el-Kader (pictured here with Ingram), who appeared in several of his films.

and buy herself a birthday gift on his behalf. But when she returned to the hospital the doctors were waiting with bad news. Ingram had suffered a massive heart attack and was in a coma. He died soon afterwards aged just fifty-eight. In a simple tribute to Ingram, O'Leary writes, 'In America, the three acknowledged masters of the silent movie were and are D.W. Griffith, Erich Von Stroheim and Rex Ingram. They were friends. The first two are familiar names. Rex Ingram is forgotten.'

CHAPTER 6

A REAL MURDER MYSTERY

"Cocaine was very prevalent, you could go into a bar in the Twenties and they would have cocaine on the bar, it was like an hors d'oeuvre." That's how a former Los Angeles District Attorney's Office veteran Tom McDonnell describes the Hollywood that Rex Ingram had found so hard to come to terms with. Sex orgies, illicit drugs, Prohibition speakeasies and corruption at the highest levels thrived in this new Hollywood. For William Desmond Taylor it was a playground. If Rex Ingram is remembered today as the embodiment of artistic ethics at Hollywood's birth, fellow Irish director William Desmond Taylor is the antithesis. He may have been one of the industry's finest directors and president of the Directors Guild of America, but Taylor is unjustly associated today only with all that was wicked about Hollywood. The body of William Desmond Taylor lay in a pool of blood on the floor of his study as his killer had left him. A bullet in the back from a handgun had ended the life of this enigmatic Irishman as strangely and as mysteriously as it had been lived. A homicide detective with the Los Angeles Police Department noted the date on a fresh page in his notebook: February 2nd 1922. It was also the beginning of a fresh page for Hollywood where the close-knit film community had so far managed to successfully keep their dirty linen well hidden from their public. As far as the cinema-going public of America was concerned, their stars and the people who made the movies were decent, moral folk who told tales of simple heroes and heroines who represented all that was fine about America and humanity. Villains were vanquished and evil was defeated in the movies of the day. Now that innocence was about to be lost forever.

Henry Peavey had a bad feeling that chill February morning of 1922 as he made his way to his employer's house in the upscale Westlake district of Los Angeles. The butler worried about the secrets he kept, of the nineteen-year-old starlet who was sleeping with his forty-nine-year-old employer, of the star comedian hooked on cocaine who spent her days and nights at the house, of the drug baron his employer had punched. Now that shady character, Sir's so-called private secretary had absconded leaving all those forged cheques.

Peavey worried that it would do his career as a butler no good, no good at all, if the police were to become involved in household business. Little could he guess how prophetic his concerns were to prove. He opened the front door of the luxurious courthouse bungalow, stepped inside and made straight for the study to tidy up before preparing a morning meal. But his employer would not be eating breakfast that morning. For there he lay, prone on the study floor, the murdered William Desmond Taylor, one of Hollywood's foremost film directors and the film town's 'gentleman'.

'He had class because he was Anglo-Irish,' Hollywood historian and author Betty Fussel said in a television interview about Taylor. 'He was the guy they would trot out in Pasadena at fancy society parties. He was the only one (in the film business) who was respectable.' But Los Angeles high society was in for a very rude awakening. And so was Hollywood. The scandal that was about to descend on the film town in the wake of this Irishman's murder would have all of America peering at the film set and gloating on the tales of decadence that made newspaper headlines. The seemingly charmed careers of some of Hollywood's brightest stars would be buried in a sea of scandal — for the first time the immunity from public scrutiny and the law that the top echelon of Hollywood society had enjoyed would be shattered. As for the unfortunate murder victim himself, that pistol shot which was heard around America ended a life more colourful, more mysterious than any of the swash-buckling characters he had ever played or directed on the silent screen.

Newspaper headlines of the day tell their own vivid story of America's reaction to the scandals that emerged about Hollywood's citizenry following the Taylor murder. The following headlines are recorded in a contemporary newsletter about Taylor's life and murder entitled 'Taylorology.' This newsletter, it should be noted, contains a vast amount of in-depth analysis of the murder and its investigation and certainly far more detail than can be dealt with here.

PHILADELPHIA INQUIRER

"A few more 'close-ups' of Hollywood and there will be a demand to close up Hollywood."

DETROIT FREE PRESS

"Those opium parties which are said to have been given in the movie centres of California must have one advantage over the ordinary kind in that no guests can be accused of impoliteness if he goes to sleep."

PITTSBURGH POST

"Only by the exercise of supreme self-restraint has Congress refrained so far from appointing a commission to go on a California excursion to investigate picture studio shenanigan."

KANSAS CITY STAR

"The roisterers who lived in the Roman empire days weren't pikers at heart. They did the best they could, but were handicapped by the fact that chemistry and drugs had not been perfected up to the Hollywood stage."

PHILADELPHIA RECORD

"'May Never Solve Taylor Mystery,' says the headline. No, but we're learning a lot about Mr Taylor and his friends."

He was born William Cunningham Deane Tanner in Carlow in 1872, the son of a military man. Throughout his boyhood and teens he constantly resisted his father's demands that he pursue a career in the British Army. To the utter dismay of his family, the young man announced that he would much prefer to be an actor and, flying in the face of his

The victim – Irish-born director William Desmond Taylor. His Holywood murder remains unsolved to this day.

father's ire, he took a job as secretary in a small Irish theatre company. Pater's response to his son's youthful rebellion was quick and decisive. The would-be actor was shipped off to America to family friends who had a ranch in Harper, Kansas, where presumably it was expected that a dose of hard work would knock the nonsense out of him. The plan backfired terribly.

Instead of buckling down to life on the farm, William Cunningham Deane Tanner bolted. He struck out for New York and its more attractive distractions. A fair knowledge of antiques helped him secure a clerking position in a city antique firm. Deane Tanner was a smart young man, tall, well built and handsome and he had a natural debonair way about him, attributes that fitted well into a high-class antiques business. By 1901, just two years after joining the firm he had become vice-president and manager of the business. That same year he married the daughter of a wealthy stockbroker. By the following year, Deane Tanner was the father of a baby girl, he was wealthy, successful and apparently happily married. But something must have been very amiss in this seemingly idyllic life.

About noon on October 23rd 1908, he left the antique business to go to lunch… and never returned. The following morning he telephoned his bank and requested that a messenger bring six hundred dollars in cash to a nearby hotel. The money was delivered and Deane Tanner was never heard of again – by that name at least.

"One day he had lunch and just disappeared," recounts veteran Hollywood producer A.C. Lyles. "One heard stories that he came searching for gold in the Klondike and worked on oil fields and wound up in Hollywood as an actor." In fact, Deane Tanner made three trips to the Alaskan goldfields but never hit pay dirt. He was shanghaied, according to one report, and forced to crew a rigger around Cape Horn. When he eventually jumped ship he clerked for the Western Railroad Company for a time, joined a mining outfit as a bookkeeper then hooked up with a touring theatre company with which he got his first stage training. That was when the fledgling actor began to hear glowing accounts of Hollywood. The more popular actors were commanding huge salaries in the moving picture business which was moving en masse to the West. Land prices were soaring and things were on the move in Los Angeles. That was where he must be.

Calling himself William Desmond Taylor, he arrived in the film town in 1917 and joined Western Vitagraph Pictures as an actor. After one of his early movies hit at the box office an article in *Movie Pictorial*, a fan magazine, said of him, 'He is an actor, athlete and Irishman and has never done anything better than his interpretation of the title role in *Captain Alvares*, but he has done things just as good. He is tall and distinguished looking, has kindly grey eyes and a mouth that bespeaks humour, and this, of course accounts for some of his great popularity in the Western Vitagraph Pictures.'

But Taylor felt he would be better suited to directing and within two years of arriving in Hollywood he got his first job behind the camera. He was a natural. With just a few directorial credits to his name he was becoming a favourite of the great Mary Pickford as well as screen star Mabel Normand, a wild-hearted beauty who electrified the screen and commanded enormous fees. He was also moulding the talent of a beautiful young ingénue called Mary Miles Minter. He had become one of the biggest names in Hollywood and, when he was elected president of the Motion Picture Director's Association, Taylor became a golden boy at Paramount Studios.

'Mr Taylor has gained a very particular reputation for human photoplays, plays of real people acting in a real way under different circumstances. He will be particularly remembered for *Huckleberry Finn*, *Tom Sawyer*, *The Varmint*, *The Soul of Youth*, *The Furnace* and a score of other pictures all of them remarkable for their reality. The reason is not far to seek. For certainly of all the present day producers Mr Taylor stands foremost in the matter of life experiences. Successively Irish student, Kansas rancher, Klondike miner, construction engineer of large industrial projects, actor and director of film features, he has encompassed an unusual segment of human activity,' wrote Ray Davidson in a 1920 article about Taylor and re-produced in 'Taylorology'.

But something sinister lurked in the life of this successful and handsome grey-eyed Irishman of the fan magazines. He was becoming enmeshed in a deadly web of intrigue that would not begin to unfold until after his murder. The first detectives to arrive on the murder scene that morning found the door of Taylor's home wide open and studio executives were carrying out boxes of booze, illegal during those Prohibition days. Inside the house, police encountered more studio lackeys huddled around a fireplace throwing papers into the flames. After expelling the studio lackeys from the crime scene the police found a stack of pornographic photographs, a set of keys that fitted no lock in the house and women's underwear that bore the initials M.M.M. Could these be the initials of the nineteen-year-old star Mary Miles Minter? The scandalmongers scented blood.

As detectives set about piecing the last hours of Taylor's life in place they discovered that Mabel Normand, the great movie star of the Keystone comedies was the last person – apart from the killer – to have seen Taylor alive. She had stopped off at his bungalow that night to "return a book," she said. After a cocktail or two Taylor walked her to her car outside the house. "Mabel," he said, "I have the strangest and most ghastly feeling that something is going to happen to me." But it seemed there was more to Taylor's relationship with Normand than she was prepared to admit.

Taylor was in love with the star. And she was engaged to be married to the man they called the King of Comedy, Mack Sennett, the Irish-Canadian genius behind the immortal 'Keystone Kops' comedies and the Mack Sennett 'Bathing Beauties'. She was also a 'snowbird,' Hollywood lingo of the day for a cocaine addict. The Irishman wasn't winning friends in Hollywood. Particularly when he decided to take on the town's drug cartel.

It was said that Taylor had tried to rescue Normand from the clutches of her drug dealers, even coming to blows with one man. The director went so far as to ask an Assistant District Attorney to investigate the Hollywood drug ring, saying he was "friendly with an actress who was paying $2,000 a month to support her habit." One report suggested that Taylor spent $50,000 of his own money to flush out the kingpins of the narcotics gang that was flooding the town with drugs.

Normand could not convince the police that she had been returning a book that night or that Taylor had been giving her French lessons, as she also insisted. What troubled the investigators were the letters. Normand had rushed over to Taylor's house after hearing the news of the murder, frantically demanding that detectives return a packet of letters she had written to Taylor. She knew where Taylor had kept them, she said. But when police went to look they found the letters had vanished. This immediately aroused suspicion that a would-be blackmailer – who knew of the letters and what they contained – was in the act of stealing them when Taylor came home. Did this blackmailer and burglar kill Taylor? Maybe. But there was no evidence of a burglary.

This was just one of an assortment of theories that would surface in the course of the investigation. Another theory suggested that Taylor's private secretary, a man called Sands, was a suspect. He had allegedly forged cheques in Taylor's name and had gone missing around the time of the murder. The Press was having a field day. It seemed that every new clue took police along a different path and every path led to a star. Hollywood was cringing.

Silent screen star Mary Miles Minter (right) pictured here with her mother Charlotte Shelby was at the centre of the Taylor murder mystery after it was revealed that the nineteen-year-old was having an affair with Taylor. Shelby, who controlled her daughter's finances and was known to carry a gun had ample motive for the shooting as Minter's studio contract could have been jeopardised if she married.

Mabel Normand, reputedly the highest paid actress in the movies in 1922, found herself besieged by reporters. And though a bystander in the scandal, she was ruined. Her career nose-dived and she became virtually penniless.

While the unfortunate Mabel Normand was fending off the press, police attention turned to the initials on the underwear found in Taylor's home. The owner of the undergarments was clearly the same person who had scrawled a note that had also been uncovered in Taylor's home. It read "Dearest, I love you, I love you" and was signed M.M.M. The scandal hounds were back on the trail – this time they were on the scent of teenage screen beauty Mary Miles Minter. When cornered Minter blurted out that she and the murdered director had intended to announce their engagement within a week. If this were true, the police now had a motive, and a suspect. Minter's mother Charlotte Shelby was a domineering and manipulative woman who handled all her daughter's money and was known to carry a gun. The fact that Minter's million-dollar film contract stipulated that she could not marry pointed towards the mother as the culprit. Did the star's mother turn to murder to protect her golden goose?

If this woman had murdered Taylor, as many investigators now believe, she would never be convicted. But she had money, lots of it, and Los Angeles and Hollywood at that time were cesspools of bribery and corruption. The District Attorney who handled the Taylor case was later sent to prison for taking bribes in relation to another investigation. Huge sums of money mysteriously vanished from Minter's bank account which her mother controlled.

The blanket press coverage of the murder could not have come at a worse time for Minter and Normand – or Hollywood. An infamous affair of 1921 was already focusing national attention on the morals of the film town and its denizens. The sensational charge was levelled that top screen comic Roscoe 'Fatty' Arbuckle had so viciously and sadistically raped a young would-be screen actress at a wild party in a San Francisco hotel that she died of internal injuries. America and the world was traumatised by the idea that this beloved, roly-poly, jolly and simple comedian, this famous moving picture star could have so bilious a private life. Were all those film folk the same? Hollywood was facing its first public relations disaster.

In one of Hollywood history's great ironies, just days before the Taylor murder hit the headlines, film company chiefs had asked William H. Hays, Postmaster General, to act as a morals and policy overseer to the film industry. It was a bid to pacify the Hollywood critics – a public relations exercise, perhaps – a statement that Hollywood could and would bear the most stringent scrutiny, and that the Arbuckle scandal was an aberration. The Taylor murder and its scandalous wake stopped that spin-doctoring dead in its tracks. Hollywood cringed as scandal after scandal, each more fantastic than the one before, was summoned from the film community's previously secret netherworld. It was there for all the world to see in banner headlines: drugs, sex, booze, bribery, pornography. For Hollywood, the wild party was over.

No arrest was ever made and the story gradually faded from the headlines. But, combined with the fall out from the Arbuckle trials – despite the fact that Arbuckle was ultimately found "not guilty" – Taylor's murder and its lurid aftermath resulted in the introduction to Hollywood of rigorous self-censorship and strict codes of conduct for its stars. Old Hollywood was dead and gone.

The ghost of the Taylor affair would rattle its chains occasionally through the years. The most sensational re-emergence came some four years after the murder, when District Attorney Asa Keyes announced that an arrest was "imminent" in the case. A short time later an embarrassed Keyes had to confess that "certain vital evidence" had "mysteriously vanished" from a locked cabinet in his office.

As time went on, those whose lives had been shredded by the affair passed away. The unfortunate Mabel Normand, once the brightest and highest paid star in Hollywood's firmament, died in ruin of tuberculosis. Mary Miles Minter, her career destroyed, lived to be an elderly lady, guarding to the end whatever secrets she knew about Hollywood's first real-life whodunnit murder mystery.

But the affair was not to be shelved without one final official attempt by the Los Angeles Police Department to uncover the truth. About twenty years ago the LAPD's technical experts re-examined the preserved physical evidence using crime solving techniques that were not available back in 1922. Nothing of consequence was found. To this day, nobody has ever been officially named as the murderer of William Desmond Taylor and the case remains open on police files.

FOOTNOTE

The shadow of the Taylor debacle fell on the careers of many in Hollywood, but perhaps none more dramatically than a brilliant Irish-Canadian called Michael Sinnott, better known as Mack Sennett, legendary film maker of the silent screen.

Irish-Canadian Mack Sennett and star Mabel Normand – victims of the fallout from the Taylor murder.

Sennett wrote of his beginnings: "My people were pure Irish at the time I arrived, weighing twelve pounds, and not considered large for my age… when (my people) left Wexford they brought over a few legends about Brian Boru, the recollection that Ireland was the centre of European culture until the Vikings sneaked up on our forefathers about AD 70, and the conviction that an Irishman can lick any ten men in the world, including ten Irishmen. But we did not bring any pixies or leprechauns with us. We left them in Ireland, where they are now in politics."

This genius who would leave the world of cinema with the immortal Keystone Kops and was dubbed 'The King of Comedy' in Hollywood was hurled into a tailspin by the Taylor murder. He was the man who loved the ill-fated Mabel Normand: when dirt flew in Hollywood it landed on guilty and innocent alike.

Sennett had left his family home in Quebec as a young man and landed in New York with ambitions to get into showbusiness. He had arrived in the early 1900s in the city of burlesque where the inimitable Little Egypt cavorted in her micro-costume and where a boy called Buster Keaton was dodging the police because he was legally too young to work in theatre. It was also the city where a talented group of pioneer film makers were planting the seeds of a new industry at the Biograph Film Company. It didn't take Sennett long to find them.

The young adventurer threw himself headlong into this wonderful new moving picture business at Biograph where his wit and natural charm endeared him to his stable mates, Mary Pickford, Owen Moore and a veteran stage actor called Lionel Barrymore, who would become the first great thespian of the early screen. When the ravishing young actress Mabel Normand joined the company, Sennett fell instantly and forever in love. There was an engagement ring, a party and toasts to the couple at Biograph, but no date for a wedding. Their hurly-burly life in the movies was just too uncertain to plan that far ahead. Besides, they were both too busy getting famous.

Sennett got financial backing for a venture to Hollywood to direct his own movies, even build a studio. Sennett and Normand were headed West and into Hollywood history. The name he chose for the outfit would become legend: The Keystone Studios. A lighting bolt of creativity hit Hollywood when Sennett went to work. His outrageous Keystone Kops cavorted and crashed their way into the hearts of film fans with their mad car chases in pursuit of bad guys. A young Englishman called Charles Chaplin joined Sennett as did the comedian Fatty Arbuckle. Sennett teamed Normand with Arbuckle and one of the first great comedy teams of the early screen was born. Hundreds of Normand and Arbuckle comedies hit the nickelodeon circuit. Audiences loved them, they were stars. Sennett was wealthy and famous beyond his dreams. Money was rolling into the Keystone venture and it was rolling into Hollywood and Hollywood was partying with abandon. Journalist Walter Wanger would say of the film town in those days, 'If you didn't take the young lady on your right upstairs between the soup and the entrée you were considered homosexual.'

As a couple in love Sennett and Normand really didn't stand a chance. They set a date for their wedding in 1915, but two weeks before the ceremony Normand suspected that Sennett was having an affair with her best friend and called the whole thing off. Devastated, Sennett lavished her with expensive gifts, doted and nursed her through an almost fatal bout with tuberculosis and vowed his undivided love. He even created a brilliant new movie for her to make a comeback in after her illness. The film was *Mickey*: it was one of the greatest hits of early Hollywood and it affirmed Normand's place at the pinnacle of the industry. But not even this triumph could soothe the actress's hurt, and she abandoned Sennett and Keystone to join Samuel Goldwyn's film company at a record salary of $150,000 a year. It all went straight to Normand's head and, as they might say today, "she went Hollywood". Her partying was infamous. She also found cocaine. Then *it* happened. Someone killed her new lover, the director, William Desmond Taylor. Her slide to ruin was nothing less than spectacular. A crushed and heartbroken Sennett looked on helplessly at the train wreck.

It was around this time that Sennett's brilliance seemed to fade. His work was becoming less inspired and he was directing just a handful of films in the time he once would have churned out a hundred. His company continued to make pictures and even provided a launch pad for such Hollywood greats as Gloria Swanson, Carole Lombard, Wallace Beery and an Irish-American crooner called Bing Crosby.

Sennett's personal decline would not be stopped. The Wall Street Crash took his fortune in 1929 and he took to directing run-of-the-mill movies to make a living. But the final nail in the coffin was the talkies. Sennett's genius lay with the silent screen and the comedy of image and action. He could not adapt to sound. A decade after the Taylor murder Sennett was an out-of-work bankrupt. He never made another movie, and died in 1960 in Hollywood.

CHAPTER 7

DESIGNS ON HOLLYWOOD – CEDRIC GIBBONS

Hollywood had survived the trauma in the early 1920s of the murder of William Desmond Taylor and the Fatty Arbuckle scandal – but it required a new and serious image as an industry of upstanding professionals who were dedicated to the art of film. It was a fact that film-making, in part due to Rex Ingram and Herbert Brenon's influence, had indeed become a true art form, so much so that it was decided in 1927 to found an organisation of professionals who would come to represent the finest and highest principles of that art. The organisation would be known as the Academy of Motion Picture Arts & Sciences. Mary Pickford and Marshal Neilan were among its founding members. So was a young, highly respected Irish-American by the name of Cedric Gibbons. This was the first real milestone in Hollywood's climb out of the lurid affairs of the earlier part of the decade as it strived for global respectability.

The meeting droned on and everybody there had an idea. It was quite an important meeting of the Board of Governors of the newly founded Academy of Motion Picture Arts and Sciences, and all in attendance were suitably solemn. They had gathered that year of 1927 to discuss a suitable design for a statuette that would be presented to recipients of the forthcoming inaugural annual Hollywood industry celebration of excellence in cinema, the Academy Awards.

One of those present didn't seem to be paying much attention to the debate about what form the statuette should take. In fact he seemed far more engrossed in whatever it was he was sketching on a note pad. This was Cedric Gibbons, the talented young Irishman who headed up the art department at MGM Studios. It was one of his movie mogul bosses at the studio, Louis B. Mayer who had recently proposed that yearly awards be given by the Academy for outstanding achievement in film and Gibbons, despite his casual air at the meeting, was anxious to please. He glanced up from the pad he'd been sketching upon and suggested to his fellow Academy governors that the award should "be a figure of dignity". He offered his sketchpad to them for perusal. On it, in the confident lines of an artist, was a drawing of a man standing on a reel of film holding a broadsword in his hands. Within minutes all members of the board approved what would become the cinema industry's world-famous icon. The figure would in time be dubbed Oscar. The drawing was moulded by sculptor George Stanley and the following May 16th 1929, at the Roosevelt Hotel, still a landmark of Hollywood today, fifteen of the golden statuettes were handed out.

Cedric Gibbons
pictured at the
funeral of actor John
Gilbert circa 1936
with his wife Dolores
Del Rio and Marlene
Dietrich (centre).

So it was that Cedric Gibbons, a legend in the world of film set design, presented Oscar to Hollywood and the world. It's unclear in Hollywood history how the statuette came to be known as 'The Oscar,' but it is said that an Academy librarian and eventual executive director, Margaret Herrick, thought it resembled her Uncle Oscar. Rumour has it that a reporter overheard the comments and the word 'Oscars' began to filter into the media coverage of the event. By 1939 the Academy was using the nickname in an official capacity.

'When a young Irishman, educated in architecture, travelled about the world to gather impressions for art work, he laid the foundation for a career that made him the most important creator of sets for motion pictures in the entire motion industry,' barks a biography put out by Metro-Goldwyn-Mayer, the studio that would be his home in Hollywood for a lifetime. 'Such was the background of Cedric Gibbons, art director at the Metro-Goldwyn-Mayer Studios, the originator of the modernistic screen sets, and whose work has had a profound influence not only on set designing for the screen, but in architecture, inside and out, which has echoed many of his conceptions in homes all over the world,' the studio biography added.

Gibbons, according to this glowing biography which was circulated with the designer's stamp of approval, 'was born in Dublin, Ireland, March 23, 1893 the son of Austin Patrick Gibbons, an architect, and Veronica Fitzpatrick Gibbons.' The note about his birthplace being Dublin has circulated widely since it was first put out by the studio in the 1930s, and to this day is very often repeated as fact in articles about the famous set designer. In fact, it appears that he was actually born in Brooklyn to Irish parents. His father was a successful architect. 'The considerable wealth of his family allowed Cedric to be educated privately by tutors. Years later he regretted having been deprived of the company of boys and girls his age,' recalled Oscar Rimoldi writing in *Hollywood Studio Magazine* in 1990. "I had very few friends and what's worse I didn't know how to make friends. I became withdrawn, reserved, and awfully lonely," Gibbons confessed.

As a young man Gibbons was treated to a tour of Europe to study the history of classic architecture in England, France, Italy and Spain. On his return to New York he was enrolled at the Students Art League, where he was awarded a Prix de Rome award as the most outstanding art student in the entire United States. Young Gibbons was proving everything his father had dreamed he would be as successor to the family's architectural business. But this was New York and it was 1912 and something new and exciting had captured the young man's eye: the moving pictures. Young Gibbons was intrigued by the medium and frustrated by the often crude and unrealistic sets that were being used in these one-reel flickers. In 1914 after two stultifying years' work as a draftsman in his father's firm Gibbons met Hugo Ballin, a painter who specialised in murals and who worked for the Thomas Alva Edison Moving Picture Studios in Bedford Park, New York. Ballin needed an assistant at Edison Studios and offered the job to Gibbons who accepted immediately. 'Gibbons introduced some innovations that greatly enhanced the realism of scenes. He soon realised that sets are not only the 'working area' in which actors perform and the action takes place, but are the most important in rating the mood that reveals historical settings,' according to Rimoldi in a study of Gibbons's life in film. His pioneer work at Edison attracted the attention of the original Goldwyn organisation in New York which brought him aboard as art director. When the company joined the movie industry's migration to Hollywood Gibbons went with them.

Now supervising the design of all the films pouring out of the Metro-Goldwyn-Mayer Studios in Culver City, Gibbons became one of the most influential forces in elevating movies from simple flickers with crude painted backdrops to new, sophisticated heights. Art departments were becoming key elements of every motion picture studio. But not only were Gibbons's innovative set designs prompting dramatic shifts in movie making; they were also influencing the tastes and styles of America. When Gibbons designed unusual lines and levels for indoor ceilings, walls and stairwells in *Our Dancing Daughters* in 1928, the style started a new trend in home design across America. And when Gibbons transformed an old barn into a modern home in *When Ladies Meet* in 1933 another fad took off. Gibbons, who wrote a chapter on motion picture set design for the *Encyclopaedia Britannica*, was the master of film design in the black and white era when he utilised a simple work ethic. The setting should not be so obtrusive as to detract from the story unfolding on the screen. But with the introduction of Technicolor Gibbons was unrestrained and wrote another chapter in Hollywood history with his fantasy of colour and whimsy in MGM's 1939 classic *The Wizard of Oz*.

This six-foot, dark-haired, blue-eyed Irishman was writing his own chapter in Hollywood legend and Hollywood lauded him for it. When honoured with the 'award for distinguished achievement for contributing the most to the motion picture industry through art direction' in 1950 by the Society of Motion Picture Art Directors, he responded with typical modesty. 'I'm deeply moved because by this award the members of my profession have praised the work of my entire career. Whenever the members of any profession, knowing all the problems and challenges a person is faced with, honour anyone for his contributions in their profession, it must be presumed the highest of all tributes.' He also generated headlines in Hollywood unconnected to his brilliant work. The town was thrown back on its heels when in August 1930, Gibbons married actress Dolores Del Rio, one of the screen's most ravishing beauties. She was at the pinnacle of her career and the focus of the world press. Gossips speculated that the reserved and withdrawn Gibbons could never tolerate life in the

public gaze. They were wrong: the marriage lasted eleven years until their eventual divorce. 'On August 29, 1944, Gibbons, forty-nine, again surprised the movie colony by marrying nineteen-year-old actress Hazel Brooks. Many thought that Miss Brooks's motives to marry the pre-eminent Gibbons were to further her movie career,' wrote Rimoldi. 'Time proved them wrong.' The young actress gave up her career to run her home and to care for her husband after he suffered a heart attack, which dramatically slowed the pace of his work at MGM where he continued working until 1956.

In the spring of that year Gibbons suffered a massive stroke that left him semi-paralysed and housebound. Though nursed and cared for by his loving wife, he never recovered and four years later on July 26th 1960, he passed away in his Westwood home where no fewer than eleven of the Oscar statuettes that he had designed stood at attention side by side, testimony to a genius.

Films for which he won Academy Awards for best art direction were: *The Bridge of San Luis Rey* (1928–29); *The Merry Widow* (1934); *Pride and Prejudice* (1940); *Blossoms in the Dust* (1941); *Gaslight* (1944); *The Yearling* (1946); *Little Women* (1949); *An American in Paris* (1951); *The Bad and the Beautiful* (1952); *Julius Caesar* (1953); and *Somebody Up There Likes Me* (1956).

◀ The vibrant colour and fantastical sets and designs for the MGM classic *The Wizard of Oz* have enthralled cinema audiences since it was first released in 1939 when a young Judy Garland set out 'to see the Wizard' on the yellow brick road. The movie earned Cedric Gibbons one of his many Oscar nominations (with William A. Horning).

CHAPTER 8

THE IRISH COWBOYS

"Y'know, there's no such thing as a good script. I've never seen one," the great director John Ford once told a young Peter Bogdanovich. "Yes, I have. I've seen ONE. This O'Casey thing I'm gonna do next. Based on his autobiographies. It's the first script I've ever read that I can just go over and shoot." Ford had been talking about a movie called *The Young Cassidy* that he indeed did "just go over and shoot" in Ireland with Irish-Australian Rod Taylor in one of his finest screen performances. Ford made Irish movies, most notably a screen version of Liam O'Flaherty's masterpiece *The Informer*, and he made Westerns – "I'm John Ford and I make Westerns," he would introduce himself once to the Director's Guild – and he loved both themes equally. He was perhaps the toughest and most brilliant of a mongrel breed in Hollywood… the Irish Cowboy. The Western was probably the first real 'genre' of the movies with the first early one-reeler, *The Great Train Robbery* produced in 1903 and general recognised as the first 'real movie' ever made. Within a few years almost all of the early studios were churning out Westerns. By 1910, as moviemakers were setting up permanent homes in Hollywood and had access to mountains, canyons, deserts and other perfect Western locations, some twenty per cent of Hollywood's entire output was Westerns. Later would come the 'cowboy' serials that packed kids into cinemas around the world. By and large, writers who had never been to the West wrote the early cowboy movies. The stories and the characters became more fantastical and often verged on the ridiculous, the cowboy 'hero' parading around in a sparkling white suit with fringes and white ten-gallon hat and the bad guy inevitably dressed in black. But that was all about to change in the 1930s with the emergence of a brash and talented young director called John Ford. The son of Irish immigrants from County Galway, Ford is generally credited with having re-invented the Western and transforming it into an authentic genre that genuinely captured the heart and soul of the real West. Another great director of Westerns, and contemporary of Ford's, Howard Hawks, was once asked if he had been influenced by Ford. He replied that he didn't know how anybody could make a Western without being influenced by Ford. He was not the only Irish movie doyen responsible for the creation of the Western as a centrepiece of the Hollywood industry.

John Ford was filming *Cheyenne Autumn* out in the wind carved mountain spires and red, eroded landscape of Monument Valley along the Arizona-Utah state line and within the Navajo Indian Reservation. The ageing director was dining after a long day's shoot with his cast, among them Patrick Wayne, son of John Wayne, one of Ford's oldest and dearest friends, Ricardo Montalban, Dolores Del Rio, Carroll Baker and Jimmy O'Hara, younger brother of Maureen O'Hara, another treasured friend. It had been a magical evening out in a magical place with songs being sung by Navajo, Irish, American and Latin.

"'Sing the national anthem, Jimmy," Ford said. It was getting late now. O'Hara knew what he meant... he sang 'The Wearing of the Green,' a song traditionally sung during Easter Week in Ireland. After the second refrain, Ford contributed a verse,' remembered the director Peter Bogdanovich in a moving and very personal insight into his old friend published in *Esquire* magazine in 1964 under the heading, 'The Autumn of John Ford'. Instead of the National Anthem, O'Hara gave Ford a rendition of 'The Wearin' of the Green'.

The account serves wonderfully to express the dichotomy that was this Irishman and classic American, John Ford. (While Ford is perhaps most commonly associated with his wonderful Westerns, his early classic *Stagecoach* among them, he would repeatedly return to Irish themes, setting to film such works as his Oscar-winning adaptation of Liam O'Flaherty's tragic drama *The Informer* starring Victor McLaglen; Sean O'Casey's *The Plough and the Stars* and, of course, *The Quiet Man*, that Irish romp about a Yank (John Wayne) returning home to Ireland, falling in love with the local lass (Maureen O'Hara), fighting her brother (McLaglen) and encountering all sorts of mischief from a cast of rogues, Barry Fitzgerald, Arthur Shields and the impish Jackie McGowran among them.

On the one hand, Ford seemed to be always in search of his Irish roots, while on the other he was singularly American, a Naval officer and perhaps the most important chronicler of the American saga on screen. His career and his life are signposted both by his efforts to explore his Irish heritage and by his monumental salutes to the land of his birth, the United States. He was born John Martin Feeney in Portland, Maine, in 1894, the son of an Irish immigrant saloonkeeper, Sean Feeney from Spiddal in County Galway. Ford's mother Barbara was from the same county, but the couple didn't meet until they arrived in their new home of Portland, Maine.

Shortly after graduating from Portland High School in 1914 Ford, still using the family name of Feeney, "left the Irish neighbourhoods of this port city" to try his luck in Hollywood, where his older brother Francis was finding considerable success as an actor in the new movie business. He stepped off the train in downtown Los Angeles, lugged his bag onto a tram headed for Hollywood, paying a dime for the twelve-mile ride through the citrus groves that blossomed around the town. He was hoping that Francis would be there to meet him as planned, but he wasn't too worried; things were going to work out well, he sensed. Francis's letters home had been filled with colourful frontier yarns of the young film town and Feeney reckoned this was just the place for him.

Francis, who had anglicised his last name to Ford for the movies, was indeed there to meet his younger brother when he stepped off the trolley at Sunset Boulevard. Across the dust road was the barn rented by Cecil B. DeMille where *Squaw Man* had been filmed just two years before. But the brothers were headed further afield to the studios of cowboy star Tom Mix, the 'Mixville Studios' in Edendale. With apologies Francis explained to the new arrival that without any experience under his belt there was not a lot for him to do in Hollywood. For the time being, young Sean would work as a stable hand at the studio. That was just fine with the young adventurer. It didn't take him long to work his way up playing bit parts, including a hooded clansman in D.W. Griffith's *The Birth of a Nation* (the studios were constantly looking for extras to do crowd work). A later move to Universal and another menial job would ultimately propel him into the apprentice directing ranks. A publicity sheet put out in 1941 by 20th Century Fox says glibly, 'Ford got 'staggered' after he was elevated from 'prop' boy at Universal Studios to the job of directing... In six years he had made two hundred Westerns – short and long 'cliffhangers,' all speedy. He had served his apprenticeship. He is still fast, perhaps faster than ever, but he is one of the most finished directors in Hollywood, and four times a winner of the Academy award for the best film of the year.'

The press release, typical of its day with a wordy and breathless style, describes Ford thus: 'In person, Ford is a hulking, rugged, soft-stepping six-footer, hidden behind a flop hat, a large pipe, rubber-tyred spectacles and an up-turned collar. He wears the same hat, worn coat and scuffed shoes – an outfit that a junkman would thank you not to fling in his cart. But there is an aura of quality about them: the hat was especially made, the coat woven of Harris tweed, the shoes of Cordovan leather.'

During that 'apprenticeship' he had become a contract director responsible for numerous Westerns, many of them starring Harry Carey Sr, the legendary Irish-American Western star. Feeney, now calling himself John Ford in the style of his brother, was becoming a respected figure among the cowboys of Hollywood who rode for the movies. These were true cowhands who years earlier had been moving herds in Montana, Colorado or Wyoming before migrating to Hollywood in search of work. If a director could gain the respect of these tough men he would have their co-operation – without which it would be almost impossible to bring in a movie on schedule or on budget. Ford, who drank, fought and played poker with the toughest of the Hollywood posse, was high in their standing. His roustabout manner would remain a trademark of the director throughout his life. 'I love Hollywood,' he once said, 'I don't mean the higher echelons, I mean the lower echelons, and the grips, the technicians.'

It was the common touch of this tall, burly son of an Irish saloon keeper that probably contributed most to his ability to make gritty, truthful accounts of the West typified by such enduring films as *Stagecoach, She Wore a Yellow Ribbon* and, much later *The Searchers*. *Stagecoach* challenged *Gone with the Wind* (which won) and *The Wizard of Oz* for best picture in the Oscar race in 1939. It should be noted that many critics felt that because *Stagecoach* was shot in black and white at a time when colour had arrived, there was an unfairly negative vote. Ironically, Ford, the man who boasted, "I make Westerns," won his first Oscar not for a Western but for his Irish movie *The Informer* made earlier in 1935. Two more Academy Awards for best direction came his way for his adaptation to screen of two great literary classics, *The Grapes of Wrath* and *How Green Was My Valley* in 1940 and 1941 respectively. *Stagecoach* would mark a milestone in cinema history in another way though. It marked the beginning of a close working relationship and friendship between John Wayne (who had distant family roots in Ulster) and Ford. They went on to make nine movies together, including of course *The Quiet Man*. It was said that *Stagecoach* in fact made Wayne's career. 'At the age of thirty-two after nearly ten years of making around eighty low-budget Westerns, the six-foot-four Wayne received new life when Ford cast him in the role of Ringo (in *Stagecoach*),' writes Sam B. Girgus in his book *Hollywood Renaissance*.

Before Ford came on the scene, the so-called Hollywood posse – riders, real veterans of the cowboy life – had to remain silent as they watched the 'rhinestone cowboys' of the earlier Westerns play acting in huge hats and brandishing shiny six-guns.

Irish tough guys of the Wild West movie: (left to right) John Ford and Raoul Walsh.

One of these early 'dude' cowboys was Dublin-born actor William Desmond (not to be confused with director William Desmond Taylor) who shifted from stage to screen in 1915 and made cowboy movies for nearly quarter of a century. 'As long as there's a man, woman or youngster of America, Westerns will be in demand. They are the cleanest, most exciting type of entertainment of all – even if we do frill up the cowboys a little,' Desmond once said.

To the audiences who paid their nickels to see William Desmond rout the bad guys, he was everything a cowboy should be in those days; brave, handsome and above all fast on the draw. Audiences saw Desmond dispatch the villains of such silent films as *Perils of the Yukon, Riders of the Purple Sage, Heading for the Rio Grande* and *Ruggles of Red Gap.*

But Ford's growing knowledge and respect for the real code of the West – and the genuine cowboys who were his friends – brought a new type of Western hero to the screen, a hero who didn't need to be 'frilled up'. Ford wanted to hear what his real cowboy compadres had to say about the movies he was making – and he listened.

Diana Serra Cary in her splendid book *The Hollywood Posse* recounts the screen cowboy days of her Irish-American father Jack Montgomery. She tells of how one scene in Ford's movie *My Darling Clementine* was totally changed on the advice of the cowboy extras. Four real cowboys were put to playing poker. The men were reluctant, explaining that a totally different card game called Jick, Jack Ginny and the Bean Gun was exclusively played in the time and place being depicted. Ford changed the scene dialogue on the instructions of the extras. The film, released in 1946, along with a clutch of other Ford films including *She Wore a Yellow Ribbon* (1949) and *The Searchers* (1956) are seen today by some critics as among the most important films ever made. Ford was ready to take counsel from the cowboys on all manner of things, from the way a man might have worn his hat in a particular part of the country to the style of his saddle or the way he wore his gun.

Yet for all his films mastery, it was as much the legend of John Ford the man that captivated Hollywood. The industry revelled in 'Fordisms': a man arrived on one of his sets with a message from the studio brass complaining that he was running five days over the shooting schedule. Ford asked the man how many pages of script he figured were filmed on an average day. "I'd say five," came the response. Ford called for a script of the movie he was shooting, flicked through it, then ripped out twenty-five pages and threw them in the air and informed the man that they were now back on schedule.

Bogdanovich recollects in his homage to Ford in *Esquire* that when filming *Mr Roberts* starring Henry Fonda things were not running smoothly between the director and the star. The studio called a conference to settle things. When Fonda rose to list his complaints Ford jumped up and started punching him. Fonda struck back and the conference became a knockdown brawl.

While respected and admired in his public life, Ford's private world was no picture of bliss. In 1920 he married Mary McBryde Smith, a woman of aristocratic Southern heritage. By all accounts their marriage met its challenges though they remained together, bringing up two children.

Ford and his wife lived separate lives. He made a habit of retreating to his room to drink and brood alone. "When he wasn't drinking, he would be drying out after a binge. Apart from his voracious consumption of written material and his deep love for his yacht, he had few interests and friends, shunning the Hollywood party circuit and even failing to pick up any of his Academy Awards in person," according to Stephen Galloway, *The Hollywood Reporter*'s senior feature writer and former film editor.

Ford continued to work into his late sixties, making his final masterpiece, *The Man Who Shot Liberty Valance* in 1962. Even today the body of his work remains unrivalled in the history of American cinema. Before he died in 1973 at his home in Palm Desert one of his last visitors was his old friend the director Howard Hawks. According to Bogdanovich the final scene of Ford's life was played out thus. Hawks had spent several hours talking with his old friend who was fading. He left the bedroom, spoke a few words with Mrs Ford, then returned to the bedroom for a moment:

> "That you, Howard, I thought you left," said Ford.
> "Just came back to say 'goodbye,' Jack."
> "Goodbye, Howard."
Hawks turned to leave.
> "Howard," called Ford after him.
> "Yes, Jack?"
> "I mean 'really goodbye', Howard," said Ford.
> "Really goodbye, Jack?"
> "Really goodbye."
The friends shook hands.

There were few in Hollywood to equal Ford in the ranks of curmudgeons, unless you include that other Irish-American giant of the silver screen, director Raoul Walsh. 'Many wild Irishmen helped brighten the history of Hollywood, but none has made greater contribution than Raoul Walsh. He has more than four hundred pictures to his credit, discovered more stars, befriended more struggling talent and been best friend and severest critic to more players than any director in the business,' chirped Hollywood gossip Hedda Hopper of Walsh.

Once when Ford was complaining on set about a bad eye, and making life miserable for all in sight of his good one, his friend Walsh, who was visiting the shoot, advised, "Jack, I have the answer to your problem."

"You do?" asked a relieved Ford.

"Sure I do. Damn, I went for years with a bum eye, gave me nothin' but trouble. I told the doctors to take the damn thing out once and for all. Have it out like I did, Jack," was Walsh's advice.

Like Ford, Walsh is celebrated for his brilliant narrative style and the vastness of the Western wilderness landscapes that his lens could capture in Westerns like *The Tall Men, Pursued* and *They Died With Their Boots On*. Like Ford, Walsh commanded the utmost respect of the Hollywood cowboy riders and stuntmen, many of whom he counted among his best friends. Walsh's spirit of adventure was probably inherited from his father, whom Walsh would claim had fled Dublin with his four brothers and Walsh's grandfather. "They had sprung the old man from jail where he had been serving time for subversive activities," he contended. 'Raoul' was the name of the captain of the ship that brought them to the United States...

"Life was good when I was a boy. I was born in New York but raised in different cities... I hated the life of the city. I ran away to sea. My uncle Matt owned a sailing vessel. We were

Walsh's career in the early movies began when he was sent by famous filmmaker D.W. Griffith to ride with Mexican revolutionary Pancho Villa (pictured with his officers above) and to film the events of the day. Walsh paid Villa in gold and often filmed as Villa's men executed Federal soldiers. Walsh's films would never shirk from reflecting such brutality in all its reality.

broke up in a hurricane so I went ashore in Mexico and joined a cattle drive across the Texas Panhandle. I learned breakin' horses, mendin' fences, and went on to Montana, where I broke in more horses for the wagons. They had tough boss fellas in those days. Toughest guys in the whole world, in Butte," an ageing and failing Walsh told respected Hollywood journalist Charles Higham for *The New York Times*.

His first taste of the movies and of war, another theme realistically explored by Walsh, came in 1911 when D.W. Griffith dispatched him with a camera to ride with the Mexican revolutionary Pancho Villa, and film all the dreadful events of that most bloody of wars. "I rode alongside Pancho all the way from Juarez to Mexico City. We paid him $500 a month and gold to let us film him… when Pancho would line up the Federales along a wall to shoot them," Walsh told Higham.

Though Griffith liked what the twenty-two-year-old adventurer had filmed, Walsh still had some way to go before gaining his director's stripes, including numerous bit parts as an actor, the best known of which was the role of Lincoln assassin John Wilkes Booth in Griffith's *The Birth of a Nation*. Later he signed on with William Fox where he learned the craft of directing while whipping cowboys into shape in Hollywood.

One of Walsh's early jobs in Hollywood when Fox was making a Western was to tour the Hollywood hangouts of the cowboy crowd and hire riders for the shoot. Usually he didn't have to look very far for the cowboys drank almost exclusively in a small bar called 'The Waterhole', a squat building at the junction of Cahuenga and Sunset where a mini-mall now stands. Walsh who "could twirl a lariat, jump through the loop, rope a steer," was not unknown to lift a shot or two of rye whiskey at the Waterhole with his cowboy friends.

If he couldn't find enough riders at the Waterhole he would ride over to the barns of the Mixville Studios in Edendale (where John Ford got his first job in Hollywood), which many of the cowboys used as free shelter. "Roll up and roll out, you bastards," was his shout. With Walsh leading the way, the posse for the day's filming would pick its way back to Hollywood, almost a six-hour ride over the hills.

Though noted for his gritty Westerns – including the first 'talking' Western titled *In Old Arizona* featuring a character called the Cisco Kid, and *The Big Trail* which gave John Wayne his first lead role – his mastery of film extended to many other themes. Walsh directed the war films *The Naked and the Dead, Battle Cry,* and *What Price Glory*, and the chillingly brutal crime story *White Heat* with a young Irish-American actor called James Cagney in the lead role of psychotic gangster Cody ("Made it Ma! Top o' the world!") Jarrett.

Walsh's movies were by the most part tough, macho and brutal. Someone once suggested he direct a romance movie. Warner Studios boss Jack Warner, for whom Walsh was working at the time, responded, "Walsh's idea of a tender love story would be burning down a whore house."

One of Walsh's personal non-Western favourites was *Gentleman Jim* which starred the Irish-Australian and real-life Hollywood buccaneer Errol Flynn in the role of legendary pugilist 'Gentleman Jim' Corbett.

The title of his autobiography, *My Wicked, Wicked Ways* says it all about Hollywood's most colourful Irishman Errol Flynn. Although he was born in Tasmania, he liked to be referred to as Irish when he was at his peak as the movies' most infamous swashbuckler. His father Theodore Thompson Flynn was a popular professor of Zoology at Queen's University Belfast and during the Blitz was Chief Casualty Officer in the Civil Defence organisation in the city. Errol Flynn shot to Hollywood fame in *Captain Blood* in 1935 and went on to play a plethora of action-man roles in such films as *The Adventures of Robin Hood, The Dawn Patrol*, and *Against All Flags* which co-starred Maureen O'Hara and Anthony Quinn. One of his best roles was in the film *Gentleman Jim* (1942) in which he played the legendary pugilist Jim Corbett. The film's director Walsh took a liking to Flynn, who greatly impressed him by going one-on-one in the movie with real boxers, no punches pulled, no stunts, no doubles. The movie made Walsh and Flynn fast drinking buddies and they were often joined in their carousing by another screen legend of Irish descent – John Barrymore, whose corpse once paid an unwelcome visit to Flynn's Hollywood mansion.

Flynn and Barrymore had been inseparable friends and Barrymore would always sit in the same place in Flynn's house as they drank and talked into the dawn. When Barrymore died, Walsh played a devilish practical joke. He talked a film extra who worked at the morgue where Barrymore was lying into lending him the great actor's remains. Walsh placed Barrymore's stiff corpse into the chair in Flynn's home that he had favoured in life, and placed a lit cigarette in the corpse's fingers. When Flynn arrived home and saw his old friend back from the dead he very nearly collapsed. He remained conscious long enough to jump into his car, clutching his chest and screech off down the Hollywood Hills in terror. When Walsh returned the body an hour or so later the mortician/movie extra, who worked regularly on Walsh's films, asked, "Where did you take him?"

"To Errol Flynn's," Walsh replied.

"Why didn't you tell me," the mortician/extra responded. "I would have put a better suit on him."

Errol Flynn (seen
here as 'Gentleman
Jim' with character
actor Jack Carson),
became close
friends with Raoul
Walsh.

Also considered a Walsh masterpiece is *High Sierra*, starring Humphrey Bogart as a desperate gunman on the run who heads into the high country to escape the law. The harrowing script was penned by John Huston, the director/writer/actor who spent many years of
his life raising a family in Ireland, including actress daughter Anjelica and director Tony
Huston. John Huston is best known today for the screen classics *The Maltese Falcon, The
Treasure of the Sierra Madre, Key Largo* and *The African Queen* and in later life *The Dead*. He
was the son of legendary character actor Walter Huston whose credits were legion from the
1930s to the early 1950s.

No account of Walsh's life and career, no matter how brief, would be complete without
mention of the fact that he discovered and launched the career of an actor who called
himself 'Rock Hudson'. Hudson's real name was Roy Fitzgerald. Walsh had been the first
to recognise the handsome young actor's possibilities after he played a bit part in *Fighter
Squadron* in 1948. Walsh put the actor under personal contract and brought him around to
see such leading producers as Hal Wallis and Walter Wanger without any luck. Then he
arranged a meeting with John Ford.

Ford knew that nobody was named Rock by their parents. He asked the young actor what
his real name was. Hudson said it was Fitzgerald, then Ford roared in rage, "Why did
you change it! Now get out!" Of course, Ford had changed his own name from Feeney.
But 'Rock Fitzgerald' was not being entertained that day by Ford. Walsh eventually sold
Hudson/Fitzgerald's contract to Universal and the rest, as they say, is history.

John Ford and Raoul Walsh may have come to typify the Irish tough guys of the Western in Hollywood, but they shared that honour with one of the great hard men of the screen. Irish-American cowboy star Tim McCoy's career spanned four decades from the 1920s to the 1960s when he appeared in his final great Western *Requiem for a Gunfighter* in 1965. McCoy, whose parents were both from Ireland, was born in Saginaw, Michigan in 1891 and took his first job as a cowhand when he was a boy. It was a humble beginning that would launch him into a career as soldier, Indian agent, Wild West show star, movie star and television talk show host. But then Timothy John Fitzgerald McCoy was not one to back away from a challenge – something his adventurous Irish father had taught him. McCoy's father was a Union Army veteran and Fenian who was wounded in a bizarre and abortive Fenian 'invasion' of Canada in 1866.

McCoy's early experiences as a cowhand out in Wyoming brought him into contact with the culture, ceremonies, language and sign language of the region's Native Americans which he learned. 'Had to,' he said. 'They didn't seem to want to learn my language, so I had to learn theirs.' This rare knowledge earned him a job as liaison between the tribes and the government's 'Indian authority'. (McCoy would later use these skills as an officer in World War II to teach Native American sign language to intelligence officers.) 'Content with life in Wyoming, McCoy never set out to be an actor. Hollywood, attracted by his legendary knowledge of Indians, came after him and he didn't resist,' recounted writer Dennis Hunt in the *Los Angeles Times* in 1978 in tribute to the then eighty-seven-year-old Western star. 'In 1923, film-maker Jesse Lasky, interested in authenticity for *The Covered Wagon* hired McCoy as a technical adviser.'

"They had been using Mexicans and Filipinos as Indians," McCoy recalled. "I finally got them to use some real Indians and from then on I was always after those film people to treat the Indians with dignity." McCoy was hired to deliver a live prologue in the movie theatres to *The Covered Wagon* in which he spoke passionately about Native American lore and society. The former cowhand became so well known for this delivery that Metro-Goldwyn-Mayer's 'boy genius,' Irving Thalberg, asked him to do a screen test. On seeing the footage of himself McCoy snorted, "I wouldn't pay a dime to go see that guy up there on screen." But MGM signed him anyway and a remarkable career in the movies was just beginning. Thalberg put McCoy in a series of silent screen Western dramas that were filmed on the Wind River Reservation of Wyoming with hundreds of Arapaho, Sioux and Shosone Native Americans. These films included *War Paint, Winners of the Wilderness* (with Joan Crawford in an early role), *California, The Frontiersman, Wyoming, Sioux Blood* and *Spoilers of the West*.

McCoy, unlike so many other silent stars, shifted effortlessly into the era of the talkies when he starred in the first 'talking serial' from Universal, *The Indians are Coming*. He moved to Columbia in the 1930s to make such Westerns as *Fighting Marshal, Two-Fisted Law, Texas Cyclone* and *Riding Tornado*. When Monogram Studios began its famous *Rough Riders* movie serial, McCoy was hired as one of the stars. A passion for politics intervened in his movie career at this point and he resigned from the serial to run unsuccessfully for a Senate seat. Following that brief joust with politics, he toured the U.S. with his own Wild West circus, appeared in his own 1952 Emmy Award-winning television series about Native American history, sign language and customs and even became a prize-winning contestant on the TV game show *The $64,000 Challenge*.

On his death in 1978 in an Army hospital near Nogales, Arizona, the tributes to his life focused almost as much on his proud career as a military man as they did on his life as a movie star, recalling that he had served with such bravery in two World Wars that he was a recipient of the Bronze Star and a citation for meritorious service, achieving the rank of

colonel. He was also awarded the French Cross of the Legion of Honour and Medaille de L'Aeronautics for his work in developing French aerial reconnaissance for the Allies.

The deep respect and knowledge of Native American lore that McCoy tried to instill in Hollywood was shared by another Irish-American cowboy star of the day, William S. Hart. 'Though he was not the first Western actor/film maker nor the last, Hart was surely one of the most important, achieving both commercial success and artistic recognition for his films,' said a 1978 tribute to Hart in the periodical *Terra*, a publication of the Natural History Museum of Los Angeles County.

Hart, whose mother Rose was an immigrant from Ireland, grew up poor, travelling from town to town around the Midwest in the 1870s with his parents. Many times the family's closest neighbours were Native Americans. His father, a miller by trade, often worked with Native Americans on reservations, milling their corn. Their children were young Hart's playmates and he learned to speak the Sioux language as a result. He also gained a life-long respect for Native American traditions and their culture.

Hart's early life was a saga of poverty and poorly paid messenger jobs. But he was good looking, a champion athlete and a natural performer and like so many other Irish, theatre seemed to offer an escape. Having paid for acting lessons by selling the trophies he had won as an athlete, he was hired as an actor with the Daniel Bandmann's theatre company, and spent his meagre wages to support his now-widowed mother and his younger siblings. It was around this time he saw one of the movie industry's early Westerns and was horrified.

"While playing in Cleveland (in 1913) I attended a picture show. I saw a Western picture. It was awful! I talked with the manager of the theatre and he told me it was one of the best Westerns he ever had. None of the impossibilities or libels on the West meant anything to him – it was drawing the crowds... I was so sure that I had made such a big discovery that I was frightened that someone (would) read my mind and find it out. Here were reproductions of the Old West being seriously presented to the public – in almost a burlesque manner – and they were successful. It made me tremble to think of it. I was an actor and I knew the West... the opportunity that I had been waiting for years to come was knocking at my door... Rise or fall, sink or swim, I had to bend every endeavour to get a chance to make Western motion pictures," Hart told in his autobiography *My Life East and West* published in 1929.

Hart called the New York Motion Picture Company and was put in touch with producer Thomas Ince (the same film-maker that Owen Moore and Mary Pickford *[See chapter 2].*had gone to war with in Cuba. This was a fortunate coincidence, for Hart and Ince had once roomed together as actors. Ince immediately agreed to hire Hart as an actor for the picture company. Hart's couple of outings in this new medium were hardly memorable but there followed two Westerns in 1915 that began to show Hart's promise; *The Bargain*, and *On the Night Stage*. Ince had contracted Hart on $125 a week, a salary that seemed to be a fortune to the actor. But then, as now in Hollywood, nothing was as it seemed. Despite the bonds between Ince and Hart, Ince was taking advantage of Hart financially. *The Bargain* turned out to be a tremendous success and Ince sensed that Hart was destined for stardom. But he had Hart locked into that comparatively paltry wage. "Although he did not begin to realise that he was being exploited until later, it is clear that Ince took advantage of their friendship from the very beginning," asserts Katherine H. Child, author of the *Terra* periodical tribute to the actor.

Hart followed his first two films with Ince with one success after another and became one of the top-name actors and directors in Hollywood. But Ince still held Hart's salary to a fraction of what it could and should have been.

Ince teamed up with Mack Sennett, Harry Aitken and D.W. Griffith in 1915 to form the Triangle Film Corporation. Hart loyally went with Ince to the new film outfit which was paying its stars, Douglas Fairbanks among them, salaries as high as $2,000 a week. Hart's $125 a week salary was doubled and Ince threw in a $50 bonus. Later Hart's salary was raised to $1,000 per week after some tough negotiations, but by now it was becoming obvious to Hart that Ince was exploiting their friendship. The result of Ince's conduct was a successful lawsuit filed by Hart against the film-maker in 1920, by which time Hart had finally achieved the earning power his status as Hollywood's top Western star and director commanded – a contract with Paramount for nine pictures at $200,000 each. The good times were here and Hart, like so many of his fellow Irish compatriots in Hollywood in those days, Owen Moore and Marshal Neilan among them, was determined to enjoy the success.

It was said that Hart 'fell in love' with most of his leading ladies and proposed marriage to just about all of them, including Winifred Westover, his co-star in *John Petticoats* who accepted the proposal. They married in December 1921 and were separated by May 1922. At the same time, Hart's films were losing the spark of authenticity and originality that had been his trademark, and he was beginning to fail at the box office. Paramount demanded that he give over control of the production of his films, which he refused. The clash led

Tough as old cowhide Irish-American silent screen cowboy star William S. Hart was one of the screen's first western heroes.

directly to his departure from the studio in 1925 to make his own films as an independent, a move that effectively marked the end of his film career.

He made one more film, *Tumbleweed* which was doomed at the box office because of a badly mishandled distribution arrangement. Hart died in 1946 without ever making another movie. He left the bulk of his estate to the County of Los Angeles with the stipulation that his home and the grounds of his ranch in Newhall, California, were to be used as a public park and museum. The home stands today as a tribute to this Irish-American film hero and as a museum of Western art and artifacts that Hart bequeathed to the people of Los Angeles.

CHAPTER 9

LOST AND FOUND IN HOLLYWOOD - THE ABBEY THEATRE

As Hollywood sought more and more reality and authenticity in the 1940s, the movie moguls stepped up the worldwide search for a new breed of acting talent that could bring to the screen renowned theatrical backgrounds. Broadway was mined — but so too were the great theatres of the world. To Hollywood came a new generation of Irish actor, a generation spawned of the country's first national theatre, the famed Abbey Players. It is one of the great inconsistencies of Irish history that the Irish — with their distinctive temperament, flair for self-expression and poetry — had no real tradition of drama. Yet Ireland has produced more writers and performers for its size than any other nation. The growth of Irish drama was stunted with the demise of the Old Gaelic Order, but with a resurgence of nationalist spirit, poetry, literature and theatre in the twilight years of the nineteenth century a new dramatic energy was born. This extraordinary artistic meld of art and nationalism was sowing the seeds for an infant Irish native theatre, The Abbey Theatre. Providing the great energy behind the renaissance were such literary and stage luminaries as W.B. Yeats, Lady Gregory, Sara Allgood, and J.M. Synge, the poet and playwright.

"We have a popular imagination that is fiery, magnificent and tender, so that those who wish to write start with a chance that is not given to writers in places where the spring-time of local life has been forgotten and the harvest is a memory only and the straw has been turned into bricks." — J.M. Synge

The fruit of this renaissance was plucked by Hollywood. And those who came from that illustrious Abbey stage to colonise the film town were easily the strangest misfits that Tinseltown has ever seen.

The gnome-like Irishman shuffled out of the laundry shop into the pounding summer heat of Sunset Boulevard in Hollywood to continue his quest. The battered tweed suit and cap that he was wearing would have been more appropriate for a chill Irish winter than the heat-wave that was choking him in Los Angeles. The man was none other than Barry

Fitzgerald, and he was on a quest for his clothes. He'd left them into some dry cleaning establishment or other on the Sunset strip and had completely forgotten which one.

Fitzgerald, the loveable little genius from Dublin's famed Abbey Theatre, the rogue priest from *Going My Way*, one of the biggest box office hits of 1944 (which co-starred Irish-American Bing Crosby) was spending his day wandering in and out of dry cleaning shops in the somewhat confusing new world he had found himself, far from his beloved native Dublin. The world and Hollywood had fallen in love with the diminutive actor and he was all at sea. Being a Hollywood movie star was new to him and so was Hollywood.

'He finds it all rather bewildering,' Fred Stanley wrote in the *New York Times* in 1945 of Fitzgerald's transplant from the boards of the Abbey to fame in Hollywood. 'He resents the disruption of his previously inconspicuous private life. He can't even browse in Los Angeles bookshops or join in a discussion with strangers at some out-of-the-way bar-room or drug store without being targeted as Father Fitzgibbon. His old clothes and cloth cap, which once kept him inconspicuous, now make him a marked man.'

Barry Fitzgerald, perhaps the most unlikely Irish star that Hollywood ever was home to, went on to win an Academy Award for the role of wily old twinkle-eyed Father Fitzgibbon, who made life a conundrum of frustration for the parish curate played by Crosby. His comment on winning the coveted honour was typical of the reluctant Hollywood recruit. "Although it's nice to know I'm getting along all right in my work… a man of my age likes as much peace and quiet as possible. If I have to go through another one of those things they'll probably discover me in Forest Lawn Cemetery."

Fitzgerald, who was fifty-six years old then, simply could not fathom what was happening to him. He was besieged by fan mail he had no idea what to do with, and was so engulfed by well-wishers and admirers calling to his home off Hollywood Boulevard that he regularly took flight. One of his favourite ports of refuge was the Hollywood home of another Irish expatriate, May Flo Gogarty, sister of the renowned Irish poet, author, politician and surgeon Oliver St John Gogarty. 'Hollywood just baffled Barry,' May Flo's daughter, the late Hollywood agent Maureen Oliver recalled once. 'He would come to our home and sit alone playing the piano for hours. But if anybody entered the room he would stop playing because he was too shy to continue.'

Oliver laughed as she remembered the displaced Abbey actor arriving at her mother's home 'in a terrible state and moaning, "I've lost all my clothes." He had taken them to a laundry but for the life of him he could not remember which one. We searched Hollywood for hours looking for his clothes, his entire wardrobe, but we never did find them. We had to lend him a suit that we dug up somewhere for him to wear to the studio because he did not have a stitch left but the old things he was standing up in. And that was at the time when he was making $75,000 a picture (then a top Hollywood salary range).'

The laundry lapse was probably not too surprising considering that the new Hollywood star, described by Tinseltown columnist Hedda Hopper as 'a gnome-like little man with shaggy eyebrows that defy gravity, training or barber shop cajolery' was gaining a reputation as by far the worst-dressed celebrity in the movie industry, whose stars in the day were pictures of sartorial elegance. He appears to have favoured tweeds (unpressed) and cloth caps. But what may have been an amusing if eccentric dress sense to some was clearly an offence in some high society quarters as Fitzgerald would discover to his amusement.

A great golfing enthusiast, Fitzgerald became a regular at a prestigious Santa Barbara club of which Avery Brundidge, former head of the Olympic Games Council, was president. Brundidge was sitting in the clubhouse one afternoon gazing out at the course when he spied an odd little figure in what he considered to be an appalling state of dress shuffling about. It was Fitzgerald. The offender was ordered off the course and out of the club by Brundidge, who didn't realise the shabby intruder was one of the biggest Hollywood celebrities of the day.

On another occasion the actor was invited to play tennis with Charles Chaplin. To be invited to Chaplin's lavish mansion was considered an 'A-list' invite. Unaware or uncaring of the social importance of an invitation to Chaplin's for tennis, Fitzgerald appeared, much to his host's chagrin, in a shaggy old sweater, shoes stained with motor oil from his motorcycle, and faded, yellow pants. Chaplin, decked out in gleaming whites, trounced Fitzgerald in straight sets. The two stars remained friends, but Fitzgerald was never invited to tennis at Chaplin's again.

For all of that, Hollywood loved the eccentric Irishman who in turn was fast assimilating into his new life. 'In Hollywood these days everyone it seems is excited about Barry Fitzgerald... (he) is in greater demand by the studios than any character has ever been in the history of cinema,' exclaimed the usually conservative *New York Times*.

It has been said that Fitzgerald's characterisations on screen have rarely been surpassed. His understanding of film was immense and he often transformed mundane scenes into magic moments. Such was the case in *Two Years Before the Mast* in which he played a ship's cook.

Barry Fitzgerald and Bing Crosby in *Going My Way* for which Fitzgerald received an historic two Oscar nominations for the one role – best supporting actor and best lead actor.

In one scene he is called upon to serve food to his bellicose captain who complains about the meal. Fitzgerald's character is called on to reply in a most insubordinate tone. They ran through the scene several times, but something just wasn't working. On the next take, instead of sticking with the scripted lines, Fitzgerald remained silent. He picked up the food, sniffed at it. Disdain was written on Fitzgerald's face and silent mutiny in his eyes. The scene was a take – it was brilliant.

The Hollywood party circuit may not have been his passion but he soon found other things to amuse him in his new life. 'Perhaps his most revealing hobby is cutting records of those radio advertising jingles,' observed a piece in *Collier's* (magazine). 'He plays these home-made records over and over, chuckling with glee at the inanities of the music and rhymes. He is making a collection of such pieces to send to Ireland to be played on the phonograph in a certain pub so that some of his old pals may enjoy this new American art form.'

It all seemed so many worlds away from the nine-to-five job as a Dublin civil servant that he held down until well into his middle years, while moonlighting at the Abbey as an actor with his brother Arthur Shields, who was equally lauded by Hollywood. Born in Dublin by the name of Joseph Shields on March 10th 1888, Barry Fitzgerald was recruited into the mundane world of government clerking upon finishing school and remained there until he was forty-one. Hardly the stuff from which Hollywood legends are made, but then very little about Barry Fitzgerald and his younger actor brother Arthur fitted any mould.

Fitzgerald, who came across his stage name through a print error on an early Abbey Players' bill, was ten years older than Arthur. The pair were inseparable as boys growing up in Dublin. The Shields family was involved with a local amateur drama group, The Kincora Players, with which the brothers got their first stage experience. But the first step to the professional footlights was taken by younger Arthur. The security of the civil service in those economically depressed and politically uncertain days kept the elder brother entrenched in his day job.

Arthur was working at Dublin publishing firm Maunsels, while going to acting classes at the Abbey Theatre in the evening. He eventually took up employment with the Abbey on a full time basis at a salary of £1 per week, a decent wage back in 1914. Barry followed Arthur to the Abbey.

The Abbey was a creative cradle for names that would be literary giants, William Butler Yeats, John Millington Synge, Padraig Colum, Sean O'Casey. Initially, Barry played walk-on parts to fill in the crowd scenes. Eventually he began to accept bigger parts. "But because he didn't want his supervisor at the day job to know what he was up to he asked the company to bill him as Barry Fitzpatrick. A printer got it wrong and the name Barry Fitzgerald appeared on the program," recalled Dublin journalist Jack Jones, a nephew of the brothers.

For seventeen years Fitzgerald led this double life until he was forced to make a decision. The Abbey was touring to London with *The Silver Tassie*, a play by a major new Irish writer, Sean O'Casey, and Fitzgerald held a leading role. Finally, but not without weighing all the pros and cons, this shining light of a great theatre resigned his clerking job.

But the brothers' lives had not been confined to the theatre in those days of turmoil in Ireland. Arthur could thank the Abbey for indirectly landing him in the thick of the Easter

Rising of 1916. Arthur was a volunteer in the Irish Citizen Army and had been issued with a handgun, Jones recounted: 'In a fit of confused logic that he never could fully explain he decided that the best place to hide the revolver that was issued to him was beneath the stage of the Abbey,' Jones would recall. 'When the call to arms came he rushed to the theatre and had the dickens of a time trying to get to his gun so that when he reached the meeting place for his particular group of volunteers they had already departed.' An officer immediately ordered the young actor into a company of volunteers that was headed for the General Post Office in the heart of Dublin. This was to be the scene of the fiercest fighting and the place from which one of the leaders of the Rising, Padraig Pearse, would proclaim to a staggered populace that Ireland, under force of arms was now a Free State. Eighteen-year-old Shields was in the thick of it. 'I got off a few shots through a window but to the best of my knowledge I never hit anybody,' he confided to his nephew years later.

Shields was rounded up with most of his fellow volunteers and interned in a prison camp in Wales until a general truce was called in 1922. "The important people were still kept in jail. The unimportant people like myself were let loose," he informed an American journalist in later life. But for now it was back to the Abbey – and to more battles.

The renaissance of Irish drama that the Shields brothers were embroiled in had kicked up a fiery young playwright out from the cracks of the cobblestones of Dublin. His name was Sean O'Casey. And Irish audiences were none too happy with how this working class writer saw them. "I remember the time we put on *The Plough and the Stars* (by O'Casey) in 1926. The second-night audience threw things so steadily it was almost worth your life to go out on the stage. We acted around the missiles for two acts but in the third act the barrage got too heavy for us and we finally ran the curtain down," Shields recounted of those tempestuous days. "W.B. Yeats made a magnificent speech, telling the audience that they were disgracing themselves in the eyes of the world…"

But even if one fiercely conservative element of Irish society was disgracing itself with violent outbursts at such unthinkable contentions as the existence of prostitutes and sex out of wedlock in Ireland, being put about by the Abbey Players, the world of theatre beyond Ireland didn't seem to care. This valiant troupe of actors, writers, poets, artists and dreamers had wrenched a new style of theatre from a long sleeping spirit, a minimalist method of acting that stressed mood, expression and form as much as it did the golden dialogue of its writers. By the 1920s the Abbey Players were being invited to tour around the world, which is how the brothers first came to America. Whistle-stop tours of the United States became a regular feature for the Abbey Players. Shields delighted in telling of one stop in Portland, Oregon, when the company was so anxious to catch a train to the next venue that the scenery was thrown eight stories from a window to the snow-covered ground to save time. "The audience was requested to remain in the theatre to avoid falling objects," the actor recounted.

But the brothers' first American screen appearance would not come until 1936 when the Irish-American director John Ford brought them from Ireland to make his screen version of O'Casey's *The Plough and the Stars*. "The reward was six weeks at $750 a week – more money than we in Ireland believed the mints produced," Barry Fitzgerald remembered. "I intended going on from there to the South Seas and around the world. But just as I was oiling up the bicycle and packing the other shirt, Mary Pickford put me under a one-year contract – and never used me. I have been in Hollywood ever since."

How Green Was My Valley (1941) Directed by John Ford. Shown from left: Donald Crisp (as Mr Gwilym Morgan), Sara Allgood (as Mrs Beth Morgan)

Following his year of inactivity under contract to Pickford, the work began to flow in for Fitzgerald. Irish-American director Leo McCarey cast him in the role of the parish priest in *Going My Way*. He had seen Fitzgerald years earlier when the Abbey had visited Broadway with Paul Vincent Carroll's classic *The White Steed*. McCarey had been so impressed with the actor's work that he had "filed me away for future reference". This was the beginning of a peculiar relationship between the eccentric actor and Hollywood, in which Fitzgerald carved out for himself an island of privacy, surrounded himself with mementos of Dublin and held an open house for any acquaintance from home, or acquaintance of an acquaintance, that would call. He shunned the town's high society parties, dressed and spoke pretty much as he pleased, while remaining one of the industry's highest paid and sought-after actors for many years. Arthur was not so quick to settle, but in 1944, more because of precarious health and the need to live in a warm climate, Arthur set up permanent residence a few blocks from his brother in Hollywood with his wife Aideen O'Connor, also of the Abbey. The film town embraced the brothers. Their most recognised film was of course John Ford's Irish romantic ditty *The Quiet Man* with John Wayne and Maureen O'Hara. Fitzgerald played the roguish matchmaker while Shields was the wily Protestant clergyman. The brothers also appeared together in Ford's *Long Voyage Home*. Other Hollywood roles for Shields included *Drums Along the Mohawk* with Henry Fonda and Claudette Colbert, and *Lady Godiva* with Maureen O'Hara. But others from the Abbey would not find Hollywood so generous a host. The legendary Sara Allgood was a case in point.

'Sara Allgood was a great – a very great – stage actress, who managed to transform many poor feature films in which she appeared into works of art,' wrote one of the most respected film historians of our day, Anthony Slide of this Abbey luminary, whom Hollywood tormented into an abyss of despair.

Allgood, known to her friends as Sally, was born in Dublin on October 31st 1893 into a family that might have been considered 'comfortable' in those days. Her father provided for his eight children through his job as a proofreader with a publishing firm. She was educated at the Marlborough Street Training College in Dublin, which she left at the age of fourteen full of dreams of becoming an actress like her idol Sarah Bernhardt. It would have been a heady dream for a working-class girl in the Dublin of the day, were it not for the existence of a small amateur drama group called the National Theatre Society that was staging works drawn from Irish history. The Society was later to merge with W.B. Yeats and Lady Gregory's Irish Literary Theatre to become The Abbey. The acclaimed Irish poet Padraig Colum would vividly remember his first sight of the teenage Allgood in her first role with the Society in Yeats's *The King's Threshold*.

"I recall one evening when some young men and women, all with office or workshop employments, gathered in a small hall in a side street in Dublin to make a third attempt to gain an audience of a few hundred for plays dealing with Irish life and tradition. Benches had been put together, a platform had been built, and amateurs… were assembled for a rehearsal of a new play by William Butler Yeats," the poet told. 'Who is the new girl?' someone asked referring to Allgood. "The new recruit had dark hair parted in the centre and a face that somehow had a doll-like contour," Colum recollected. "Suddenly she had taken on an extraordinary dignity. The voice was resonant; it had a deep and moving quality. And the girl was making something significant of what she had to do. I saw Yeats turn to W.G. Fay (a key founding member of the Abbey and that play's director) (and say), 'Fay, you have an actress there.'"

Allgood would become one of the great Abbey actors, hailed by theatre critics world-wide for her creations of some of the immortal characters that would be born of O'Casey, Yeats and Synge, most notably the title role of Juno, the poverty-stricken but proud wife and mother in O'Casey's classic work of tenement life in Dublin, *Juno and the Paycock*. She would later reprise the role on screen under the direction of Alfred Hitchcock in a British production that would pave the way for Allgood's call to Hollywood and to a way of life for which she was utterly unprepared.

By now an internationally recognised actress, a veteran of the London and Broadway stages and with several British films to her credit, including Hitchcock's *Blackmail*, Allgood was summoned to Hollywood for the pivotal role as mother to Lady Emma Hamilton in the classic *That Hamilton Woman*. This "earnest" person, as the poet Padraig Colum had described her, an actress who held her art above all, came to a Hollywood that in 1939 was perhaps at its most capricious, and deserving of its new moniker 'Tinseltown'. A new word had entered the lingo; that word, as Allgood would learn to her eternal regret, was 'bankability'.

Allgood could never come to terms with the fact that her talent would now take second place to her drawing power at the box office when it came to the casting process. For a moment fickle Hollywood had the welcome mat out for the Abbey actress, and briefly she had her hour in the arclight. 'The delay in Miss Allgood's arrival in American film is strange,' piped the *New York Herald Tribune* following the release of *That Hamilton Woman* in 1941. 'Consider these facts. She has an international reputation on the stage. Hollywood has never had enough good actresses of her type, and Miss Allgood for years has been interested in doing film.'

Her most singular triumph came with a major role later that same year in John Ford's screen adaptation of *How Green Was My Valley* co-starring Barry Fitzgerald and a rising Irish screen star Maureen O'Hara. Allgood was nominated for an Oscar for her work in the film which garnered no fewer than six Academy Awards that year. Then something happened that is simply inexplicable. Hollywood shut the door in Allgood's face.

Despite her monumental talent, glowing praise from the critics and an Oscar nomination, the offers of good roles for the now middle-aged actress dwindled to a trickle. "Sally went to Hollywood with high hopes. Being the great artist that she was it was a great shock to her, to say the least, to be treated in a high-handed manner," the actress's niece, Mrs Pauline Page, confided to Anthony Slide, one-time director of the Margaret Herrick Library of the Academy of Motion Picture Arts & Sciences. "I'll never forget one thing she said to me when I was in her beautiful Spanish home in Beverly Hills. She hadn't been getting much work and Mr Bernie (Allgood's agent) was urging her to give a big party and invite important people to it. Sally was dreadfully depressed and later said to me, 'I could never do a thing like that. I could never prostitute my art.' Another thing she said to me, 'When you go back to your home and your family, you can think of me sitting alone… afraid to go out for fear I should miss a call to work.'"

Allgood did play some small parts in a number of movies, usually for 20th Century Fox, after that but the characters were mostly clichéd Irish maids or old Irish mothers, roles which never allowed her to display her true worth on screen. Her final role in Hollywood came in *Cheaper By The Dozen* (1950), a 20th Century Fox production. "The salary is cut to the bone, but no matter, it's activity, and that's the main thing," Allgood wrote to a friend, Gabrielle Fallon, in Dublin. It would be her last letter home. A heart attack took her that same year as she 'waited for the phone to ring' in Hollywood.

'For those who saw her even once on the screen or on the actual stage, the announcement of the death of Sara Allgood is bound to leave a deep sense of loss,' lamented Padraig Colum.

If Allgood had become a victim of that all too common affliction that continues to bedevil the industry today – a dearth of strong roles for mature actresses – her male colleagues from the Abbey had no such torments. The brothers Fitzgerald and Shields were working in major roles regularly, as was another member of the Gaelic sanctum, Dudley Digges, during the 1940s. Though Digges, also a founding member of the Abbey, landed in Hollywood as a mature, reluctant visitor of fifty-one years, he went on to star and feature in more than fifty movies, including the 1930 version of *Mutiny on the Bounty* and a 1931 production of *The Maltese Falcon*.

Born in Dublin in 1879, Digges got his first training at the Abbey which he joined in 1901 and where he and Allgood formed a lifelong friendship. Barry Fitzgerald revered Digges whom he credited for encouraging him to take those first walk-on roles at the Abbey so many years before.

Digges was one of the first of the Abbey troupe to emigrate to the U.S. when he joined the Manhattan Theatre and later became a central figure in the formation of the famous New York Theatre Guild in 1919. Appearing in more than 3,500 performances with the Guild, Digges was a lauded Broadway actor, praised for his dynamic stage presence and remarkable voice, a gift that Hollywood craved most when the talkies arrived in the late 1920s. To its horror, the movie industry discovered that the voices of many famous silent-screen names were completely unsuitable for the talking pictures. Hollywood careers were crashing left and right as swashbuckling actors squeaked lines in high-pitched nasal tones and beautiful sirens muttered indistinct words in heavily accented European or Bronx accents. When the call went out to from Hollywood for 'actors who could speak lines,' Digges was among the first recruits.

But the instant fame that Digges achieved in the Hollywood of the Thirties and Forties with its glitzy premieres, industry parties and carefully managed hierarchical system did not sit easily with this balding, somewhat rotund and mature stage thespian. He joined his fellow Abbey veterans nightly in homely get-togethers, mostly at Fitzgerald's house, and surrounded himself with books, mostly Irish classics. A constant disappointment to journalists seeking headlines, Digges told one writer, "I'm really a dull fellow. I've managed to get through life without important or exciting incident. What I have to show I show upon the stage. I don't have adventures and I don't make headlines." But he did make movies, great movies, with such milestones as *The General Dies at Dawn* (1936), *Valiant is the Word for Carrie* (1936), and *Raffles* (1940) among his myriad credits.

'Ireland is his first love, the stage his second,' *The New York Times* wrote of Digges in 1944, so it was perhaps fitting that his final role came not in Hollywood but on Broadway in the original production of the Eugene O'Neill classic *The Iceman Cometh*, in which he created the role of the saloon keeper. One evening during the run of the play he confided in a friend, "Do you know that this play gives me about forty-three years in the New York Theatre?" He never mentioned Hollywood. "I've just been sitting here thinking how lucky I have been to keep with good things and good people." He died of a stroke just a few months after the final curtain of the production following a long bout of failing health. He was sixty-eight. An obituary in the *Daily News* said simply, 'He delighted American audiences for forty-three years with his stage and screen characterisations.'

If Digges felt out-of-step in Hollywood in his day there was one place in the film town he could always call home, and that was Barry Fitzgerald's house. A centre of hospitality for many a friend from the old days in Dublin, Fitzgerald and Shields lived most of their later lives in California. While Barry stayed on in Hollywood, Arthur set up home in Santa Barbara, California, which he festooned with pictures of Dublin, old Abbey posters and playbills.

The brothers remained inseparable in their self-imposed exile, but parted ways when it came to leisure activities. Barry was a motorcycle fiend and loved nothing more than gunning his Harley Davidson through the Hollywood Hills with an Iroquois Native American pal, Gus Tallon. Arthur, on the other hand, preferred the more leisurely pursuit of stamp collecting. Common to both was their love of old friends and they continued for many years to provide open house for many others from home who would wander through the film town. One such was a fiendishly handsome young actor from Cork, Kieron O'Annrachain, known to the world of international theatre and film by this time as Kieron Moore, Playing the dark-eyed bully Pony Sugrue, he gave Sean Connery almost as good as he got in that Walt Disney celebration of Ireland of the shamrocks, *Darby O'Gill and the Little People* with Jimmy O'Dea playing the king of the Leprechauns.

Moore, another who first trod the boards professionally at the Abbey, was born in Skibbereen in County Cork, the son of a fiercely nationalistic Gaelic-speaking family. It was an inheritance that burned deep. "Even today, although I think in English now, I say my prayers in Irish," Moore would confess to Walt Disney publicist Joe Reddy many years later when he called Hollywood his home in the 1950s.

It was Moore's passion for the Gaelic language that led him to the Abbey Theatre when he was still in his teens. He wrote, produced and acted in an Irish language play that went

Abbey actor Kieron Moore in *Anna Karenina* (1948) with Vivien Leigh (as Anna Karenina)

on in a small theatre in Dublin just around the corner from the Abbey. The production closed within the week and Moore and his backers were out of pocket to the tune of £30, a vast sum in a city where a working man brought home £2 a week, if he was lucky. In a desperate, almost naïve attempt to recoup the enormous loss for his backers, Moore, who was then just seventeen years old, fired off a letter to the Irish Taoiseach Eamon De Valera, explaining the predicament. De Valera, a voice in the movement to restore the Gaelic language, sent Moore a personal cheque for £30 by return mail.

Subsequently he was summoned in to see Frank Dermody, director of the Abbey. "The message I got was to come in and audition for a secondary role in an Irish language production. It was the first time I met Frank Dermody (a powerful figure in Irish theatre), and I was terrified."

Moore was cast in leading role in the production. "I was good, but not fantastically so," Moore remembered of that career-defining moment. The role led to the offer of a full-time job at the Abbey, with Moore playing lead roles and bit parts ("there was no star system at the Abbey," Moore explained) in a variety of productions from William Butler Yeats's *Kathleen Ni Houlihan* to *The Lost Leader*, a Gaelic version of *Tristan and Isolde*, and *The Rugged Path* in which Robert Clark, head of Associated British Picture Corporation spotted him. A summons to a screen test in London followed – and that's when the trouble began.

Moore threw some clothes in an old suitcase and was off to London. The British film company was so impressed by Moore's presence in the film test that he was offered a seven-year contract. The excited seventeen-year-old sent word home to Ireland of the great news and received by return a flat 'permission refused' dispatch from his father. Still legally a minor, Moore could not sign that passport to the silver screen without his father's consent. Bitterly disappointed but now utterly consumed with determination to pursue his acting career, he doggedly planted himself in London.

He scraped by with work in repertory theatre and managed to get some film work. His performance in a production of Sean O'Casey's *Red Roses For Me* earned him a contract with Alexander Korda's film company. This time there was no parental veto barring his way and Moore was no longer the gangly youth who had left Dublin with a dream and a cardboard suitcase. He was a swarthy, tall, confident leading man who knew his way around a film sound stage. 'He has dark brown curly hair and large liquid eyes. Although his name and upbringing are as Irish as the shamrock, he could be mistaken for a Spaniard, an Italian, a Frenchman or a South American,' one enamoured journalist wrote of him.

His reputation grew on the British screen, with such films as *Anna Karenina* in which he co-starred with Vivien Leigh, and *A Man About The House* in which he played an Italian. Moore quickly drew the attention of Hollywood. Roles in American films incuded 20th Century Fox's *David and Bathsheba* and Columbia's *Ten Tall Men*, and of course Walt Disney's *Darby O'Gill and the Little People*. Though Moore was feted by the studios and had regular encounters with Hollywood, he never settled down in the film town, preferring to commute from his home in England, much in the same way as a bevy of other former Abbey actors whom Hollywood briefly courted.

Among these of course is Jackie McGowran, the rubber-faced genius who was the embodiment of the Beckett actor on stage and who showcased his talent for comedy and off-the-wall characters in such films as *Darby O'Gill and the Little People* and the Warner Brothers-Seven Arts Release *Two Times Two* with Gene Wilder and Donald Sutherland. More substantial films included *Doctor Zhivago* and *Lord Jim*. He also appeared in Ford's Irish movies *Young Cassidy* and *The Quiet Man*.

Another fleeting Abbey visitor to Hollywood was Denis O'Dea, who was married to fellow Abbey luminary Siobhan McKenna. O'Dea played mostly character roles in the Hollywood productions in which he appeared and his credits include *The Informer, Odd Man Out, The Mark of Cain* and the role of Doctor Livesey in the RKO-Walt Disney Technicolor version of *Treasure Island*.

29-130

The story of the Abbey players in Hollywood and their diverse experiences with the siren would not be complete without mention of Una O'Connor. The Abbey graduate, born Agnes Teresa McGlade in Belfast in 1880, had made her mark on the London and New York stages before arriving in the film town in 1924 to recreate for the screen her stage role as the housekeeper in Noel Coward's *Cavalcade* for Fox Films. O'Connor was to prove no less an enigma in Hollywood than any of her fellow Abbey players.

A curious biography put out by RKO Studios in 1946 would say of her, 'When she went (from Hollywood) to New York in 1945 to do a stage play, she lost her apartment and since has lived at a hotel in Santa Monica. She drives a car back and forth to the studio. She is a teetotaler and never serves alcohol at any of the informal gatherings at her home. The friends she assembles at her home don't play cards either but spend their time in the discussion of art, books, and topics of the day… Steak and kidney pie is one of Miss O'Connor's favourite dishes. She cannot swim, but bathes in the ocean and loves to lie on the sand and let the breakers toss her about. She has a keen sense of humour, is reserved, but friendly if someone else takes the first advances; likes to have her fortune told with tea leaves; is never lonely as long as she can be outdoors in beautiful scenery or has a good book, believes that gremlin is a modern name for the Irish "little people".'

O'Connor, who died in New York in 1959 aged seventy-eight, included among her credits such films as *Random Harvest, The Plough and the Stars, Lloyds of London, This Land is Mine, The Sea Hawk* and *The Bells of St Mary's*. She also appeared in numerous films by horror genre director James Whale including *The Invisible Man* and *Bride of Frankenstein*.

J.M. Kerrigan was another former Abbey actor to whom Hollywood beckoned. First appearing in Ford's *The Informer* playing the Dublin joxer who befriends Victor McLaglen's Gypo Nolan after he's been paid for informing on his best friend, Kerrigan settled in Hollywood permanently in 1935. Kerrigan was assigned mostly character roles, including parts in numerous John Ford films. He also appeared in *Gone With The Wind*.

The Abbey Theatre clearly was a breeding ground for a diverse group of passionate actors who would come to Hollywood, some to stay and thrive, some to pine and wilt. But all of them, in their own way, left an indelible imprint in the town's legendary history.

◀ Darling of the Abbey stage and lauded screen star Una O'Connor in *Bride of Frankenstein* with Boris Karloff.

CHAPTER 10

ON THE RUN IN HOLLYWOOD — GEORGE BRENT

Clark Gable, Bette Davies, James Cagney, Carole Lombard, Joan Crawford – these names from Hollywood's 'Golden Years' heyday have become part of the lexicon of Americana. Their marquee names are today associated with the apex of Hollywood's most fruitful years. Cast into this potpourri of talent was an Irishman who would come to symbolise the melding of cultures and accents that would be the lifeblood of the movies. He was the greatest movie star of his day. His American accent was indefinable – yet perfect. He was a big, handsome and talented lad from Galway… and he has been credited as one of the most important screen actors of his era. His name was George Brendan Nolan – better known as George Brent. The Hollywood legend would confess that he was born in Galway – and was an IRA man on the run.

The Irish Sea was turbulent beneath an overcast night sky. A fishing trawler complained on her moorings in the swell. Her skipper strained his seaman's eyes to pierce the dark along the harbour wall. He was anxious for any sign of the special passenger he'd been ordered to spirit out of Ireland. Clandestine night boardings on small boats by nameless men on the run were not unusual in those troubled times following the country's War of Independence in the early 1920s. A man appeared on the pier above the vessel.

"Are we set?" The voice was that of a youth.

"Get aboard and be quiet about it," the skipper ordered.

The young man nimbly jumped on deck and a crewman tossed off the moorings. The noise of her throbbing engine was drowned by the wind and surf as the trawler moved slowly out to sea.

The passenger was a Galway boy with a head of waving black hair and a sturdy, square-set jaw. His name was George Brendan Nolan and he was fleeing Ireland a wanted man. One day in the not too distant future he would be safe, rich and one of Hollywood's busiest and most talked about movie stars – known to the world as George Brent. That at least is how Brent would recall his departure from Ireland.

Brent, a big handsome lug of an actor, who once had a brief fling with Dublin's Abbey Theatre, was Warner Bros. Studios' answer to Clark Gable, rival MGM's resident star in the 1930s. It has been said that Brent's career in Hollywood was overshadowed by Gable and by his other screen rival Tyrone Power, whose great-grandfather was a popular Irish-born comedian. Power was named for the family's original home in County Tyrone. Power, a dark-haired, tall 'Adonis' of the screen, is best remembered for such screen successes as *Blood and Sand*, *The Sun Also Rises*, *Lloyds of London*, *The Rains Came* (in which George Brent co-starred) and *Witness for the Prosecution*, his last picture.

Brent's starring roles throughout a long and illustrious Hollywood career are legion, not least of which is his portrayal of the surgeon who falls in love with a dying Bette Davis in the classic romantic tragedy *Dark Victory*. He shared star billing in his movies with such Irish-American screen legends as James Cagney, Pat O'Brien and Merle Oberon (whose surname was taken from her father – O'Brien), as well as Barbara Stanwyck, Joan Fontaine, Hedy Lamarr and Ruth Chatterton, whom he famously married. Yet, somewhere on Hollywood's twisting road, the name George Brent has faded from the list of legends upon which he more than earned his place.

Born in Shannonbridge near Galway in 1904 he was orphaned at the age of eleven and was shipped out to New York with his sister, his elder by three years, to live with an aunt. Howard Sharpe claimed in a series of articles about the star's life that was published with Brent's cooperation and approval by *Photoplay* magazine in 1939, that Brent returned to Ireland during the Civil War. The article reads, 'By the time he was eighteen and a fully fledged New York kid, the 'Troubles' back in Ireland had reached a bloody pitch and he decided he had to go home to play his part.' That's where the mysterious figure of a Catholic priest, whom Brent would refer to in the telling of his story as 'Father Dan,' enters the story. Father Dan, "a brilliant Irishman with the cause of Eire as the main purpose of his life," as Brent described him, invited Brent to join him on a journey back to Ireland. The priest, whom Brent had met and befriended at meetings of an Irish cultural group called the Pearson Club, had accepted a teaching post in Dublin. Brent, according to his own telling, had a brief stint at Trinity College before being expelled after a "shindig". Then came a sojourn at The Abbey "lugging props" and appearing in walk-on parts, Brent would recount. Sometime later, according Brent, he was recruited as a "dispatch carrier" for Michael Collins. He would claim that his involvement with Collins resulted in a warrant for his arrest being issued and as a consequence he was forced to flee the country on a fishing trawler. Twenty years later he would say that he again returned home in the 1940s and found a most inhospitable atmosphere. "We went back to Ireland, just outside Dublin, and rented a lovely old house just a few years ago. We lasted two months. We almost froze to death. And you couldn't get anybody to do anything, everything was mañana. I shipped my Rolls Royce over and they scratched the doors; they thought it belonged to a British official. I had a helluva time getting it repaired."

Brent had come a long way from the day when he first applied for a job with a touring theatre company in New York and was taken on, principally because of his imposing stature, good looks and a commanding voice. Changing his name to Brent, an adaptation of his middle name Brendan, he honed his craft in more than three hundred productions with various stock companies before the first big break came. He was cast in the lead role of Abie in *Abie's Irish Rose* with the stock company. His reviews were glowing and caught the attention of Hollywood. But his first year in Hollywood was a disappointment. Director Erich von Stroheim wanted him for the lead role in a major movie but the studio chose an actor with more screen exposure. Then Brent was tipped for the lead in another major movie, *The Man Who Came Back*: he lost the role when the studio decided to make the movie as a vehicle for Charles Farrell and Janet Gaynor. Brent was getting a taste of how fickle Hollywood could be, but he chose to tough it out and accepted numerous second-rate roles without complaint. Brent was hired ('loaned out') to do a 'read in' on a movie called *The Rich Are Always With Us*. He was not testing for a role himself, but was merely there to feed lines to the actors who were auditioning for the Warner Bros. movie.

The following day, as the casting director studied the tests, Ruth Chatterton, star of the picture, bustled into the screening room, announcing that she was there to personally peruse her potential leading men. The projector flickered and George Brent's image appeared on the screen. "Oh, that's just the feed man," somebody mumbled dismissively. But Chatterton, the highest-paid star of the day, had already seen enough. "Where has this man been all my life?" she shouted.

Warner Bros. wanted to know the same thing! The studio decided that this "Big Irish fellow" could be their answer to MGM's big star Clark Gable. Brent was offered a seven-year contract at $250 a week. "I was flat broke and it was a heaven sent deal," Brent recalled. Like most seven-year contract players working within the Hollywood studio system in those days, Brent found that he was on an exhausting treadmill. Though he was cast in a pivotal role alongside Chatterton in *The Rich Are Always With Us*, he was required to simultaneously play in another picture being made at the studio. Brent would never forget this exploitation.

"You signed those seven-year contracts and they had you. There was nothing on earth you could do about it, nothing," he would complain. "For years, I was working six days a week, and until midnight on Saturdays if the film was behind schedule. It wasn't until a few years later, when I was established, that I would say 'No more night work and never again on Saturdays.' And you never had any script options: you were sent a script on Thursday, you began rehearsals on Monday, you started shooting on Tuesday, you just didn't have any time. I was making *The Rich Are Always With Us* at the same time that I was making *So Big*."

Brent's shooting schedule that year (1932) continued at the same hectic pace, with the studio starring him in no fewer than six pictures, including the memorable *Miss Pinkerton* which saw him playing an heroic detective opposite Joan Blondell. But 1932 was a banner year for Brent in other respects. Hollywood society was all abuzz when he disappeared with Ruth Chatterton. There was pandemonium at the studio head office. The cry went up, 'Where was their most expensive starlet? Where was George Brent? Could the rumours be true? Were they together? Who could have let this happen?' Well, a Justice of the Peace had allowed it. Brent and Chatterton had run away to be married. The event caused a sensation in Hollywood. Brent, despite his growing screen success was still a 'bit' contract player on just $250 a week. Chatterton was a star and earning well in excess of $10,000 a week. But the publicity provided a boost for Brent's career. His appearance with his new wife (whom he would later divorce and then re-marry three times), just a month after the wedding in *The Crash* – a movie set around the Wall Street Crash – thrust him into the limelight. Despite the publicity the studio continued to cast him in mediocre pictures. Curiously, Brent would not cast off his second-rate status until a divorce from Chatterton three years later. The movie that marked this elevation was *Living on Velvet* in which he co-starred with Kay Francis. This was the first of a series of Brent/Francis pictures made at Warner Bros., which included such vehicles as *Stranded*, and *The Goose and the Gander*. One critic wrote of *Living on Velvet*: 'Mr Brent's penchant for comedy is an excellent antidote for Miss Francis's penchant for heavy tragedy. He keeps her from taking her art too seriously.'

It seemed that Brent's persistence and sheer good luck had finally paid off… though Brent had little regard for luck. "You hear too much of 'the luck of the Irish,' for, believe me, they run into as much 'unluck' as anybody else," he informed one interviewer. He went on to make six films with Barbara Stanwyck over the next few years, including *Baby Face* and *The Lady Eve*. But perhaps the highlight of his career was played out alongside Bette Davis with whom he co-starred in eleven films over a remarkably productive twelve-year span. Among the most acclaimed of these films are the classics *Jezebel* and *Dark Victory* which co-starred another Irish screen great, Geraldine Fitzgerald. The fact that Brent found himself co-starring with another Irish actor is not at all remarkable, considering the galaxy of Gaels who populated Hollywood in the 1930s and 1940s. He also co-starred with Irish Americans James Cagney and Pat O'Brien in the enduring screen tale of America's Irish war heroes in *The Fighting 69th*.

The star roles were now pouring in – *The Spiral Staircase*, *The Great Lie*, *42nd Street* and *Till We Meet Again* – and Brent had gained the reputation as the hardest-working actor in Hollywood, 'a solid, dependable performer,' as the *New York Times* described him. "At one point I made thirteen films in eleven months," Brent boasted, adding, "and then there were the interviews and nightclubs…" And Brent was no shirker of the nightclub circuit. He may have worked hard, but he played hard too. 'The actor has at various times escorted a great many of Hollywood's most beautiful and charming women,' wrote one of the town's gossip columnists, around the time that Brent was making one of his best-known movies. But Brent was nothing if not discreet about his romantic life. 'He has probably been father-confessor to more beautiful women than any man in Hollywood. George is so much safer than a diary – no one can ever pump him – if you get too inquisitive about things, George

Two great Irish stars of the Hollywood screen Geraldine Fitzgerald and George Brent in *Dark Victory*. Pictured with Bette Davis (shaking hands with Brent) and Fitzgerald in cocked hat.

George Brent
(right) was the most
unlikely Irish-born
movie star of all. He
hid a secret past
behind a perfect
American accent.
George Brent in one
of his best-known
Hollywood films,
Jezebel with Bette
Davis and Henry
Fonda.

just looks at you and through you and past you – and you gain nothing. In this day and age, there is something quaint and old worldish about a man who behaves that way. Today it's sophisticated to spout. Tearing down people's characters has replaced dominoes as an after-dinner amusement,' wrote Hollywood columnist David Hanna. 'George Brent has never gotten into trouble by talking too much.'

Brent's discretion was perhaps as much admired by his peers as his talent. 'Bette Davis has been heard to say that she is always delighted to work with George. He is so good-natured and no matter what you may say in an off-guard moment (to him) you can forget it. There are never any repercussions. George has the habit of forgetting – in fact he is the perfect forgetter,' declared Hanna. 'During the period when George was so attentive to Bette and the news hounds spread every conceivable rumour about the pair, George's silence aroused the admiration of a great many Hollywoodites, especially Bette's friends. The result is that George and Bette are still the best of friends with a mutual regard for each other that is hard to match,' the writer added.

Aside from *Jezebel* and *Dark Victory* (both with Davis) and *Till We Meet Again*, Brent's films didn't win him the fame that Gable and Power enjoyed. Years before the stardom days Brent and Gable had appeared together in a Broadway play. Men's fashion of the day dictated the hirsute facial look and slicked-back hair. So the clean-shaven Gable was intrigued by the attention his pal Brent was receiving by way of a well-groomed moustache and decided to grow one himself. Brent would forever claim that Gable stole his moustache to make it in the movies.

In his time Brent was one of the most lauded Irish screen stars in Hollywood. There was never a trace of his Irish accent on screen and he never played any stereotypical 'Irish' role. George Brent retired from films in 1954 to spend a brief period raising horses back in Ireland with his fifth wife Janet. He ended his days living alone in San Diego with a small black dog named Skippy as his only companion. Some nights, if one of his movies was playing on television he would sit up to watch. "But only if they are on at a reasonable hour," Brent commented in old age.

"God," Brent once said in retirement, not long before his death from natural causes at the age of seventy-five in 1979. "There must be fifty (of my films) I haven't seen. But looking back, I'm glad I was in the business then and not now. George Raft talked me into doing an automobile commercial a few years ago. He said it would be an easy day's shooting. It was the hardest two days I ever worked in my life."

CHAPTER 11

HOLLYWOOD'S 'GLORIFIED MISSUS' – GREER GARSON

It was the late 1930s: Hollywood was at the zenith of its 'golden age'. It was boom time for the studio czars, the talkies had come a decade before and by now movie sound was a perfected art. Hollywood movies were being exported to more countries than ever before. The search for talent continued to expand. Hollywood was no longer waiting for immigrant actors, directors and talent to shuffle up to its door. It was now actively head hunting. London, where the natives spoke a passable form of American, was a particular favourite of the studio movie moguls.

Louis B. Mayer was in a particularly buoyant mood over dinner that evening in London. His full cheeks were a happy pink as he enthused about his beloved Hollywood and all it would offer his guest, a stunningly attractive young stage actress called Greer Garson. Mayer, head of Metro-Goldwyn-Mayer Studios, was expansive of gesture over the table as he painted a picture of bliss and success that was in store for his ravishing dinner guest.

It was late in the 1930s and the Hollywood 'star system' was in its heyday. The call to Hollywood for a London stage actor was a heady temptation. Garson toyed with her food as she listened to the studio mogul. That evening's performance in her latest West End show, *Old Music* had left her too exhausted to eat and focus on her host's conversation at the same time.

"Greer, you belong in Hollywood," Mayer insisted.

The actress considered this for a moment. She thought of her mother, who was not getting any younger and was in poor health. Then there was the fact that she had worked exceedingly hard to get to this pinnacle of success on the London stage. Did she really want to abandon civilised society for Hollywood?

Garson thanked her host most profusely for a wonderful evening, for the compliments, for his interest, and refused his offer of a magic carpet ride to Hollywood. Mayer would of course have his way in the end. He convinced Garson that the climate of Southern California would be most beneficial to her mother's health. Greer Garson came to Hollywood, one of its most reluctant émigrés, but destined to become one of its most enduring and respected stars. Mayer's battle to convince his latest discovery to come to

Hollywood, which went on long after that night at dinner, would make dinner tales for years to come.

Greer Garson was born in 1904 to Nina and George Garson. She spent her childhood in County Down, where as a seven-year-old she once created a huge scare for her parents and neighbours when she went missing from the family home. The crisis ended when the manager of a touring theatrical company performing nearby delivered the missing one safely back to her family. The child had decided to become an actress and her 'interview' with the bemused theatre manager had made her late for tea. Many years later, Garson would identify that moment as the beginning of her theatrical ambitions. "I did a recitation at a town hall in Ireland. And everyone applauded. And smiled at me. And that was all the encouragement I needed."

Upon her father's untimely death when Garson was still a child, the family moved to London where Garson grew up. She was a particularly bright scholar and after secondary school wanted to attend the Royal Academy of Dramatic Arts in London. Her mother vetoed the idea and Garson ultimately graduated from London and Grenoble Universities. Following a brief period working at a London advertising firm, Garson signed on with a Birmingham theatre company. Here she gained some basic training in stage craft before being cast in the role of a scantily clad 'Island Girl' in George Bernard Shaw's *Too Good To Be True*, which the company was taking on tour around England… in winter. The severely underdressed trainee actress was struck down by tonsillitis and was rushed to a country hospital while an understudy took over her role for the rest of the tour. Three weeks later, fully recovered from her illness, Garson headed for London. She was jobless and broke. As Garson would recount years later, she was taking tea in the Women's Club in London one afternoon when a fashionably dressed lady approached her. "I hear you are an actress," was the stranger's opening remark. "I have written a play and I believe you are the girl for the lead role."

It seemed to be an opening line that many a young actress had heard before. But the stranger was none other than novelist Sylvia Thompson and she had indeed just completed a play which was getting serious backing for a West End opening with Laurence Olivier headlining the bill. The play was *The Golden Arrow* and the role Garson had been given was "the perfect introductory part for me, that of a gay and vivacious American girl." The show's financiers had other ideas. They refused to risk a West End opening with an unknown actress in a pivotal role. Olivier went to war on Garson's behalf and threatened to find alternative financing if this newcomer was fired. "Having Larry as a friend was the luckiest thing that happened to me," Garson would recall. Olivier won the day and Garson made the cast. The critics hailed her and her stage career was launched.

Success followed success and her admirers were legion. Fans became an all-too-frequent part of backstage life, so when a Mr Robert Ritchie sent his card to Garson's dressing room during the run of the Gilbert Miller production of *Old Music* she told the messenger, "If it's stockings, tell him I don't need any today." The messenger hesitated. "I, eh, I believe Mr Ritchie has a message from Mr Louis B. Mayer, Miss Garson." The message was an invitation to dinner that night with the Hollywood mogul. Following dinner and an after-theatre party, Mayer was still being turned down by Garson, despite a firm offer of $500 a week – an unprecedented offer for a relatively unknown and untried actress. But Garson, who remained extremely close to her widowed mother was not prepared to go to Hollywood without her. Throughout his many conversations with Garson, Mayer had been impressed

Greer Garson complained of being typecast by Hollywood as prim and proper. Pictured here with Irish-Australian legend of the screen Errol Flynn in *That Forsythe Woman*.

by her dedication to her mother. Mayer insisted that Mrs Garson should absolutely come to Hollywood. "The California sunshine will add ten years to her life," Mayer promised. That was the argument that clinched it and Greer Garson was off to Hollywood – but it wasn't going to be the joyride that Mayer had promised, not yet anyway.

Garson was left to cool her heels for almost a full year in Hollywood while Mayer and his team tried to figure out what to do with her now that they had her. 'Her beauty – sunny-red hair, blue-green eyes, milk-white skin – had caused the conservative English drama critics to forget the play and hunt for adjectives to describe her: 'devastating,' 'scintillating,' 'magnetic'… But in Hollywood, the city that combs the world for glamour, the boys just couldn't see her, in fact they came within one day of letting her get away from them entirely,' hooted one fan magazine article on Garson in 1941.

The writer was referring to the fact that Garson's initial contract at MGM was for just one year. After her year of inactivity, Garson wasn't much interested in what Mayer had to say anymore. She was homesick and longing to work. "It was the most difficult and unhappiest year of my life," she once said. It was around that time that director Sam Wood was in search of an actress to play Mrs Chips in the movie he had been assigned to, *Goodbye Mr Chips*. Garson forever insisted what happened next was true – as did Sam Wood.

Wood was working late in a projection room over at MGM, bleary-eyed from looking at screen test after screen test of some pretty big names who were looking to play the lead in his next movie – the role of Mrs Chips. A new test flickered onto the screen, a girl appeared; she was notable for her high cheekbones, she wore no lipstick or makeup of any kind. The image hovered in front of Woods, the girl walked across the screen, an image of tall dignity. Suddenly the projection room hatch flew open and the projectionist shouted down, "Excuse it, Mr Wood, that dame ain't even on the (screen test) list." Wood looked up at the operator, "Mistake hell! That's Mrs Chips."

'Her contract was within a week of expiring when she was offered the role of Mrs Chips in *Goodbye Mr Chips*, that was to make her a star. Initially, she turned it down fearing that Mrs Chips' death twenty minutes into the film would make the role insignificant. She was persuaded otherwise and found she had made cinema history for her depiction of the woman who draws out the scholarly title character, played by Robert Donat,' recorded Jonathan Leake writing in the London *Times* in 1996.

Garson was hailed for her portrayal as Mrs Chips in the 1939 adaptation of James Hilton's novel, of a shy man devoted to school life and only emerging from his shell when he meets the future Mrs Chips – Garson. It earned Garson the first of seven Oscar nominations. She received five more nominations in as many years for portrayals of women in self-sacrificing roles including *Blossoms in the Dust* in 1941, *Mrs Miniver* the following year, *Madame Curie* and *The Valley of Decision* in 1945. It was in *Mrs Miniver* that Garson emerged as a heroic icon for World War II, playing the brave and resourceful English housewife who holds her family together during the blitz of London. It was also the film that won her an Oscar for Best Actress. Garson's reign in Hollywood transcended the introduction of Technicolor to the screen which began with *Blossoms in the Dust*.

'Because Greer Garson has red hair and green eyes, her next appearance on the screen was set back two months. Ever since the Irish actress appeared in Hollywood directors and cameramen have been saying that Miss Garson and Technicolor should be joined,' recorded an article in *The New York Tribune* in June of 1941. The union caused more complications than anyone could have suspected. *Pride and Prejudice* was the logical film for Miss Garson's introduction to colour. Once the picture was in production, it was too late. Then Miss Garson did a stage stint for the British War Relief Society in Noel Coward's *Tonight at 8.30*. All Hollywood saw her and none but colourblind persons missed seeing that Miss Garson had something in her Titian locks. About that time Metro-Goldwyn-Mayer had found a vehicle for Miss Garson in *Blossoms in the Dust*, a dramatic theme inspired by the life of Mrs Edna Gladney, superintendent of the Texas Children's Home... The script was ready and a date set when Miss Garson's red hair entered the picture. Karl Freund who photographed *The Good Earth* was called in to make a conventional colour shot of Miss Garson, her first...they shot a few feet of film in colour that was to be used in an advertising trailer. A few minutes after Freund viewed the results of his camera artistry he was banging on the office door of director Mervyn LeRoy, who rushed to the office of producer Irving Asher. It was decided that anything but Miss Garson in colour was doing Miss Garson and the public an injustice... it was a lot of trouble to show off Miss Garson's red hair (but) after this the star and Technicolor will be associated permanently,' the newspaper article trumpeted.

Her transfer to colour came when Garson's career was at its zenith. Just a year prior she had won audiences and critics over with her portrayal of Elizabeth Bennett in MGM's adaptation of Jane Austen's *Pride and Prejudice*. The production reunited her with friend and mentor Laurence Olivier. 'Greer Garson is Elizabeth Bennett,' wrote Bosley Crowther in his *New York Times* review. 'Dear, beautiful Lizzie' stepped right out of the book, or rather out of one's fondest imagination; poised, graceful, self-contained, witty, spasmodically stubborn, and as lovely as a woman can be.' *Pride and Prejudice* premiered at the Radio City Music Hall on July 26th 1940, and ran for a record four weeks. Garson was the undisputed 'Queen of the Lot' at MGM – but she was not at all happy. The 'Greer Garson' that audiences identified as the brave, silently suffering, smart, charming and dedicated wife was not the Greer Garson who was complaining to anybody who would listen about the parts Mayer was giving her.

"Now I am the glorified missus of M.G.M.," she announced to reporter Philip Scheuer. "Mrs Gladney in *Blossoms in the Dust*, Mrs Woodruff in *When Ladies Meet* – Mrs Miniver... You see I've always played mean gals on the stage – with lovers most of whom I shot, and illegitimate babies. All the parts that Bette Davis seems to get in the pictures."

"I've been bebustled to death," Garson complained to Edwin Schallert, drama critic of the *Los Angeles Times*, in 1944. "As far as I'm concerned, 'MGM' means 'Metro's Glorified Mrs'," she complained to yet another writer, Theodore Strauss in the *New York Times Magazine*. "I'm tired of playing forty-eight-year-old matrons. I was not born with a bustle," she railed. Strauss wrote, with a flair not untypical of Hollywood journalism of the day, 'If Miss Garson now rebels against the connubial role, the wedding ring and purring domesticity, no-one should be greatly surprised. There is rebellion in her blood – a fact which even determined her being born in County Down, Ireland, far from the celestial banks and braes of Scotland. Her forebears – she is a direct descendant of Rob Roy MacGregor – migrated to Ireland shortly after the clan was proscribed for kicking up bloody ructions with too alarming frequency... '

A press leak put out by the studio around the same time seems to reflect the mood of battle that Garson, by now one of the highest-paid stars in Hollywood, had created:

'Sometimes she's been very wrong; her boss, Louis B. Mayer almost had to call the Marines to make her do *Mrs Miniver* and it turned into her greatest success. Greer admits her mistakes − but the point is she never stops pitching, giving every job all she has. And her boss, Louis B. Mayer, who's chronically at dagger's point with Greer professionally, admires and respects her. One Christmas, not long ago, he said how he felt with a custom Continental convertible, with red leather seats − a $5,000 token of esteem.'

But for all her complaints, Garson was not about to break out of the good wife roles just yet. *That Forsythe Woman* in 1949 saw her cast yet again in the mould that she so frequently and loudly rebelled against. This time she was playing opposite Errol Flynn and Walter Pidgeon, with whom she had previously co-starred in *Mrs Miniver* and *Madame Curie*.

'Garson emerged as one of the most heroic icons of World War II in 1942 as Mrs Miniver, a film which earned her an Academy Award as best actress. She made twenty-five films, fourteen of which played Radio City Music Hall for a total of eighty-three weeks, a feat unmatched by any other actress. In 1949 Garson married Col. 'Buddy' Fogelson, who owned the Forked Lightning Ranch in Pecos, and the actress turned her energies towards philanthropy,' according to *Films and Videos* magazine in 'Remembering Greer' in 1977. Her marriage to Fogelson, an oil millionaire marked Garson's semi-retirement from Hollywood and her battles.

"Living with Buddy has broadened my life. I've shared the excitement of sitting up with him all night waiting for a gusher to come in and answering fan mail for a horse." She still remained in touch with her agents in Hollywood but suitable parts were rare. She played Eleanor Roosevelt in *Sunrise at Campobello* in 1960 and the mother superior in *The Singing Nun* in 1966. Her last screen role was, ironically, as the wife in *The Happiest Millionaire* the next year. But she never lost her love for the stage and her appearances on the boards at the Greer Garson Theatre on the University of Santa Fe campus.

Garson and her husband donated millions of dollars to the arts and to the University of Santa Fe in scholarships and building funds. Garson once said, "I'm suspicious of people who say they had it tough starting out and add that they wouldn't have it any other way. Believe me, I would have had it some other way. So that's why I'm doing this, to give young aspiring artists some sort of helping hand."

Greer Garson Fogelson died on April 6th 1996. Upon her death in 1996 *Daily Variety* reported, 'Irish-born actress Greer Garson, (who won her Academy Award) for the World War II drama died April 6 in Dallas of heart failure.' An obituary in the *New York Times* recorded, 'Greer Garson was born on Sept. 29 in 1905, in County Down, Northern Ireland.' Subsequently, a piece in the London *Times* on April 7th 1996 would report that researchers at the University of Ulster had found some evidence that Garson had been born in Essex, England but conceded 'some of her family did live there (Ireland).' Shortly before her death Garson wrote to a friend, "May I just say that it is Buddy's hope and mine that after we have left the scene, you will think of us sometimes and continue to keep alive and growing the good things that have been started. Our hearts are full of love for the Land of Enchantment (Hollywood) and for our friends and neighbours who live there."

CHAPTER 12

THE 'IRISH MAFIA' – O'BRIEN, TRACY AND CAGNEY

The 1930s and 1940s marked a period when the craft guilds of Hollywood such as the Screen Actors Guild and the Directors Guild continually battled the studios on behalf of their members' rights, while forging milestone clauses for contracts and film workers' rights. Legendary Jimmy Cagney is infamous in Hollywood history today for his landmark battles with Warners that rattled the entire studio system. Cagney was also the lead pack member of a group of Irish-American movie stars in that period known as 'The Irish Mafia'. The sway that this group held over Hollywood social life was enormous. The most famous of the 'Irish Mafia' were Cagney, Pat O'Brien and Spencer Tracy, three lifelong friends engaged in Hollywood's power struggle between the might of the studio and the rights of the people who worked for them.

Pat O'Brien and his best friends James Cagney and Spencer Tracy came from Irish immigrant beginnings. "Being Irish in America was not to me as a kid as tough a job as it had been in my father's day… (but) there was still a carry-over of the cartoon Irishman of popular imagination who had a red fringe of beard, a clay pipe upside down in his wide ape's mouth, spoke in 'begorras' and 'bejabers' and Pat-and-Mike dialogue," recalled O'Brien. He would come to be one of Hollywood's most enduring stars, playing mostly Irish characters of all hues. O'Brien was born in Milwaukee, Wisconsin in 1899. His mother's family, the McGoverns, were immigrants from Galway. His father's family came from Cork. He was born William Joseph O'Brien. He later changed his first name to Pat "in admiration" of his grandfather Patrick O'Brien, who had been shot and killed when attempting to stop a saloon brawl, according to the actor.

O'Brien grew up in a predominantly Irish neighbourhood of Milwaukee where he became a boyhood pal of Spencer Tracy. They were classmates at Marquette College. A small role in the drama class of the college convinced O'Brien that he would have a career in acting. He took off for Broadway with little more to his credit than top billing as Charley in his university's production of *Charley's Aunt*. Tracy, meanwhile, was at odds about what he would do with his life. His father John Edward Tracy, "a God-fearing Irishman and a devout Catholic," was the sales manager at the local Sterling Motor Truck Company. An

evening out at the theatre with O'Brien started Tracy thinking that he too might give the profession a try. The two young men decided to give New York and Broadway a shot.

This was the New York of the Jazz Age, speakeasies and the Ziegfeld Follies, bathtub gin, and hundreds of doors – the closed doors of producers and agents upon whom they called in search of theatre work. They shared a room together in a boarding house on New York's West Side. Jobs were scarce in that year of 1923, and the pals helped each other out as best they could. Tracy made some spare cash by sparring in a Bowery boxing club. The pair would read lines from plays to one another at night against a backdrop of shouts from other boarders to "stop the noise!"

O'Brien found a job with a stock company in New Jersey and Tracy continued to hit every theatre agent in New York until he finally ended up at the Theatre Guild which was rehearsing a play called *R.U.R.* Some young actors who could play robots were needed. There were no lines and faces were covered by masks, but the pay was $15 a week. After *R.U.R.* closed Tracy was back pounding the pavement. O'Brien returned from his theatre tour after the show folded. The stock company could not afford to pay O'Brien the last few dollars owed him, so he settled for the tuxedo that had served as his costume in the play, remembered O'Brien in his autobiography *The Wind at My Back*. O'Brien's introduction to Hollywood came by way of a call from Howard Hughes to star in a movie version of *The Front Page* after O'Brien had successfully played in a stage version of the newspaper adventure yarn. Hughes wanted O'Brien to play Hildy Johnson, the hard-nosed reporter determined to get out of the newspaper business and settle down to married life as an ad executive. O'Brien was on his way to Hollywood, with a $750 contract in hand – and a $250 a month salary increase guaranteed. Hughes may or may not have realised it, but O'Brien had not in fact played Hildy in the stage version. He played Walter Burns, Hildy's cranky old boss. Nor had O'Brien even appeared in the Broadway stage version – but in a production in the provinces. Hughes's representative had asked only if this was the same Pat O'Brien who had played in the stage production of *The Front Page*. That much was correct.

Hollywood was an adventure for O'Brien, but as he would later lament, "I had come out to Hollywood too late to share the early marble swimming pool age, the kingdom of Mary Pickford and Douglas Fairbanks, when custard pies first flew, and Mack Sennett's Keystone Cops brought the Model T into film art. I would often see a shabby D.W. Griffith, inventor of American film storytelling, lonely in a bar hoisting a few, forgotten and neglected, and Charlie Chaplin was becoming more and more full of social protest. Saddest sight was F. Scott Fitzgerald (another Irish boy) the hero of the Jazz Age of the Twenties trying to write screenplays; you would find Scotty numbly staring into the sunlight at the Garden of Allah Hotel with cronies Bob Benchley, Monty Woolley; all promising each other they would soon go on the wagon."

O'Brien conceded that he was never a glamorous person – but that was okay because he reckoned that the glamour was gone from Hollywood by the time he arrived at the beginning of the sound era. Hollywood's tempestuous infancy was drawing to a close and the stars were moving their residences out of town, to the west, to Brentwood, Westwood, and following Mary Pickford's early lead, to Beverly Hills. Hollywood in those days for Pat O'Brien was a canvas of sadness. He bemoaned the waste of genius that he saw all about him in the faces of the likes of John Barrymore, cartoonist Milt Gross, Griffith, Scott Fitzgerald, artist John Decker; a crowd, he observed, who all soon slid to Forest Lawn Cemetery.

Spencer Tracy, meanwhile, had been forging along in stock companies around the country and had finally come to play the role of 'Killer' Mears in *The Last Mile*, a play about a prison break, at the Theatre Guild in New York. The production went on to standing room only and the rave notices for Tracy brought Hollywood calling.

Tracy went to Hollywood on a one-picture contract to make *Up the River*, a clever spoof of prison pictures directed by John Ford. Critics hailed it as the best comedy of the year. Tracy received glowing praise as a screen newcomer to watch out for. A young Humphrey Bogart was no slouch in the film either. Fox signed Tracy to a five-year contract and immediately set him to work in second-rate movies. Tracy was furious and frustrated by the studio's policy. Stories began to circulate the town about his tempestuous nature, his clashes with studio brass, drinking binges and frequent disappearances from the studio. Among the movies from that period known as his 'Fox' era were such forgettable films as *Bottoms Up*, *The Show-Off* and *20,000 Years in Sing Sing*. When the contract with Fox expired, Tracy signed on at MGM where a smart management team clearly saw his star potential. It was MGM that gave Tracy the picture that would plant his name atop the Hollywood A-list of actors – *San Francisco* with Clark Gable and Jeanette MacDonald. In the movie, set against the great San Francisco Earthquake, Tracy plays an idealistic Catholic priest, Father Tim, a foil to Gable's devil-may-care character Blackie Norton, the owner of Barbary Coast saloon. Tracy's smouldering, angry performance was brilliant and it made him a star. Right on the heels of *San Francisco* came *Fury*, Fritz Lang's dark picture about mob violence.

It was a milestone film for MGM, a box office smash and it cemented Tracy's already strong presence in Hollywood.

Later came *Captains Courageous* in which Tracy played a mystical Portuguese seaman who befriends child actor Freddie Bartholomew. The character of Manuel was almost a mirror image of Tracy's own – happy on the outside, gregarious, but with a religious and brooding core. The performance won Tracy his first Academy Award. A second Oscar came for his portrayal of yet another Irish priest, Edward Flanagan founder of a poor boys' home in Nebraska. The movie, *Boystown*, featured a young Mickey Rooney as a wayward youngster. Tracy had an inscription set into that second Oscar which read, 'To Father Edward J. Flanagan, whose great human qualities, kindly simplicity and inspiring courage were strong enough to shine through my humble efforts.'

Though Tracy had his problems with Hollywood in the early days with Fox, days when he frequently was overwhelmed with bouts of depression and heavy drinking, he eventually came to represent the embodiment of strength and stability in the tempestuous film town, with a coterie of devoted friends and family at his side, including of course Katharine Hepburn his partner in later years and until his death.

O'Brien was also in full flight in Hollywood at the time that Tracy was at his most successful, but would never be in the same league as his old friend. O'Brien's best-remembered roles include Knute Rockne, Hildy Johnson, and a string of tough-talking Irish priests and soldiers; Major Cavanaugh in *The Iron Major*, another priest in *Fighting Father Dunne*, Colonel Paddy Ryan in *Bombardier*, Gorman in *The Last Hurrah*, in which he co-starred with Spencer Tracy, who had insisted on O'Brien for the role.

Spencer Tracy and Katharine Hepburn in a scene from *Keeper of the Flame* (1942)

Then there was the first of what became known as the Cagney-O'Brien movies, *Here Comes The Navy*. One of the great screen partnerships was about to begin, and it involved two Irish guys who could not have been more different. Cagney was a private man who rarely drank and was not very talkative. O'Brien loved good company, enjoyed his Irish whiskey but never drank to excess, loved to spin a tale and was not completely happy until he was singing one of the many Irish songs in his repertoire.

In Warner Bros.' *Here Comes The Navy* Cagney played Chesty O'Connor, a tough kid who comes to blows with Biff Martin, played by O'Brien. The movie, shot mostly aboard the U.S.S. *Arizona* in 1934, very nearly put an early end to the careers – and lives – of both actors when a scene went terribly wrong. O'Brien was hanging from a rope suspended from a dirigible. The script called for Cagney to shinny down the rope to 'rescue' O'Brien. Unfortunately, O'Brien lost his grip on the rope. Cagney, who had his legs wrapped around O'Brien, took both their weights as they slid down the rope. He held on long enough to break the impact of the fall. A witness later reported that he had seen 'smoke' coming from Cagney's hands, which resembled hamburger after the accident.

It was the beginning of a friendship that would last for the next fifty years. Cagney, whose father was a second-generation Irish saloon keeper and alcoholic, and whose grandmother on her mother's side was also Irish, was described by O'Brien as a "far away fella," a misfit in Hollywood. But a group of close, intelligent and witty friends kept Cagney afloat in those strange waters, among them O'Brien, Frank McHugh and Spencer Tracy. Others included Ralph Bellamy, Frank Morgan, Lynne Overman and Allen Jenkins. Columnist Sidney Skolsky labelled the group the 'Irish Mafia'. It was a catchy but blatant misnomer because of the group only O'Brien, Tracy, Cagney and McHugh were of Irish ancestry.

The chemistry of Cagney and O'Brien on screen worked again in *Devil Dogs of the Air*. This film also featured Frank McHugh, who had come to Hollywood from vaudeville and was often mistaken as being first-generation Irish because of the brogue he employed in movies that included *Going My Way* with Barry Fitzgerald in 1944. The three were teamed together again that same year by Warner Bros. in *The Irish In Us*, in which they played brothers.

Cagney's explosive bantam cock, tough-as-nails street smart wiseguy played well off O'Brien's calmer, more mature, slower, rock of stability character perfectly, but never more brilliantly than in *Angels With Dirty Faces*. Here O'Brien played yet another Irish priest, Father Jerry Connelly, who must convince Cagney's hoodlum character Rocky Sullivan to scream and cry like a coward on his way to the electric chair, so that a gang of street urchins will cease to view Rocky as their idol. The classic is probably the best-remembered and most intense of the Cagney-O'Brien films, the film that created one of the great unanswerable questions in Hollywood history. When Cagney's character, Rocky, breaks down on the walk to the chair, a screaming, snivelling coward, was he doing the right thing by Father Connelly or was he really a coward at the end?

The Fighting 69th (1940), a fictional account of a real Irish regiment of World War I, brought another teaming of the Cagney-O'Brien chemistry. But this time not only were Cagney and O'Brien called to action, but just about every Irish actor in Hollywood was signed up for the movie including Frank McHugh and George Brent... and another Irish-born Hollywood veteran, Creighton Hale.

Kiss Tomorrow Goodbye (1950) starring James Cagney

Hale was born in 1882 in Cork by the name of Patrick Fitzgerald. His father was a singer/actor who used to tour Ireland with a travelling 'fit up' company playing from town to town. The young Hale got his first acting training with that company in Ireland. His first trip to America was with a theatre company headed by Lady Forbes Robinson. He stayed on in the U.S. when the tour ended and found his way into the new picture company called Famous Players in New York. He went on to enjoy a very successful career as a character actor and sometimes silent movie cowboy in Hollywood.

'The Irish Mafia' continued for many years to meet regularly for good food, some drink, and fine conversations in one or other of their homes. It was a tradition that lasted until, one by one, the members made their final bows in this life. Cagney was the last to depart in 1986, surviving Pat O'Brien by just three years. Tracy had died years before in 1967.

Of the three, Cagney was perhaps the most ill-at-ease in Hollywood. His battles with Jack Warner made headlines. Here was a man who stood his ground against the studios in his ongoing fight for what he considered a fair wage for his talents, at a time when the industry's bosses could make or break a career with a flick of the pen and a phone call. One journalist said of him, "He has too much Irish red hair on his head to be the fair-haired boy in Hollywood."

So much has been written about Cagney, about his studio fights, the role he played in founding the Screen Actors' Guild, his unsurpassed acting abilities, his glorious dancing in *Yankee Doodle Dandy*, his passionate loyalty to his friends, his retirement to an 800-acre farm to raise horses and cattle, that it would be inappropriate to try to do justice to his entire career in a few words. But it would be fair to reflect on the strong Irish immigrant background and early work ethic that came to drive him in his Hollywood days to battles royal with his studio bosses and the pursuit of the highest standards in his work.

Born James Francis Cagney on July 17th 1899 on New York's Lower East Side, Cagney was a fighter from the beginning. He had to be to survive the family's poverty and the stark reality of life on 96th Street in Yorkville, the tough neighbourhood to which the family moved when Cagney was eight years old. "It seems as I look back, that there was always crepe hanging on a door or two somewhere on the block. There was always the clanging of an ambulance bell. Patrol wagons came often…"

The Cagney clan, also known by their original name, the O'Caignes, James Cagney would recall, "was surrounded by trouble, illness, and my dad's alcoholism, but we didn't have time to be impressed by all those misfortunes." Time meant money, and money meant food, as far as the young Jimmy Cagney was concerned. His mother, a woman of Irish and Norwegian parents, instilled in him the importance of an education. Hard work was just a fact of life. During one vacation from Stuyvesant High, he wrapped bundles at Wanamaker's Department Store, worked as a switchboard operator and a pool hall attendant at night and on Sundays sold tickets for the Hudson River Day Line. His attitude to Hollywood was born out of that tough boyhood in Yorkville where he had fought with and beaten the toughest bullies in the neighbourhood. In fact he was such a good street fighter that he seriously considered professional boxing as a career – an idea quickly quenched by his mother. Instead, he scraped for a living in one low-paid job after another, until he heard he could make $35 a week in vaudeville.

A friend happened to mention one day that there was an opening for a chorus line player at Keith's 86th St. Theatre, and when Cagney heard what the job paid he wasted no time in getting over there. The fact that he had not even a modicum of stage training and that his only claim to a theatrical skill was his ability to dance 'The Peabody' did not deter him. At the audition Cagney did his 'Peabody' routine and threw in a few moves he had seen another hopeful demonstrate. Much to his surprise, he got the part. Much more to his surprise was the fact that he would be required to wear a dress for the role. The male chorus dancers in the show, *Every Sailor*, were playing female characters. For $35 a week Cagney would have worn a hula skirt. The career of the toughest, two-fisted gangster the screen would ever see began in drag. Other small vaudeville roles followed, including a show called *Pitter Patter*. Cagney fell head over heels in love with Willie, a fellow player. Willie's actual name was Frances Willard Vernon and she was a stunner, as far as Cagney was concerned. She was sixteen when Cagney spotted her arriving for work in the chorus line of the show – "all dressed up and let out for the day," was how he would remember her. Together they would pound the Broadway pavements in search of work, share the grinding poverty, which seemed to be their inescapable lot and encourage each other through the hard times that lingered over the ensuing years. On the strength of regular paycheques for their parts in a show that toured the vaudeville circuit, *Lew Field's Ritz Girls of 1922*, they were married and moved into the Cagney family apartment in Yorkville.

It was hardly an auspicious beginning, but Cagney was more determined than ever now to make a success of this new 'job' he had found. In time, the parts grew bigger, the shows more important. He began to appear in 'legitimate' plays and learned through trial and error the skills of his craft. "In vaudeville, by persistent trial and error and unremitting

James Cagney plays a leading role in real life as a fighting member of the Screen Actors' Guild – pictured here with fellow Guild directors.

hard work, the performer learns how to please an audience," he maintained. It was a show called *Penny Arcade* that marked the turning point for Cagney, despite the fact that the production bombed and closed. Al Jolson (*The Jazz Singer*) loved *Penny Arcade* and bought the screen rights which he sold on to Warner Bros. with the proviso that Cagney and Joan Blondell, who co-starred with Cagney in the stage version, would reprise their roles in the screen version. The title was changed to *Sinner's Holiday*. James Cagney was on his way to Hollywood.

The three-week contract at Warner Bros. at $500 a week with which he arrived in Hollywood was quickly extended to seven years and a starting salary of $400 a week. Two more films followed the same year and then *it* happened. The grapefruit that Cagney angrily squashed into the face of Mae Clark in *The Public Enemy*, his fourth film role. That grapefruit shook up Hollywood and put the name of James Cagney on the map. The film, shot over just sixteen days at a budget of $150,000 in 1931, paved the way for a new kind of screen character – an angry, tough and sometimes all-too-human persona that brought a collective intake of breath from a public weaned on clean-cut heroes. Other stars would follow Cagney's lead, including Edward G. Robinson, Paul Muni and Humphrey Bogart.

Cagney revealed later that his character in the film was based partly on a gangster named Earl 'Hymie' Weiss, who threw an omelette in a girl's face. "I don't think we could afford an omelette," he later joked. Cagney's sometimes brutally realistic screen portrayals of hoodlums throughout his career were in fact often based on real characters that he had known back in the Yorkville days, he would confess in later life.

Cagney followed *The Public Enemy* with a series of hit gangster movies interspersed with musicals, and, in sixty-two films over three decades, he proved himself the most versatile of screen stars, alternating between the hardest of the screen's tough guys to the light-footed characterisation of George M. Cohan in the musical *Yankee Doodle Dandy*, the warmly patriotic musical tribute to the great showman. The performance won Cagney an Academy Award in 1942. It was Cagney's favourite film and prompted him to announce that he wanted most to be remembered as a dancer. "Once a hoofer, always a hoofer," he said.

To most he will probably be best remembered as Cody Jarrett the gangster who pushed the crime movie genre to new levels – literally – when he died on top of an exploding oil tank in Raoul Walsh's *White Heat* screaming "Made it Ma! Top of the world!"

Cagney the star commanded the respect and adulation of fans around the world. Back in Hollywood however, his boss Jack Warner, head of Warner Bros. Studios was definitely not one of Cagney's fans, despite the gold mine for the studio that Cagney represented. Warner had discovered early on in their relationship that Cagney the man was just as tough as any of the hardened characters he brought to life on screen. Cagney knew full well his value to the studio when his films first began to hit in 1931. He demanded a salary increase to reflect his status. Warner steadfastly refused and Cagney, ignoring threats of what would happen if he did not fulfill the terms of his contract with the studio, took off for New York declaring that he would give up acting and look for another job. It became a knockdown battle of wills, but nobody who knew Cagney doubted for a minute that he would be true to his word and would walk away from the movies for good rather than back down. The new star made himself scarce all through the summer of 1931 and agreed to return to the studio and Hollywood only when Warner reluctantly offered to increase his salary to $1,400 a week. Upon the return of the prodigal son to Warners, he was immediately cast alongside Loretta Young in *Taxi!* another popular success. Then came the 1932 melodrama *The Crowd Roars* in which he played a racecar driver. The Cagney star continued to rise with these two movies. After playing a down-and-out boxer in *Winner Take All* Cagney, still insisting he was grossly underpaid, took another hike back to New York. This time he stayed away for six months while the battle over his salary raged amid lawsuits, threats and insults doled out to the delight of the press. Again Cagney vowed that he would give up his screen career. He had always fancied becoming a doctor, he said. Medical school sounded like a good idea. The row was eventually settled when an arbitration panel granted him $3,000 per week, and Warner Bros. agreed that he would only have to appear in four films per year.

The studio boss put his star to work in one tough guy picture after another, *Hard To Handle*, *Picture Snatcher* and *The Mayor Of Hell* before allowing him a respite in *Footlight Parade*, the first film in which Cagney could show off his skills as a hoofer.

The feud with Warner erupted once again in 1936 when Cagney rebelled against a role cast by the studio. When he refused to take the part the studio put him on suspension. Cagney sued and won a court victory that stunned the industry. The practice of suspending actors who refused to take roles they felt were unsuitable or could damage their careers was common in the industry. Cagney had broken this powerful studio weapon. It was a pyrrhic victory, for Cagney found himself unofficially blacklisted at the other major studios and, after a year without work, signed on with a 'B'-level movie company, Grand National. Both films which Cagney made at his new studio failed to reach the box office heights that he had expected, and he realised he needed Warner as much as Warner needed him. A truce was agreed and Cagney came back to Warner Bros. with one of the richest contracts a star had ever signed in Hollywood to that point. He would earn $150,000 per picture for five years plus ten percent of the gross over $1.5 million dollars. In addition, he had story refusal rights on his film projects. As a kicker he negotiated a 'happiness clause' which allowed him to break his contract if he deemed his relationship with the studio to be 'obnoxious or unsatisfactory to him.' Cagney was a hero among his peers. He was the giant-killer, the street fighter who took on the studios and won. And he was unselfish in his support of other actors, becoming the president of the Screen Actors' Guild and an icon of courage in the constant battle between the creative talent and the executive branch in Hollywood.

Through it all, Cagney never viewed his brilliant career in Hollywood as anything more than a job he did well and liked, a job he once said entailed the ability to "walk in, plant yourself, look the other actor in the eye and tell the truth." But it was also a job that required him to spend long hours locked in dark sound stages, hours he would much preferred to spend on the farm that he had bought. He longed to be out in the fresh air among the horses that he was now breeding so successfully in upper New York State. Cagney was growing older, and he wanted nothing more than to enjoy the fruits of his work. The day of decision finally came in 1961 on the set of the Billy Wilder-directed *One, Two, Three*. He decided to quit. "I walked out of the sunlight and into the dark studio and said to myself, 'this is it.'"

Throughout his retirement, producers tried to lure Cagney back to the screen, but he turned down every role offered, including *That Championship Season* and *The Godfather: Part II*. Then *Ragtime* came along. After twenty years of retirement out in his "sunlight," James Cagney was giving a return performance – the Hollywood happening made headlines around the world. But it had been a chance meeting in a restaurant with director Milos Forman that had brought it about. Cagney was lunching with an actor, Treat Williams, who was keen on playing Cagney in a planned movie about the great man's life. Cagney was introduced to director Miles Forman who casually offered him a part in his upcoming film *Ragtime*... any part he wanted. Cagney read the script, picked his part and that was it. The great 'Jimmy' Cagney was coming back to the screen – but not to Hollywood. The movie was filmed in England where Cagney and the ever-present rock of his life, his wife Willie, were treated like visiting royalty. On arrival in London to begin filming they could see throngs of people outside their limousine holding signs that read, 'Welcome to London: We Love You, Jimmy.' For Cagney, an old man now and suffering poor health, it was pure joy. He may have once craved privacy and the sunlight on his farm, but he had never realised how a part of him would always hanker after a life among the throng. But something else, something very special for Cagney, would make this trip to film *Ragtime* all the more thrilling – none other than Pat O'Brien and his wife Eloise had also been cast in the movie. The old-timers kicked up some dust in London. The highlight of the trip for the reunited friends was the Queen Mother's command-performance birthday party at the London Palladium. When Cagney made an unscheduled walk-on the Queen Mother led a standing ovation. Later, when she met the performers back stage the Queen Mother had a few private words with Cagney. Asked what she had said to him during the moment Cagney replied, "How the hell should I know?"

CHAPTER 13

STEPPING OUT IN HOLLYWOOD – THE IRISH HOOFERS

Perhaps one of the most enduring film genres is the Hollywood musical in which such unforgettable Irish-American legendary song and dance men as Gene Kelly, Donald O'Connor and George Murphy made their names. They were following a tradition of dance that Irish immigrants had first introduced to the New York musical stage generations before. Irish dancers were legion in those early vaudeville days. One of the first recorded exponents of Irish dance in America was the popular hoofer of the nineteenth century, Kitty O'Neil. Later, Harry Kelly and John Kennedy speeded up the old steps and introduced a fast tap motion that was a precursor to modern tap. From Kitty O'Neil to George M. Cohan and other Irish hoofers such as Irish-American vaudevillian James Barton, or Paddy Shea who could dance with a glass of beer on his head and never spill a drop, dance evolved to the point of perfection and grace on screen that would be epitomised by Kelly and his cohorts. You don't have to look too closely when watching spectacular captured moments of cinema such as Kelly's immortal *Singin' in the Rain* or O'Connor's 'wild, uproarious' dancing in the same film to see the Irish roots in the work of these second- and third-generation Irish Hollywood hoofers.

"You know, I don't think I've ever been so proud of anything as I am of this," Gene Kelly confided. The year was 1990 and the great man was slowed only a little with age, but graceful as ever in manner and movement and twinkling still in those smiling eyes. He was talking about the arrival in the mail not long before of his Irish passport. Few people knew it then or now, but Kelly had gone back to his roots to become a citizen of Ireland, birthplace of his people. The authors had called on him on the occasion of his being named that year's recipient of the Ireland American Fund's Person of the Year honours in its Irish Heritage Awards. This most worthy organisation raises great sums of money for non-sectarian activities in Ireland from education to employment schemes, arts and cultural groups and other good causes. Its annual Heritage Awards dinner had become a highlight of Hollywood's calendar of social events. Kelly talked about his newly acquired Irish citizenship and his deep and genuine passion for all things Irish. "I'm so very grateful to Declan Kelly (then Ireland's Consul

Kelly pictured with 'Irish Mafia' star member Spencer Tracy in a scene from *Inherit the Wind*.

General in San Francisco) for all his assistance. I had mentioned to him that it had always been my dream to become an Irish citizen and he said, 'Well, aren't you Irish?' I hadn't realised until he told me that the fact that my grandparents were Irish qualified me. He did everything for me and here I am, a fully fledged and documented Irishman. Now my next move is to buy a house in Ireland, nothing too fancy, where I can live, for part of the year at least. I'm already in the process of doing that," Kelly revealed.

Here was a man revered, honoured, lauded, feted the world over for a career that has left a deep groove in the history of the motion pictures, the art of the dance and the American musical, the man who will live forever 'dancin' and singin' in the rain.' But at that moment news of the Ireland American Fund's Heritage Award seemed to make him most proud. "That's the greatest honour I could ever wish for," said Kelly.

President George Bush stated on the occasion of the award presentation. "Over the years, Irish-Americans have made many outstanding contributions to our Nation, excelling in business, government, the arts and in countless other fields. The beloved Irish-American you salute at this dinner has won the respect and admiration of his colleagues in the entertainment industry and charmed millions of fans around the world. A gifted and versatile artist, Gene Kelly has distinguished himself as an actor, singer, dancer, producer, and director. He has generously shared with others his wealth of talent and creativity, and he is a most deserving recipient of your recognition and praise…"

President Ronald Reagan, himself an Irish-American man of the screen, said of Kelly at that time "… Gene Kelly exemplifies what it means to live life to the fullest and to share one's talent with the world – in the Irish spirit."

Suffice to say that with Donald O'Connor as the evening's honorary chairman and with tributes flowing from such Irish-American entertainment industry show business legends as Merv Griffin and Pierce Brosnan, this was a night when the emeralds came out in Hollywood, and no more fitting an honoree could there have been than Eugene Curran Kelly who was born on August 3rd 1912, the third of five children. The Kelly family epitomised a buoyant, confident America that had not yet seen a World War and was more than a decade away from the Great Depression. They were a close-knit, hard-working, respectable American family who lived in the Sacred Heart Parish area of Pittsburgh's Highland Park. Their father, James Patrick Joseph Kelly and his wife Harriet were the children of Irish immigrants. But they were American now and spoke only occasionally of the family's roots – two hardy, happy-go-lucky, tough and enterprising Irishmen, one a Curran, the other a Kelly. But when James and Harriet did talk about their fathers, what stories unfolded.

As soon as he was old enough to comprehend, young Gene listened to the family legends of emigration. A principal character in these stories was his mother's father Billy Curran who had landed in New York from Derry in 1845, on the run, by family accounts, from the English authorities. Billy Curran decided to head for the coalfields of Huntington, West Virginia, but due to some quirky map reading ended up in Huntington, Pennsylvania. Undeterred by this basic geographical error, he decided to make the most of things, and it wasn't long before he met and married the daughter of a well-to-do family. Billy Curran proved himself a smart businessman and, with his wife's financial backing, built a thriving general store business. He used the profits from this enterprise to move his family to Pittsburgh where he opened a saloon. Some years later he would be murdered by muggers as he locked up the bar after closing.

The Kelly side of the story was no less intriguing with tales about grandfather James Kelly, a blacksmith, arriving from Ireland into America with a change of clothes and his blacksmith's hammer as his grubstake. Later, he settled in Peterborough, Ontario, where Gene Kelly's father James was born. The Kellys weren't rich. They weren't poor either, but they were damn close to it. Kelly described their neighbourhood as being as near to a slum as it was possible for a decent neighbourhood to be, according to author Clive Hirschorn in his book *Gene Kelly*. The part of town that the Kellys called home was a tough, harsh place populated by first-generation Eastern European immigrants, steel workers for the most part, who based a man's worth on how much liquor he could hold, how hard he could work and how well he could fight. The Kelly clan made the most of things though, and Gene Kelly and his brothers learned pretty quickly how to take care of themselves in a brawl.

In the midst of this melting pot of immigrant turmoil James Kelly slogged out a living as a travelling salesman to provide the best income he could for his family, while Harriet strove to instill in her children a passion for learning and a respect for hard work and common decency, an inheritance that would one day sustain Gene Kelly in the fickle environment of Hollywood. Gene Kelly, a small boy in stature, dreamed of becoming a professional baseball player. But his mother had other ideas and packed him and his brother Fred off to music and dancing lessons, all laced up in Buster Brown suits and providing perfect targets for the local bully boys. The bloody noses and black eyes collected on those Saturdays became so regular a feature that their mother took to sending them to classes in a taxi. "I hated dancing… I thought it was sissy. (But) I bless my mother now for making me go…" Kelly would later confess. Kelly attended Pennsylvania State College to study journalism but the Depression forced him to quit and take a job teaching gym at Camp Porter, a YMCA camp near Pittsburgh. Meanwhile, he worked up a dance act with his brother Fred for local amateur nights. The $5 and $10 prizes funded a return to college for Gene. It was during

Gene Kelly pictured with Donald O'Connor and Debbie Reynolds on the cinema poster for the classic *Singin' in the Rain* (1952). He is the most famous of the Irish-Americans who graced the screen and stage in America over the past century. One of the proudest moments of his life was when he received his Irish passport. He planned to retire to Ireland where his grandparents were born.

that lean period of the Depression that Kelly set up his own dance school – a venture that began when two friends asked him if he would give them dancing lessons. They had seen how popular Kelly's dancing prowess made him with the girls. He charged fifty cents an hour and within a few months had more than fifty pupils.

His reputation as a gifted dancer and congenial teacher quickly spread and he was offered a job with a well-established dance academy as a substitute instructor. He was supposed to stay for just one week, but remained teaching at the academy for seven years. "I know why they liked me," Kelly later said of his pupils during those days, "it's because I remembered how I was called 'sissy' when I started dancing. I tried to make the boys enjoy it – to make it seem like real sport." Meanwhile Kelly had become a leading light in the academy's theatre group and he was loving every minute of it. The stage bug had bitten and dreams now turned to the theatre.

He gathered together some of his best pupils – by now he was running two dance schools – and pulled a touring show together playing fireman's carnivals and charity benefits. They were a hit and Kelly decided it was time to head for the big time… and New York. With a few hundred dollars and the offer of a small choreography assignment in a Broadway show, Kelly kissed his mother goodbye at the train station and charged off to follow his dream. The year was 1937. Broadway and the world would not have too long a wait before this brilliant young Irish-American would burst into their midst.

His first big break came when he was cast in the chorus of Cole Porter's *Leave it to Me* in 1938. This was the production that rocketed Irish-American songster Mary Martin to fame and young Kelly, garbed in Eskimo furs, was one of a chorus of suitors told by Martin that her "heart belongs to Daddy". *Leave it to Me* had made him a card-carrying member of the fraternity of dancers and singers referred to fondly in the business as 'Broadway gypsies'. Broadway greenrooms were his stomping ground and touring the country with new shows became a way of life. In Chicago he met Irish-American theatre legend John Barrymore, by then crippled with drink; he rubbed shoulders with Orson Welles who had trod his first steps on stage in Dublin's Gate Theatre and was a champion and sponsor to many an Irish actor.

There was another Irish-American genius abroad in New York then. He was a heavy drinker but that was par for the course for writers then and moreso, people believed, if the writer was Irish. John O'Hara fitted that bill neatly. But New York adored him and his edgy, bone-shaving 'Pal Joey' stories they had read in *The New Yorker*. It was 1940 and George Abbott and Rodgers and Hart, the producer kings of Broadway, were planning a musical based on O'Hara's 'Pal Joey' stories. Broadway was abuzz. A theatre happening was in the making – and 'who would play Pal Joey?' was the question of the day.

Kelly had gained sufficient attention by now to be a contender. The producers knew he could dance, and how, but could he sing? Audition time and Kelly thought he'd play it clever. He headed madly into one of Rodgers's compositions, 'I Didn't Know What Time it Was,' without any clue as to the musical complexities of the ballad. He mangled it. Rodgers listened, didn't visibly wince, and then politely asked the intruder if he could possibly try something else. Kelly didn't hesitate. He launched straight into a hopping, jumping version of 'It's The Irish In Me' as his feet tapped out a hint of an Irish jig. He finished, paused, decided not to wait to hear 'Don't call us…' moved stage left to exit – and then it happened. An indistinct shout from the back of the theatre and a shuffling little man emerging from the darkness. Kelly was transfixed. The shout came again, only this time it was distinct. 'That's it. Take him.' The man shouting was none other than John O'Hara himself. That song, 'The Irish In Us,' had won the day and Kelly would never look back.

Kelly was a sensation in the show and Hollywood was beckoning. A contract offer from David O. Selznick brought Kelly to Los Angeles in early 1942. But Hollywood decided he should not dance. "You're a great actor. This nonsense about your doing musicals, that's fine. You can do them for a hobby," Selznick told a flabbergasted Kelly during an interview in the producer's office. "I have a property for you. You are going to play the priest in *Keys of the Kingdom*." Kelly hated the story and he finally convinced the boy genius producer, as Selznick was known, that he was not right at all for the part. The role eventually went to Gregory Peck, yet another famous Irish-American striding out in Hollywood. Peck (whose cousin Thomas Ashe was one of the leaders of the Easter Rising in 1916) was a frequent visitor to Ireland where he owned property and was a staunch supporter of the Ireland American Fund in Hollywood.

Meanwhile, Selznick still insisted that Kelly was in Hollywood to act – not dance. And to that end he cast him as a Scottish doctor in the same movie. Kelly was appalled but he made the best of it and even studied with a voice coach to perfect a Scottish accent. But it was a bad idea from the start and eventually Selznick realised his mistake. But rather than putting Kelly to work at dancing, he sold half his screen contract to MGM while also 'loaning' him to the studio to play Judy Garland's leading man in *For Me and My Gal* in 1942. Selznick later also sold the second half of Kelly's contract to MGM. George Murphy also starred in the movie, though relations between Kelly and Murphy were said to be sour because Murphy believed that he should have been playing Kelly's part. Murphy's role was much less colourful and far more forgettable than Kelly's.

Arthur Freed, one of Hollywood's great musical producers, and the man behind *For Me and My Gal*, had first promised the role of Harry Palmer to Murphy. But he later changed his mind and asked Kelly to take the role. He believed that the character of Palmer was very similar to that of Pal Joey, in which Kelly had been such a sensation on stage, and that Kelly could give the role "more scope". Even though Kelly personally had nothing to do with this decision, Murphy worked himself up into a dark and festering mood over losing the far more interesting role to the newcomer. The movie's director, the great Busby Berkeley was not too thrilled with Kelly either, because he had wanted Murphy in the role of Harry Palmer and he resented being overruled on the issue. Judy Garland, though still only twenty, was a seasoned professional and had an immediate rapport with Kelly. She came to the rescue. Throughout the entire production, Garland worked hard as keeper of the peace between Kelly and the moody Murphy. (It should be noted that Berkeley soon realised how talented Kelly was and changed his attitude entirely. In fact he would provide Kelly with his first real education of staging and shooting dance scenes on film.)

Murphy, a Universal Studios official biography would warble, was 'one of old Erin's most outstanding gifts to Hollywood – as Irish as the Blarney Stone.' Well, you get the picture. Born in New Haven in 1904, the son of Irish-American parents, Murphy wasn't afraid to wear his heritage on his sleeve. "Every actor should kiss the Blarney Stone," he announced the year he received the 1958 medallion of the Friendly Sons of St Patrick. Murphy attended Yale, where he played quarterback on the football team in his freshman year but due to poor grades, was suspended from the team and never did finish college. Murphy worked a plethora of odd jobs from coal mining in Pennsylvania, where he was badly injured in a mine accident, to a runner for a Wall Street brokerage. It was while working in New York that he met Juliette Henkel, an amateur dancer who taught him how to dance. The couple later married and began to perform in nightclubs around Broadway which led to Murphy's first break into the big Broadway productions including *Good News*, *Of Thee I Sing* and *Anything Goes*. Years later when Murphy had become a United States senator he confessed how he had acquired a dress suit which helped him get his first Broadway role. "Maybe I shouldn't tell this on myself with all the flap about Congressional ethics. But I went into this place, got fitted and tried the suit on. While the tailor was in the back room for a moment I simply took off wearing the poor guy's creation."

George Murphy pictured with Shirley Temple (centre), and Edna May Oliver in a scene from *Little Miss Broadway* directed by Irving Cummings in 1938.

Murphy made his debut in Hollywood in the film *Kid Millions* and went on to appear in more than forty-five movies including *For Me And My Gal*, *Little Miss Broadway*, *Battleground* and *The Powers Girl*, opposite such actresses as Shirley Temple, Judy Garland and Elizabeth Taylor. Much like Ronald Reagan, it is more for his political career than his long career at MGM that Murphy is remembered today. As a U.S. senator he was considered more conservative than most Republicans of his day. Prior to his Washington days he had entered politics, again just as Reagan did later, through his executive involvement over sixteen years with the Screen Actors' Guild. Murphy was the tough guy of the Guild, "coming in when the going was rough," according to one fellow board member in that period, who said that Murphy had taken on suspected racketeers who looked to be trying to muscle into the Hollywood unions. He exposed evidence that organised crime was shaking down some studio chiefs, and he orchestrated a strong campaign to keep them out of the crafts unions. Murphy served as president of the Screen Actors' Guild from 1944–45. When he died in 1992, an obituary in the *Los Angeles Times* referred to the so-called Communist witch-hunts of the Forties and noted that '... (Murphy) formed the Hollywood Republican Committee to "combat the general belief that all Hollywood actors and writers are left-wing."'

Nobody in Hollywood was unaffected by the Communist witch-hunt that Senator Joseph McCarthy, another Irish-American, had started: not even Gene Kelly. While Murphy was busy hunting Communists in Hollywood, Kelly and his young wife Betsy were becoming disheartened, along with so many others in the film town, at what they perceived to be an unholy injustice abroad in the land. Kelly joined a group of actors and directors, John Huston and Willie Wyler at their head, who flew to Washington, D.C.

in October of 1947 to register their concern. Other members of that now famous mission included Humphrey Bogart, Richard Conte, Lauren Bacall, Paul Henreid, June Havoc, Danny Kaye, Evelyn Keyes and Sterling Hayden. Kelly would later make it very clear, when asked straight out by the American Legion if he was a Communist, that he was not and indeed had no sympathies at all with Communism. His trip to Washington with those others of conscience had been something Kelly insisted he simply "had to do".

Meanwhile, back in the business of Hollywood and that movie that brought Kelly and Murphy nose to nose, *For Me and My Gal*, things somehow worked out just fine in the end. The red-hot tensions between Kelly and Murphy seeped through into the final cut which added drama to the final film. A full page advertisement was taken out by MGM's publicity department in the *New York Times* after the film's premiere. It announced that a new star had burst onto the cinema scene – and his name was Gene Kelly. The fact that the advertisement appeared in the *New York Times* was particularly thrilling for Kelly because, deep in his heart, he still considered Broadway his real stomping ground. If *Pal Joey* was one Broadway legacy that helped Kelly find his way in Hollywood, a young actress and hoofer called Betsy Blair was another. Kelly had married the bright, beautiful and talented Blair – whom he had first met when he choreographed a song and dance show at the Capitol Hotel in New York. The show, Billy Rose's *Diamond Horseshoe* laid claim to the "prettiest showgirls in New York." Kelly and his new wife, who was just eighteen, were madly in love. They were in Hollywood and Kelly was a rising star. The world was at their feet; or so they thought. Despite the praise heaped upon him for his brilliant performance in *For Me and My Gal*, there followed several films for MGM that totally failed to showcase his talents – movies such as *Thousands Cheer* (1943) and *Pilot No. 5* the same year. Once again, Hollywood failed to see Kelly's real potential. He was loaned out to Columbia Pictures which cast him opposite Rita Hayworth in the wartime glamour musical *Cover Girl*. Given a free hand to create a new dance number for the film, Kelly used numerous lighting and optical effects to devise the now classic routine in which he dances with a superimposed image of himself. The film was a huge success, largely because of this one phenomenal routine, and finally the folks in the boardroom back at MGM were getting the picture. MGM immediately cast Kelly alongside Fred Astaire in the all-star *Ziegfeld Follies* movie. Next came Kelly's milestone movie, *Anchors Aweigh* in 1945, co-starring Frank Sinatra. The film was a showcase for Kelly's brilliance and earned him his first and only best actor Oscar nomination. By the time *Anchors Aweigh* was released Kelly had gone off to play his part in World War II by joining the Navy – an experience he would endure but not relish. Most of his fellow recruits were ten years younger than him and Kelly felt out of place. Despite the age difference, Kelly was fitter than any of the youngsters with whom he bunked.

"You're as solid as a Sherman tank," a Navy doctor had commented when Kelly was enlisted. "How do you keep so fit?"

"Oh, just making pictures," Kelly replied.

Kelly served with distinction in the Navy's photographic division, often heading up Navy film assignments as a newly promoted lieutenant. And when the war ended, he headed back to Hollywood, convinced the town was waiting with bated breath for its young dancing star's return. But Hollywood hadn't changed a whit since the Irish director Rex Ingram had returned from World War I so many years before to a cold shoulder. Kelly discovered that his name had been all but forgotten, and he would have to begin all over again. His first assignment back in Hollywood for MGM – with which he was still under contract

– was in *Living in a Big Way* in 1947 opposite Marie McDonald, a low-budget comedy that afforded Kelly no music or dance scenes. Later came the Vincente Minnelli-directed music and dance extravaganza *The Pirate*, in which Kelly was once again playing opposite his good friend Judy Garland. Kelly's swashbuckling prowess in *Pirate* led to him being cast as D'Artagnan in George Sidney's 1948 production of *The Three Musketeers*, a rough and tumble film which saw Kelly prove his athletic abilities in some spectacular fencing scenes and other dangerous stunts which he carried out himself. He was worried that audiences would by now be familiar with his very unique dancing style and movement, and would easily spot a stunt double. It was while cavorting through *Musketeers* that Kelly and his pal Stanley Donen, whom he had known since *Pal Joey* days, developed a story idea for a new film. It was the quirky yarn of three baseball players who moonlight as vaudevillians. When Arthur Freed rowed in, the idea became a reality and the name of the project was *Take Me Out to the Ball Game*, which would once again see Kelly and Sinatra working together, along with Jules Munshin as the third ball player. Sinatra would remain forever grateful to Kelly – his wild Irish slave driver, as he called him – for being so patient and driving him so hard to become a dancer. Kelly had a reputation as a hard-working, self-driven, ambitious genius with a black temper that sometimes flashed momentarily then vanished as quickly. But behind it all, when the workday was done, the warm side of Kelly could be seen. "All the hoofers from the MGM lot would come to Gene's for the Saturday jam sessions. I shall never forget Gene doing his Irish best behind the bar, while Lena Horne – and then it was Judy Garland – sang, and Andre Previn played piano. Oscar Levant taught me how to smoke, nervously, and Stanley Donen slept," remembered Leslie Caron.

He was becoming one of MGM's leading stars by now, but Kelly had more in his bag of tricks – much more, as Hollywood and MGM would soon find out. The movie would be called *An American in Paris*. Kelly's long-time cohort Arthur Freed would produce, Minnelli would direct and Alan Jay Lerner had penned the screenplay for this story based on the Gershwin orchestral 'tone poem'. Kelly's character in the movie, Jerry Mulligan, is described as the 'archetype character of his on-screen persona – enormously likable, charming, sensitive and romantic.' The film remains today as the consummate monument to MGM's golden days. *An American in Paris* won six Academy Awards in 1951 including Best Picture, and Kelly won a special Oscar for his contribution to the art of choreography on film. Some observers feel that the enormous impact of *An American in Paris* overshadowed the brilliance of his next film – but history would seem to indicate otherwise: the film was *Singin' in the Rain*, the movie in which Kelly would be teamed for the first time with a young Irish-American hoofer called Donald O'Connor.

O'Connor, one story has it, was so in awe of the older and far more established Kelly that one day in rehearsals for *Singin' in the Rain* Kelly, in one of his notable black tempers, accused O'Connor of being out of step in a dance routine. O'Connor apologised and they went back to work. But the routine was still 'out of whack'. Then Kelly realised that he had been the one out of step. Instead of being humble about the situation, Kelly worked himself up into an even worse temper and demanded to know why O'Connor hadn't told him right out that he was the one in the wrong. O'Connor said nothing – he worshipped Kelly. It was a measure of Kelly's stature that O'Connor should have been so in awe, for O'Connor was no slouch in showbiz terms himself. He was the only twenty-six-year-old dancer in Hollywood then who could claim that he had been twenty-five years and six months in show business: a child of the stage, quite literally.

The O'Connors were a family theatre act of acrobat displays and song and dance routines during the heyday of vaudeville. O'Connor's mother was working on stage until two days before

he was born in 1925, and back in the act two days after he was born. O'Connor made his own debut on stage at the age of two months in a brief appearance and became a regular part of the O'Connor family act, complete with salary at the age of thirteen months. His mother had insisted that "if he works he gets paid," even if he was only a baby. The child's job was to come out from under the stage, jump over the footlights and be swung onto the stage by his older brother. O'Connor's father, John E. 'Chuck' O'Connor, a native of County Cork, was an acrobat. At one point in his varied career he was one of Ringling Brothers' principal 'leapers' for years, hurdling over elephants and high barriers. He headlined a trampoline act, danced, and also did sideshow professional boxing, taking on all-comers. O'Connor's French mother was a tight-rope walker, circus bareback rider and, of course, a dancer.

O'Connor was just six months old when his father died, but his mother, Effie Dubuque O'Connor, kept the family act together with Donald and his older brothers Jack and Billy. The family toured the vaudeville circuit, town to town, theatre to theatre with its song and dance act while the youngest O'Connor received a basic elementary education from his mother. The Depression brought hard times to the O'Connors as it did to all the vaudeville players, and at one point they were paid as little as $6 for a one-night stand – a dramatic drop in fortunes for the family that in better days had commanded more than $1000 a week. The family act eventually found itself in Los Angeles in 1938 appearing in a Hollywood theatre. O'Connor agreed to take part in a charity act with one of his brothers for a relief association drive at the Los Angeles Biltmore theatre when a talent scout spotted him and he was give the role of Bing Crosby's kid brother in the movie *Sing You Sinners*. He was just thirteen years old when put on contract at Paramount at a salary of $250 a week. He made eleven pictures in his first year with the studio including *Men With Wings*, *Sons of the Legion*, *Death of a Champion*, *Million Dollar Legs* and *Beau Geste*. "I was everybody's son," O'Connor recalled of those parts. But when the pint-sized thirteen-year-old sprouted and added a foot to his height in a single year, Paramount dropped his contract.

The O'Connor family act went on the road again, playing one-night engagements around the country. Tragedy struck the family again when older brother Billy died of scarlet fever in 1939. But the family act played on. Since the days when the act included Donald's two brothers, father and a sister, the O'Connors were now reduced to Donald, one brother, and his mother. The money that had been saved from O'Connor's year at Paramount was dwindling and vaudeville was being murdered by the moving pictures. Work was in short supply, pay was low and things were getting desperate. The family was playing a date in the 'sticks' of Peru, Illinois, when a wire came from Universal Studios. Donald O'Connor's work at Paramount was remembered and the studio was in search of talent. He was summoned to Universal and a contract that offered him $200 a week.

Among the pictures in which he appeared during the next few years were *Mr Big*, *Top Man*, *Chip off the Old Block*, *Follow the Boys*, *This is the Life*, *The Merry Monahans*, *Bowery to Broadway* and *Patrick the Great*. A review in the *New York Times* said of his work in *Mr Big*, 'O'Connor, now eighteen was drawing very positive reviews.' *The New York World-Telegram*'s opinion was that *Chip Off The Old Block* 'makes Donald about the funniest young man around right now.' *Variety* noted that in *This is the Life* 'O'Connor continues to demonstrate his versatility as a screen entertainer in singing, dancing and acting.' O'Connor had just renewed his contract with Universal for five years in 1944 when he was drafted into the Army. The day before his induction O'Connor and his seventeen-year-old sweetheart Gwen Carter, were married. Their daughter Donna was born two years later. During his two and a half years of service in the Armed Forces O'Connor staged hundreds of shows for the servicemen. After his release O'Connor returned to Hollywood where a mule called Francis was waiting for him. O'Connor's so-called *Francis* films, a series of pictures in which he appeared with a trained mule, made millions at the box office and included *Francis*, *Francis Goes to the Races*, *Francis Goes to West Point* and *Francis Joins The WACS*. It was in the middle of the Francis series which was in and out of production over several years that O'Connor found himself working with his idol Gene Kelly in *Singin' in the Rain* in the role of Cosmo Browne.

'Donald O'Connor has never been as good again, and in his famous 'Make 'Em Laugh' routine, dances, clowns, and sings as if his artistic life depended on the success of it. Every trick in his repertoire is aired afresh and the cumulative effect is devastating in its virtuosity,' commented Hirschorn in his Kelly biography.

Kelly, Murphy, O'Connor: each had his individual style, and they had little in common save their Irish backgrounds. In Kelly and Murphy's case this was certainly not sufficient to pave over their innate differences. Hollywood provided a spawning ground for Murphy's political ambitions. For O'Connor Hollywood was the first permanent home he had known, and for Kelly, Hollywood provided the stage for a genius that some say was way ahead of its time. Gregory Hines, a dance star of a later generation, during a tribute to Kelly at an American Film Institute ceremony to honour the star, recalled, "One night I invented a dance step. And then a few weeks later I turned on the TV and saw *Take Me Out to the Ball Game*. Suddenly I saw Gene doing the step (I thought) I'd made up."

As for Kelly, well he never forgot that his first ambition was to play professional baseball. "The Pittsburgh Pirates," he once joked, "lost a hell of a shortstop."

CHAPTER 14

INTEGRITY AND HOLLYWOOD – GERALDINE FITZGERALD

Hollywood had seen its fair share of rebellious Irish by the late 1930s. Directors Rex Ingram, Herbert Brenon and William Desmond Taylor were some of the most vocal stalwarts of artistic independence in an emerging studio system. Greer Garson added an early Irish female voice to the fray with her stinging public jibes about the roles in which MGM was casting her. James Cagney had put Warner Bros. Studios boss Jack Warner on the ropes in successive bouts over salary claims. When yet another Irish talent appeared on the scene, Hollywood rolled out the welcome mat. The newcomer's name was Geraldine Fitzgerald. A new chapter in the story of Hollywood's famous battles with its stars was about to be written.

Warner Bros. Studios was planning a movie triumph with its production of *Dark Victory* in 1939. Humphrey Bogart and Bette Davis were heading the bill. Irish star George Brent was also headlining. But that was not what had all of Hollywood talking. The chatter around town was centred on a virtually unknown Irish girl who was set to co-star opposite Davis. Some were saying that the new kid on the block would be blown off the screen by Davis, and would find herself on the first boat back to Ireland by the time the movie wrapped. The gossips would eat their words, for the actress they were maligning was Geraldine Fitzgerald, the Irish girl who would give Hollywood a lesson in integrity. *Dark Victory* would become Fitzgerald's grand debut in Hollywood. Her portrayal of the loving and faithful friend to Davis' character, a young woman dying of a brain tumour, was hailed as a brilliant performance. Fitzgerald hardly had time to take a breath before she was cast that same year as Heathcliff's spurned wife Isabella Linton in Samuel Goldwyn's *Wuthering Heights*. She received an Oscar nomination as best supporting actress to Laurence Olivier's Heathcliff and Merle Oberon's Cathy. Olivier would later confess "I saw (*Wuthering Heights*) on TV the other night and, you know, it was a bloody awful film. Geraldine Fitzgerald is the only thing that still holds up in that one."

Hollywood was at her feet and stardom beckoned but Fitzgerald was not impressed. In fact she wanted out of Hollywood and out of her contract with Warners for at least six months of every year so that she could pursue her first love – her stage career. "I desperately wanted to continue in theatre," she would explain. Jack Warner was not impressed. But Fitzgerald, whose career was rooted in Dublin's progressive Gate Theatre, didn't seem to care much what Jack Warner thought. Not then anyway.

"There's something of the banshee about her," director Lloyd Bacon once said of Fitzgerald, comparing her to the netherworld spirit of Irish legend that heralds the coming of death. In this case, the only thing the banshee was heralding was a long, bitter and fruitless war of wills with Jack Warner that would leave Fitzgerald emotionally exhausted. "I truly, honestly thought that film studios were trying to make masterpieces, and that when they didn't they were terribly upset. I was not just naïve, I was crashingly stupid. Countless people – friends like Humphrey Bogart, Bette Davis and Vladimir Sokoloff – tried to explain the commerciality to me, told me to play the game Warner's way. I would not listen." The lines were drawn in the sand for one of Hollywood's most infamous clashes between head office and its talent. "I fought with everybody…" she later regretted. But Fitzgerald was bringing something to the fight that Hollywood knew little of by this time – a little thing called integrity.

She was born in Dublin in 1914, the daughter of solicitor Edward Fitzgerald and his wife Edith. There was a family joke in the Fitzgerald household that their name would be immortal 'because a distant relative named James Joyce had used the name of her father's law firm, D&T Fitzgerald, in *Ulysses*,' recounted Gerald Nachman in the *New York Post* in a 1965 account of Fitzgerald's life. In those childhood days in Dublin she would accompany her aunt, the renowned stage actress Shelagh Richards, to rehearsals at the Abbey Theatre. The poet W.B. Yeats once ordered her and some other children ejected from the theatre with the cry, "Get those little beasts out of here." When she finished school in Dublin, Fitzgerald enrolled at the National College of Art in Kildare Street. She studied under Sean Keating who would later serve as president of the Royal Hibernian Academy. "When I was nineteen and ambitious, I finished art school," she would remember many years later. "I went to Sean Keating and asked him, 'Where would you suggest I go now; Paris or Rome?' He looked at me thoughtfully for fully two minutes before he answered. Then he said, 'My dear young lady, I suggest you go off and get married.'" Fitzgerald took the hint. A few days later she announced to Shelagh Richards that she had decided on an acting career instead. Richards set about giving Fitzgerald her first formal stage training. This consisted of rigorous exercises in voice production and breathing which continued for many months – with no sign of a real part in sight. That was soon to change.

The young actress made her professional stage debut at Dublin's Gate Theatre, whose artistic director from 1931–36 was Denis Johnson – Shelagh Richards' husband. Fitzgerald joined the avant-garde theatre at an opportune time in 1932, for the Gate was headed then by Michael MacLiammoir and Hilton Edwards, leading lights of the literary renaissance that was ablaze in Dublin. They cast Fitzgerald in a role in a production of *Blood and Sand* in which she made a strong impression with the critics. That was followed by more substantial roles at the Gate. The attention she received earned her significant roles in numerous British films over the next several years, including *The Turn of the Tide* (Rank 1934) and *The Mill on the Floss* (Standard 1939). Though Fitzgerald was never thought of as a stunningly beautiful screen presence in the classic sense, her patrician beauty combined with eyes which were, according to one journalist 'strangely bright and a little frightening,' created an intense screen persona. One journalist would write of her, 'The delicate features and the glittering eyes probably explain Hollywood's difficulty in type-casting her…'

Off-camera and off-stage Fitzgerald had met and fallen madly in love with a debonair young British horse breeder-cum-songwriter called Michael Lindsey Hogg, whom she married in 1936. But Fitzgerald was not about to take the advice that Sean Keating had given her in Dublin a few years previously. She may have gone off and got married – but she had no intention of settling down. Far from it, America was beckoning.

"I truly, honestly thought that film studios were trying to make masterpieces, and that when they didn't they were terribly upset. I was not just naive, I was crashingly stupid…" so said Irish star Geraldine Fitzgerald – seen here in *Wuthering Heights* (1939) as Isabella Linton.

"I looked toward America when I was a girl," she told Phil Casey in an interview for the *Washington Post* in 1972. "I read *The New Yorker*, and that was considered very daring, very avant-garde in those days." She already had a friend at court on Broadway, a dynamic young actor who had taken the first steps of a tempestuous career at the Gate Theatre. He had toured Ireland when he was a teenager and ended up at the door of MacLiammoir and Edwards at the Gate when he was just eighteen. Though unconvinced by the brashly confident young man's claim to considerable acting experience back in America, he impressed the pair sufficiently by his voice, stance and intelligence. The legend of Orson Welles had begun. By the time Fitzgerald was ready for Broadway, Welles was heading his own company in New York. The Mercury Theatre was about to put on a production of *Heartbreak House*, and he called Fitzgerald in for the production. Critics were particularly favourable to Fitzgerald whom they described variously as 'lovely' and 'admirable'. The notices did not translate into a big paycheque however. "My husband had gone back home on business, and Orson asked me how little I needed to eat and go on living at the Algonquin (Hotel). I came up with the sum of seventy-eight dollars and fourteen cents a week, after much figuring," the actress recalled of the period. What she didn't figure on was the note that would arrive at her dressing room door at the Mercury – a calling card from Hollywood.

A producer from Warner Bros. had taken in her impressive Broadway performance and wanted to recruit her to the studio. But if Warners expected the young newcomer to gush at such good fortune, they were mistaken. Fitzgerald had some unusual demands, the oddest of which was that she should be released from her contract with the studio for at least six months a year to pursue her stage career.

Jack Warner could understand why Jimmy Cagney had fought so hard for huge salary increases – in his mind money was something one fought for. Fitzgerald saw Warner as a philistine. "I wanted to continue in theatre. Orson had built a little world around himself, and I wanted to be with these people, or with the Gate again. I was really a fanatic about my relationship to the performing arts, indentured, as I was, to this demon which I thought was called 'integrity'. The demon's real name was 'dumb'." At the height of her stand-off with Warner – and with Hollywood in general – Fitzgerald turned down an offer from David O. Selznick to test for the role of Melanie in a little movie called *Gone with the Wind*. "I would not bend and see the possibilities in a role that was not my first choice. I mean, I would play Scarlett O'Hara or nothing," Fitzgerald admitted years later.

Inevitably her 'demon' brought down the wrath of Jack Warner, who punished her with second-rate roles in mediocre films. Fitzgerald's truly auspicious beginning in Hollywood seemed now to be dying on the vine, as Warner doled out one dull role after another. Fitzgerald was getting a taste of the studio system and how easily it could crush even the most determined ideals. She was gaining a newfound wisdom and knowledge of Hollywood and its workings. She began to wonder if it would not be wiser to make her peace with the studio. Fitzgerald confided her thoughts to her friends. "People of super intelligence would say, 'Darling, not you, it's artistic prostitution.' I'd say, 'Fine, if I'm in a brothel, I want to be the best whore in the house.' It was too late. Of course I don't exactly have regrets because you cannot change the past. But if you ask me, did I suffer for my mistakes, I'd say 'yes, deeply.' I finally saw it. No one had ever thrown away good breaks with such monotonous frequency. I felt totally alienated, frustrated… and I had to sit by and watch everyone else play parts that I knew could have been mine."

'Geraldine Fitzgerald is the critics' delight,' wrote Edwin Schallert, the *Los Angeles Times* drama editor in 1944, 'they recognise her as a highly competent actress, an extremely attractive and fascinating woman, but complain that as yet the 'luck of the Irish,' so renowned, doesn't seem to attend her. There are coming within her horizon neither the parts, the pictures, nor even the plays that are fitting to the gifts that she possesses. It is regrettable, [not] to say vastly irritating. However, Miss Fitzgerald herself is neither in revolt nor complaining. She is patiently waiting for time to take its course. She had exactly one rebellion at Warners, where she is under contract, which led to her going to the stage. It resulted chiefly in that normal suspension which is incorporated in practically all actors' contracts.'

Humphrey Bogart once told Fitzgerald that movies were like slot machines. If you played long enough, you would eventually hit the jackpot. In Fitzgerald's case, the jackpot had already been hit with *Wuthering Heights* and *Dark Victory*. There were other chances, other parts that could have represented that Hollywood payoff, including a movie with her friend Bogart; *The Maltese Falcon*. She turned down the role and Mary Astor stepped in. "I wanted to go off and do theatre somewhere. I was a fool. I stuck to my Irish logic instead of saying 'yes' to everything. I fought Jack Warner for better parts, and I finally lost," she confessed to an interviewer. But 'lost' would hardly be an apt description of Fitzgerald's remarkable career. From Dublin's Gate Theatre to Broadway, to Hollywood and back to Broadway again, she won serious plaudits and a Tony nomination for her stage directorial debut with *Mass Appeal* starring another sometimes Irish Hollywood colonist Milo O'Shea in 1980 at the Manhattan Theatre Club. Of that and subsequent theatre directing assignments Fitzgerald commented wryly in an interview in *Backstage* magazine, "… the experience of being an actress-director has made me more reasonable and understanding in both roles. When I am acting now, I also better understand the problems of other actors, since I have developed a certain perspective about the difficulties an actor can get into."

Fitzgerald may have jousted with Hollywood and in her own words "lost". Despite the setbacks she leaves in her wake a host of great American screen performances, one of which was the role of Edith Galt who became the second Mrs Woodrow Wilson in the Darryl F. Zanuck film *Wilson,* the 20th Century Fox screen biography of the former U.S. President. The studio had one big problem when it came to Fitzgerald. 'Should an Irish-born actress portray this American woman?' writes Schallert. The journalist tells how Fitzgerald negotiated with the studio. "'Let me make a test, and if it doesn't look obscene, then maybe I'll be fitted for the part," (she volunteered). So she assumed the (role) of Edith Galt and went through a scene with Alexander Knox as the mature Wilson, and as soon as Darryl Zanuck viewed this she was in. But it took an actual photographic test to convince.'

Later memorable Hollywood performances from Fitzgerald came with such movies as *Watch on the Rhine, Uncle Harry, The Pawnbroker, Rachel, Rachel, The Last American Hero* and more recently as Art Carney's childhood sweetheart in *Harry and Tonto.* She surprised critics with her outrageous comedic antics in *Arthur* with Dudley Moore and *Easy Money* opposite Rodney Dangerfield in the latter part of her career, which she spent commuting from Broadway to Hollywood. Numerous television performances also marked this stage of her career. The ABC presentation of *The Moon and Sixpence* brought her back together with her old friend and mentor Laurence Olivier. Her true fame today lies with that dedication to her thespian art rather than her worthy Hollywood career.

Upon her death *The Guardian* newspaper commented, 'When Geraldine Fitzgerald, who has died aged ninety-one, directed her Tony-nominated production of *Mass Appeal* on Broadway in 1981, she explained: "I was forgotten, so I had nothing to live up to. It was the best thing in the circumstances. I could start at the bottom learning the new craft of directing." It was a modest statement from someone remembered by film fans as a 1940s Hollywood star.'

It seems fitting to record that one of her proudest achievements was her work to promote street theatre in New York. "I've always believed that theatre should belong to everyone, like water, air, fire," she told a *New York Times* interviewer when in 1968 she collaborated with a Franciscan monk, Jonathan Ringkamp, a fellow member of the New York City Council on the Arts, to bring theatre to the people.

There can be little said or recalled to surpass the tribute paid to the actress/director by journalist Howard A. Coffin when he penned the words for the *Philadelphia Inquirer* in March, 1975, 'She's an enchantingly free spirit who roams… fast on her facile intellect and voluble Irish charm.'

CHAPTER 15

IN THE HOLLYWOOD JUNGLE - MAUREEN O'SULLIVAN

Ireland's great tenor Count John McCormack was about to star in a new movie called *Song O' My Heart* and offered to help 20th Century Fox in the search for a new talent to play his daughter. Legendary Irish tenor John Francis McCormack was born in Athlone on 14th June 1884. He trained under the great Italian maestro Sabatini in Italy and made an early landmark operatic bow in London in *Cavalleria Rusticana*. He was soon being hailed worldwide, including America where in 1917 he became a US citizen.

In mid-life McCormack moved into Moore Abbey in County Kildare, while also buying a picturesque hill spot overlooking Hollywood called Runyon Canyon which today is open to the public. It provides spectacular views of Hollywood, while also providing a wilderness hiking landscape with signs that warn of rattlesnakes and wildcats. McCormack reportedly loved living at Runyon Canyon and even filmed *Song O' My Heart* there in 1929. McCormack used the money that he made from the movie to build a spectacular home that he named 'San Patricio', (St Patrick in Spanish). The sad remains of the home, including its skeleton-like foundations stick out of the beautiful landscape today like spires. McCormack and his wife lived there until they returned to Europe in 1938. McCormack would also be instrumental in the discovery of Hollywood's latest star – Maureen O'Sullivan.

Maureen O'Sullivan, daughter of army officer Major Charles O'Sullivan, had a privileged childhood growing up in Boyle, County Roscommon where she was born in 1911. "Our nurses (she had a younger brother and sister), were always being fired. They would threaten dire things if I told mother that they had been talking with the soldiers, but I guess I was a young scamp because I always told on them," she would recall in later years. She was educated at the Convent of the Sacred Heart in Roehampton near London, where she formed a close bond with the daughter of John McCormack. She also made friends at the convent with future screen star Vivien Leigh. Later came finishing school in Paris, and an introduction to the social whirl – of high society balls, theatre, opera and motoring trips through France with her fashionable young friends.

Maureen O'Sullivan (third from left as Jane Bennett) in *Pride and Prejudice*, with Greer Garson as Elizabeth Bennett), Laurence Olivier (as Mr Darcy), and Bruce Lester (as Charles Bingley)

She did not appear to have any great interest in the movies or theatre. "I once played the part of a 'good fairy' in a Shakespearean play. But I am sure that the audience suffered as much as I did." So when an invitation came for a dinner at the luxurious Shelbourne Hotel in Dublin, where she was living with her family after finishing school, O'Sullivan paid little attention to the fact that the famous Hollywood film director Frank Borzage was dining in the same hotel restaurant. The name meant absolutely nothing to the girl who had now blossomed into a ravishing young woman. Borzage was in town to cast for his latest movie *Song O' My Heart* with none other than John McCormack, the father of O'Sullivan's old school chum. O'Sullivan noticed some whispering and furtive glances in her direction from some diners. One man in particular seemed to be paying her rather too much attention.

"Who is that man?" she asked her escort for the night.

"Why – that's Frank Borzage, he's directing the McCormack picture," she was informed.

A few minutes later, the actress recounted, a waiter brought over a calling card from Borzage with a scribbled note asking permission to speak to her. She looked over at Borzage and nodded. In what would almost seem to be one of Hollywood's more fantastic tales of instant stardom – though it has been validated in numerous first-hand accounts – Borzage asked her to test for the female lead in the McCormack vehicle for Fox. She made the test, got the role and was a sensation. The film was made mostly on location on the County Kildare Irish estate of John McCormack. The role led initially to a contract at the Fox studios in Hollywood for O'Sullivan.

"Her success in Hollywood was immediate, but soon she found it had come too quickly," attested Howard Strickling, a well-known Hollywood publicist of the day. "The demand studios (Fox) had made for her services when she first arrived was followed by a lull. For a while it appeared that she was another girl who had been rushed to stardom only to be rushed back into oblivion." In fact she made several films for Fox during that early period. But they were minor parts, the most notable probably being *A Connecticut Yankee in King Arthur's Court* in which she provided the romantic interest for Yankee Will Rogers when he is transported back to King Arthur's Court.

That was when an offer came from Metro-Goldwyn-Mayer. The studio was looking for a fresh new face to play opposite strongman Johnny Weissmuller in its new jungle adventure *Tarzan the Ape Man*. The pairing of this new Tarzan and Jane would become one of the most enduring screen partnerships of all time. It also landed the former convent girl in hot water with some of the more extreme conservative elements in the country at the time – and also with a chimp.

The chimp was Cheetah, Tarzan's primate pal. "Cheetah, that bastard," O'Sullivan told *People* magazine of the simian star, "bit me whenever he could." In another interview with the *Los Angeles Times* in 1953 the actress complained, "At times I was fearful about working with the animal, because he would bite me. Cheetah liked Johnny Weissmuller, which is probably the reason why he hated me, because he was jealous."

She went on to play Tarzan's Jane in five more jungle films, in which she caused something of a sensation with the very revealing costume provided by the MGM wardrobe department. "It started a furore," she recounted. "Letters started coming in. It added up to thousands of women objecting to my costume. In those days, they took those things seriously. I was offered all kinds of places where I could go in my shame to hide from the cruel public ready to throw stones at me. It's funny. We were unreal people, and yet we were real."

'If anybody has a right to talk about nudism it is Maureen O'Sullivan,' purred the *Photoplay* writer Winifred Audolette in 1934. 'Tarzan's mate says she was never so miserable as when forced to go raw.'

'To be forced to go around with practically no clothes on for eight hours a day on a freezing winter [day] and to stand knee-deep in what I am sure was melted ice water and to hear the sound man yelling, "I can hear your teeth chattering, Miss O'Sullivan, you'll have to control them".'

For the record, O'Sullivan's younger sister Sheilah once clarified that O'Sullivan had never actually performed in the nude. The impression that she had arose because of one particularly daring and erotic underwater scene in which 'Jane' swims naked. A body double was in fact used in that and other sub-aqua scenes in which O'Sullivan appears to be nude.

Though the six Tarzan movies – the first talking *Tarzan* pictures – that she made with Weissmuller became a point of irritation for the actress in later years, particularly the never-ending gossip about that skimpy sarong, she was particularly proud of the fact that 'Tarzan' author Edgar Rice Burroughs said of her, "I am afraid I shall never be satisfied with any other heroine in my future films."

Maureen O'Sullivan played many classic roles on the big screen in Hollywood but is more often remembered for her portrayal of Tarzan's Jane in a series of MGM 'jungle movies'. Pictured here with co-star Johnny Weissmuller. 'Boy' actor – Johnny Sheffield, and Cheetah.

There was a point where O'Sullivan seriously considered doing some more *Tarzan* movies, which MGM was begging her to take on. "But first I asked my oldest boy Michael (then eight years old) if he would like to see his mother swinging through trees with the monkeys. 'Mother,' he answered, 'I would be ashamed.' So that took care of that."

O'Sullivan admitted to feeling aggrieved sometimes when her body of work was overlooked for the brief *Tarzan* stint. Her films included such MGM notables as *Tugboat Annie* with Marie Dressler and Wallace Berry, *The Barretts of Wimpole Street* with Norma Shearer, *The Voice of Bugle Ann* with Lionel Barrymore, *A Yank at Oxford* with Robert Taylor, *Let Us Live* with Henry Fonda and *Pride and Prejudice* with fellow Irish star at MGM Greer Garson, *The Big Clock* directed by her husband John Farrow in 1948, and *David Copperfield* with W.C. Fields.

Often the roles that came her way did not give O'Sullivan the scope to do the best she could, some critics believed. 'She was… perfect as Elizabeth Barrett's younger sister Henrietta in *The Barretts of Wimpole Street* (1934), as David's child-wife Dora in *David Copperfield* (1935) and as Kitty in the shadow of Garbo's *Anna Karenina* (1935),' the London *Times* would write of her. 'She was the female lead in Tod Browning's *The Devil Doll*, but this gave her little to do but scream and look vulnerable.'

In *The Thin Man* she was never going to be 'Norah Charles,' but an innocent bystander with third billing. In the Marx Brothers' *A Day at the Races* she was half of the romantic sub-plot; in *A Yank at Oxford* she played second fiddle to Vivien Leigh, which never got anyone very far; and in *Pride and Prejudice* she was back to being a younger sister, this time of Greer Garson.

One of O'Sullivan's best films of the 1930s must have been James Whale's *Port of Seven Seas*, a moving remake of Pagnol's Marseilles classic *Fanny*, where she played Madelon 'with much charm and occasional pathos,' the London *Times* tribute continued.

She retired from films in 1942 to devote her time to her family but continued to live in Southern California. In the 1950s O'Sullivan toyed with some television roles including host of a series called *Irish Heritage*. In the 1960s after the death of her husband O'Sullivan moved to New York where she made a sensational comeback in the play *Never Too Late* playing opposite Paul Ford as a suddenly expectant middle-aged wife. She and Ford also appeared in the movie version of the comedy. Her debut Broadway performance led to an active career on the stage in later life. She went on to star in a string of successful productions from *The Subject Was Roses* to *Keep It in The Family, No Sex Please We're British* and the revival of Paul Osborn's *Morning at Seven*. Woody Allen cast her in her most 'luminous screen role,' as the *New York Times* described it, when she appeared in Allen's 1985 hit *Hannah and Her Sisters*. Her daughter Mia Farrow played one of her children in the film. She admitted that working with her daughter for the first time "made both of us nervous, but once we started shooting, it became just two actresses doing their parts." The role saw O'Sullivan, let her hair down as the "boozy old flirt with a filthy mouth," as her screen character describes herself. Hailing her performance in the film, Vincent Canby of the *New York Times* wrote that she 'never had five minutes of screen time to equal her work here.' The actress was seventy-five years old. A year later O'Sullivan's name was back in lights in Francis Ford Coppola's *Peggy Sue Got Married*.

O'Sullivan spent much of her later life married to construction company executive James Cushing while travelling between homes in New Hampshire, Schenectady and Phoenix, while visiting her thirty-two grandchildren. She was eighty-seven when she died at Scottsdale Memorial Hospital near her home in Phoenix in June 1998. Her daughter, Stephanie Soghoian said she thought her mother had died, quite simply, of old age. "She embodied all the things you hear about Irish people," her agent John Springer said of his old friend. "She was warm, generous, kind and loving." Her daughter Mia said she was a mother who had always been "full of fairy tales".

CHAPTER 16

IRISH SCREEN ROYALTY – MAUREEN O'HARA AND GRACE KELLY

Maureen O'Hara was dubbed 'The Queen of Technicolor,' at a time when Hollywood was perfecting the system of shooting films in colour. By the 1940s the Technicolor movie had arrived. It was the perfect medium for Maureen O'Hara. 'It is her hair, in fact, which most critics refer to first – before any assessment of her acting ability is even attempted – flaming, naturally curly, Titian shot with gold. Pale white skin, attractively freckled, with a blush the deepest crimson – the perfect Technicolor complexion' wrote one admiring journalist of O'Hara.

Maureen O'Hara

Hollywood fell in love with O'Hara from the day she arrived, and has never fallen out of love with her. Much of O'Hara's appeal across more than six decades of stardom has been her willingness to share a joke. She laughed louder than anybody in the ballroom at the Beverly Wilshire Hotel when a compilation of her movies was screened during a presentation to her of the American Ireland Fund's Heritage Award. There was O'Hara, Ireland's most endearing movie star, whacking and thumping an A-list of Hollywood's leading men from Tyrone Power to John Wayne. In every single scene she was walloping some movie star. The sight gag was actually an extension of a humorous send-up orchestrated back in the 1940s by some of the same legendary leading men of the screen. She was starring in one of her earliest Hollywood films *The Black Swan* in 1942. Journalist Sara Hamilton had taken a flying visit to the 20th Century Fox lot where O'Hara was working. 'They kept telling me what a nice girl Maureen O'Hara was,' began the reporter. Then she encountered Tyrone Power outside the sound stage with a swollen lip. '"Maureen hit me," he mumbled as best he could… directly inside the sound stage we met a huge bearded, red-haired giant who turned out to be George Sanders, holding his head and twirling around like a waltzing mouse. "Maureen hit me with a bottle," he moaned… On the set just then limped John Wayne. "Got a bum leg?" we asked. 'No, I just never got over the shove Maureen gave me in *To the Shores of Tripoli*. Dislocated my sacroiliac."' Of course it was all a gag and O'Hara thought it hilarious.

Maureen O'Hara who had arrived in Hollywood with her mother not long before this, took some things about the town very seriously however. Her first directive to her new studio bosses was that she would do "No Leg Art!" By this O'Hara meant that the bubble baths that were becoming popular costumes for pneumatic actresses in the movies in the 1940s were definitely off the page. "I come from a very strict family. I can't do some of the things other actresses can because my folks in Dublin would think that I had turned out all bad. And I want to keep their love. I promised my mother I would never do 'leg art'." Hollywood reporters sneered that O'Hara was acting as her own Hays Office, but O'Hara paid no heed. She was determined to be her own woman and Hollywood could like it or lump it.

"I don't believe anybody reckons with the fight that's in me," she swore to Philip Scheuer of the *Los Angeles Times* in 1945. "I don't tear my hair out, but when my chance comes, I promise you that I will surprise a lot of people. They don't know I can act. But I know it – and as long as I know it, nobody is going to stop me."

Nobody did stop this undaunted, redheaded maelstrom, and her career in Hollywood is the stuff of legend. The list of her friends from the great John Ford to John Wayne and Henry Fonda, reads like a role call of Hollywood's finest. She was busy promoting her 2004 auto-biography *'Tis Herself* until her retirement in Ireland, and was ready and willing to do the TV talkshow circuit of New York and Los Angeles with the energy of a twenty-year-old. Who can forget Maureen O'Hara giving testimony before Congress in 1979 when urging the striking of a medal for her dear friend John Wayne. Her voice shaking, her eyes filled with tears she proclaimed the words that should be struck for Wayne: "He was an American".

She was born Maureen FitzSimons in Ranelagh, Dublin, on August 17th 1920. Her father, Charles FitzSimons owned and managed a business in Dublin, and also part-owned the football team Shamrock Rovers. As a twelve-year-old she was enrolled in a "reputable school of elocution". Two years later she entered the training adjunct of the Abbey Theatre and was soon being used in small roles in the main theatre venue. A chance meeting with producer Harry Richman led to a screen test in London that won her brief appearance in the British film *Kicking the Moon Around*. But O'Hara was at first reluctant to leave Dublin for the film role. "While I was mulling the matter over, a group of us went up to Mitchell's of Grafton Street for coffee. It was a famous gathering place for actors. May Carey, whom we all called 'Mama,' a very fine actress equivalent to say Dame May Whitty, urged me to go. She said that I could always return… so mummy and I decided to go to London."

Then came one of those extraordinary fated events that seem to come by chance but which in reality are the result of hard work and preparation. In O'Hara's case hard work had been a hallmark of her teenage years. She had received a degree from the London College of Music and was the youngest student ever to complete the London Guildhall School of Music drama course. So when the great British stage and screen actor Charles Laughton saw a brief cut from one of her scenes in *Kicking the Moon Around* he offered her a contract with his Mayflower Pictures production company. Laughton's Mayflower company, in which he was partnered with producer Erich Pommer, needed a box office hit badly having suffered through two flops. Alfred Hitchcock was signed to direct Laughton and O'Hara in a film based on Daphne Du Maurier's novel, *Jamaica Inn* that same year, 1939. It was Laughton who insisted she change her name from FitzSimons to O'Hara. She became an overnight sensation with the London premiere of the film. Soon after the release of *Jamaica Inn* O'Hara travelled with her mother and Laughton to America. Laughton, who had grown very fond and protective of his protégé, had insisted on her co-starring with him in his next film,

Maureen O'Hara with John Wayne during the filming of *The Quiet Man* directed by John Ford in 1952.

The Hunchback of Notre Dame, an RKO production that would become a classic and a huge hit of its day. Laughton had split with Pommer after *Jamaica Inn* and was now under contract to RKO. He strong-armed the studio into signing O'Hara for the part of the spirited gypsy girl Esmeralda who entrances Quasimodo (Laughton) against the backdrop of fifteenth-century Paris. O'Hara was a sensation.

'The contrast between Laughton as the sad but pathetic hunchback and O'Hara as the fresh-faced, tenderly solicitous gypsy girl, is Hollywood teaming at its most inspired,' commented one critic. Laughton, one of the most lauded masters of screen characters, described O'Hara as "in truth, a character actress". The observation may appear scant on flattery but Laughton was in fact raising O'Hara onto the exclusive pedestal of the industry's 'serious actors'. John Ford, who would later become a powerful force in her career, said the same thing, but much more succinctly. O'Hara, said Ford, was simply "the best actress in Hollywood".

RKO wasted no time in placing Hollywood's latest Irish arrival on a full-time contract. They put her to work on a handful of films that failed to live up to the promise of *The Hunchback*. One of these was *A Bill of Divorcement* (1940), a remake of the original version that starred a young Katharine Hepburn. It was probably a bad choice by RKO as its rising star's first movie immediately following her acclaimed performance in *The Hunchback* because, like most remakes, critics and audiences were pedantic in their judgement. But John Ford was hovering in the wings and in 1941 he cast her in his movie *How Green Was My Valley*.

'A young and lovely Maureen O'Hara (as Angharad Morgan) moves through the picture like a breath of spring,' wrote film critic Julian Fox of O'Hara's presence in the Oscar winning screen adaptation of Richard Llewellyn's novel about the villagers of a Welsh coal mining valley. 'A creature of the valley and yet outside it, she gives the impression of something wild, something free, at once ambitious and unsettled, and then romantically grateful for the lure of hearth and home.' Fox continues. 'It is a performance of wistfulness and charm and her strange tempestuous beauty is caught to perfection by Arthur Miller's fluid camera. *How Green Was My Valley* is a film which is almost beyond praise.'

O'Hara shrugged off the praise that came with that performance when she was just twenty-one, deferring instead to her director. "John Ford was the only one who had faith in my ability as an actress," she stated. O'Hara's next venture was the swashbuckling *The Black Swan* in 1942 with Tyrone Power. Director Henry King made what might have been a third-rate pirate formula into a celebrated cutlass-wielding romp. O'Hara proved herself feistier than Power or even George Sanders, the villain of the movie.

Though O'Hara undoubtedly had some less-than-extraordinary films, particularly during the RKO days, things were moving pretty fast now. She was required now to do just one movie a year for RKO – the rest of the time would be spent at Fox. Studio boss Darryl F. Zanuck was, as one Hollywood reporter put it, 'convinced that she is now headed for great things in the movies. He bases his opinion on her performance in *How Green Was My Valley*, and also on what she will look like when the Technicolor cameras focus on her chestnut-red hair and milky complexion.'

Zanuck called it just right – O'Hara was about to become Hollywood's resident 'Technicolor Queen,' as she would soon be dubbed in the new era of colour movies that was now dawning. The dubious title was not something O'Hara particularly relished. "I did get identified with Technicolor, and that bothered me, because many of the great roles at that time were still being made in black and white. I was cast for so many years in pirate pictures." At the time of this "hoop skirts and bonnet," period as she described it, O'Hara would spell out her wish list of roles: "No more duchesses, countesses and great ladies… bangs and parasols! Instead, the kind of women that Greer Garson and Irene Dunne play. Women who are alive – not living today, necessarily, but – well, alive."

Although her career did include numerous heroines of the high seas and higher adventure from *Sinbad the Sailor* with Douglas Fairbanks Jr and Anthony Quinn, or *Against All Flags*, with Errol Flynn, she also played the more sculptured characters of Louise Cody, opposite Joel McCrea's *Buffalo Bill*, the disbeliever of Santa Claus in the Christmas classic *Miracle on 34th Street*, the harassed homemaker in *Sitting Pretty*, the estranged wife of an embittered cavalry officer in Ford's *Rio Grande*, the loyal matriarch in *Spencer's Mountain* and a French schoolteacher in Jean Renoir's *This Land is Mine*, once again playing opposite her former mentor Laughton.

O'Hara was a major Hollywood star when she met and married a handsome young army officer and movie director Will Price. "*Jamaica (Inn)* was always lucky for me because that was the movie that brought me to America, and if I hadn't come to Hollywood, I would not have met Will." They had a daughter Bronwyn.

Legendary Irish beauty – "the Queen of Technicolor" – Maureen O'Hara embraced by John Wayne in
the poster advertising Irish evergreen *The Quiet Man*.

O'Hara's reputation as a rock-solid professional on set matched her sensible approach to life in fickle Hollywood. "I've been looking for some time at the motion picture stars who have lived sensibly, wisely and modestly in Hollywood and are living comfortably now. I've also looked at the stars who spent all their money, lived high and rich. Many of these, too many, are working as extras today," said O'Hara in a *Photoplay* interview in 1952. O'Hara observed that "there is nothing in life more forlorn than the big ex-star. There is nothing more forgotten. I feel so sorry for them I'll stand there until my feet ache listening to them talk as they all talk, using the same identical words about their 'day.' Just recently, on the set of *Against All Flags* one of them told me 'In my day, I wouldn't have done this scene as Flynn did it. In my day, we would have…' My heart begins to ache as they go on and on and on about their 'day' which, but they can't face it, is their yesterday. Didn't they realise that every day must end?"

O'Hara had just completed filming in Ireland at the time of one of her most memorable films. In John Ford's *The Quiet Man* the magic of her partnership and deep friendship and affection for John Wayne bursts from the screen. They had already been paired in numerous films, not least of which were the John Ford westerns *Rio Grande* in 1950 and *Fort Apache*. While *The Quiet Man* has been criticised for being much too 'folksy' and blatantly stage-Irish it is nonetheless a worthy canvas for O'Hara's perfectly honed screen craftsmanship. 'Their quieter scenes together are a triumph of emotional growth and control, their fussing and feuding is a glorious riot. They are like Laurel and Hardy in a field full of leprechauns,' one film writer observed of the performances of Wayne and O'Hara. When Ford had decided to make *The Quiet Man* in Ireland, the job of location scouting for the film fell to a young Dublin barrister called Charles FitzSimons, O'Hara's younger brother. Later a television producer in Hollywood, FitzSimons – who also had a significant role in *The Quiet Man* – remembered vividly his sister's absolute professionalism on the very physical shoot. "In the scene where Wayne drags Maureen across the fields with the crowds following and cheering she actually hurt her back very badly and had trouble with it for a long time after, but she never complained, not once, just continued on and finished the scene. John really did drag Maureen for all he was worth. She was in considerable pain for the remainder of the production but never made anything of it," he said. In another scene, O'Hara broke a wrist bone when she slapped Wayne during a 'love scene'.

Once in the late 1950s when there seemed to be fewer important roles coming her way she commented stoically, "The Irish, although they sink into the depths very easily are, basically, a happy people. Very few Irish people go to psychiatrists because whatever happens to them, they accept it." As usual, the tenacious O'Hara prevailed and by the end of 1960 she was back as big as ever, in the hugely successful British tongue-in-cheek spy movie *Our Man in Havana*, making a charming foil to Sir Alec Guinness's wily Wormold, the vacuum cleaner salesman who gets caught up in the espionage game. The following year came *The Parent Trap*, a Disney release that co-starred Hayley Mills and Brian Keith. O'Hara's brother Charlie FitzSimons produced her next picture, *Deadly Companions* with Sam Peckinpah directing. *Mr Hobbs Takes a Vacation* followed the next year, with James Stewart. She teamed again with Henry Fonda in 1963 on *Spencer's Mountain*, twenty years on from *The Immortal Sergeant*.

O'Hara's life took off in another direction in 1967 – literally – when she married pilot Charles Blair whom she had met more than ten years earlier. In 1956 she returned to Ireland for the first time since the war. Blair, an Air Force hero who held a transatlantic flight record, was her pilot on that journey. "This man was everything John Wayne ever

The daughter of a self-made Irish-American millionaire, Grace Kelly was the epitome of
beauty on the screen and the toast of Irish-Americans everywhere.

played on screen," her brother Charles said of Blair. O'Hara went into semi-retirement from the movies to set off on a new and great adventure with her husband. Together they ran Antilles Air Boats from their home in St Croix, in the Virgin Islands. Their company began with one Navy surplus aircraft and finished with a twenty-seven plane commercial fleet that grossed some $5 million a year. The great adventure ended in disaster on September 2nd 1978, when Blair died as his amphibious aircraft crashed into the sea. "I didn't have time to sit in a corner and cry," O'Hara would recall. "I was left with an airline to be run and 156 employees to be paid every week and 125 scheduled flights a day, which had to be flown." O'Hara had become the first woman ever to run a U.S. airline. Later she sold controlling stock to Resorts International but remained the company's president until 1981. Though still emerging occasionally from her home in Ireland, O'Hara today lives the quiet life with her family, though she continues to receive thousands of letters and e-mails from fans across the globe.

O'Hara's own words in an interview conducted by her friend and young co-star so many years before in *How Green Was My Valley* serve to sum up best this most illustrious career. Roddy McDowall interviewed O'Hara for *Premiere* magazine on the occasion of the film's fiftieth anniversary. O'Hara said of her career, "Ronald Colman once said to me, 'look, if you are proud of one in every fifteen movies, consider yourself lucky.' And out of the fifty-five (as of 1991), I'm proud of much more than one in fifteen. But one time a critic did criticise me for playing so many diverse roles. I did slapstick comedy, I did sophisticated comedy, I did adventure, I did westerns, I did family comedies, I did high drama – and I think that's something to be proud of, not something to be ashamed of."

Grace Kelly

If Maureen O'Hara was the fiery 'Queen of Techicolor' then Grace Kelly was surely the 'Ice Queen' of cool blondes. However, in her case fantasy became fact when she became a real-life Princess! Grace Kelly's heritage was pure Irish on her father's side. Hollywood columnists and publicists would never let that drop – despite the fact that it had been several generations of Kellys before her who had actually come from Ireland. Nonetheless, she was the darling of the Irish societies and clubs in America and she herself rarely missed a chance to talk about her ancestry.

She was born in Philadelphia, Pennsylvania one of four children of John Brendan Kelly Sr, a.k.a. Black Jack Kelly, and Margaret Katherine Majer Kelly. Her father was one of ten children of John Henry Kelly and Irish-American Mary Costello, whose family hailed from County Mayo. Jack Kelly came from the poorer side of town, and started work at a local mill at the age of nine. A few years later he worked for one of his brothers as a labourer in a building business. The personable, handsome young man would eventually expand the business into one of the most successful in the city. He was also a popular local hero having won Olympic gold as a sculler.

Hollywood gossip columnist Hedda Hopper loved to spin a yarn that she said had come from Grace Kelly about the senior Kelly. Having proven himself as a rowing champion in the U.S. he was invited to England in 1920 to participate in an important rowing event. 'At the last minute he was rejected,' wrote Hopper who went on to state that he had been thrown out of the race because he was Irish. Some time later after winning the Olympic gold Kelly – or so the gossip writer claimed – sent his 'victorious green rowing cap to the King of England with his compliments.' Tales of this nature seemed to swirl around Grace Kelly in her early Hollywood years when literally 'no publicity was bad publicity' for a starlet on the rise.

Kelly's road to stardom and Best Actress Oscar began with dramatic classes at school as part of what can only be described as a privileged childhood, the daughter of a self-made millionaire. Upon leaving high school she auditioned for the American Academy of Dramatic Arts in New York and was accepted. She attended classes while moonlighting as a fashion model. Her graduation role at the Academy was in *The Philadelphia Story*. Her work and diligence at the Academy drew the attention of numerous producers, TV producer Delbert Mann in particular. He cast her in the first of scores of television roles that she would play while living in New York. She had just turned twenty when she received an offer from Hollywood producer Stanley Kramer to star opposite Gary Cooper in *High Noon*.

Almost immediately the town's writers were all over the 'Irish' angle. One writer prattled, 'Grace is half-Irish and half-German, and that may very well account for her personality. The vivacious, fun-loving qualities of the Irish, combined with the more serious German nature, have given the girl – born in Philadelphia on November 12, 1929, charm that few young women possess.'

Kelly followed *High Noon* with a starring role in the John Ford-directed steamy jungle picture *Mogambo* with Clark Gable. Kelly told Hedda Hopper, "*Mogambo* had three things that interested me: John Ford, Clark Gable and a trip to Africa with expenses paid. If *Mogambo* had been made in Arizona, I wouldn't have done it." The MGM movie also brought her a seven-year contract with the studio. She received a Golden Globe Award as best supporting actress and an Oscar nomination for that role.

Kelly next came to the attention of director Alfred Hitchcock for the meaty role of Margot Wendice in Hitchcock's now classic adaptation of *Dial M for Murder* with Ray Milland. Kelly was no sooner on the set than the same gossip prattle began to appear. Louella Parsons, whose column was syndicated worldwide, wrote in 1954, 'Grace Kelly, the honey-haired, blue-eyed, twenty-one-year-old charmer from Philadelphia, has come up faster than any girl who ever stepped foot in movieland – and that includes Ingrid Bergman... Grace is an Irish girl brought up strictly by a Catholic mother and father who were horrified when the columnists started writing about her rendezvous with Ray Milland...' There had indeed been gossip about a liaison between Kelly and Milland.

For Kelly 1954 was to prove a pivotal year. She began work on the movie *The Bridges at Toko-Ri* with William Holden and was also offered co-lead in Hitchcock's upcoming thriller *Rear Window*. The director had been considering Kelly for the major part of Lisa Fremont, a wealthy Manhattan socialite and model, since first working with her on *Dial M For Murder*. Kelly recounted, "All through the making of *Dial M for Murder*, he [Hitchcock] sat and talked to me about *Rear Window* all the time, even before we had discussed my being in it." Hitchcock created screen magic between Kelly and co-star James Stewart in the film and both received glowing reviews.

Kelly was to go head-to-head with the powerful studio system when she insisted on going up for a role she wanted badly in *The Country Girl* that was casting at Paramount. MGM balked at the idea of lending out their hottest new star to the rival studio. Producer William Perlberg, who worked with Kelly on *The Bridges at Toko-Ri* and *The Country Girl*, would recall in an interview, "With all her quietness and sweetness, Grace is a very determined girl. She made up her mind that she wanted to play in *Country Girl*. When MGM told her she had to come back to them and star in *Green Fire* opposite Stewart Granger, she said, 'Either I do *Country Girl*, or I go home, give up my motion picture

career and never make another picture.' She really went after her role in *Country Girl* herself."

The studio reluctantly agreed to her demands and she went on to win an Oscar for her performance as the wife torn between an alcoholic husband, Bing Crosby, and lover William Holden. She later went on to fulfill her contractual obligations to MGM and starred opposite Granger in *Green Fire*. The shoot in Colombia was by all accounts extremely arduous and was described by Kelly as "awful". The movie was a box office flop.

The gruelling work schedule continued for Kelly when she next flew to France to star opposite Cary Grant in yet another Hitchcock film *To Catch a Thief* (1954). The following year she returned to France to attend the Cannes Film Festival, when she was invited to Monaco to meet the late Prince Rainier III, then ruler of the tiny principality that lies just a short drive from Cannes. After returning to America to begin filming on *The Swan*, Kelly would remain in touch, and when Rainier came to the U.S. a short time later they would meet again. By now the media was rife with rumour that Rainier was seeking a wife. It emerged that under an old treaty with France that he had to produce an heir or his principality would become part of France. Rainier did indeed propose to Kelly and formally asked her father for her hand in marriage. The media madhouse that ensued was unprecedented. The big question was whether or not Kelly could marry a prince and still continue her career. The answer of course was 'no'. Friends in Hollywood lined up to say their farewells, knowing full well that they most likely would never socialise with her again. Hitchcock was not at all pleased at her decision to marry the prince, and declined an invitation to the wedding in Monaco. The rest of Kelly's life is of course enmeshed in

Grace Kelly and James Stewart in a scene from *Rear Window* (1954) directed by Alfred Hitchcock.

history. She would bear the Prince three children: Princess Caroline Louise Marguerite; Albert II, Prince of Monaco; Princess Stephanie Marie Elisabeth.

On September 13th 1982, while driving with Stephanie to Monaco around the hairpin turns of a section of coast road called the Moyenne Corniche, Princess Grace, then fifty-two, appeared to lose control of the Rover 3500 she was driving. Kelly was always uncomfortable behind the wheel of a car. The vehicle plunged over a steep slope and careened down about 110 feet. Though badly injured, Stephanie survived the accident. Grace Kelly never regained consciousness. Medical examinations showed that she had suffered a stroke. The American Film Institute has ranked Kelly No. 13 amongst the greatest female stars of all time.

CHAPTER 17

STARVATION TO STARDOM - STEPHEN BOYD

"In order to work in this industry, one must be as versatile as possible. Most of the good roles are for American characters, often from a particular part of the United States, and as a professional, one is really required to be able to fulfill that requirement. There are so few roles for Irish actors playing Irish characters these days. Besides, it would be far too limiting to simply seek out Irish roles." This was the great character actor Joseph Patrick Burns who was born in Oldcastle, County Meath, and who passed away in 2006. A friend of the authors, he had spent three decades in Hollywood playing parts in film, television and theatre that required him to command nuances of accents associated with different states in America – and occasionally Irish or Scottish, Welsh and Scandinavian. Irish actors were being hired in the late 1950s and early 1960s for their craft and skill… and screen 'presence.'

In previous decades, many American actors, Victor McLaglen in particular, built careers with their own home-made Irish dialects. J.P. maintained, and rightly so, that times had changed, and it was now crucial that Irish actors in Hollywood be versatile. We have only to look at the remarkable career of Stephen Boyd to bear that out.

Stephen Boyd blasted into Hollywood legend as the villain of villains, Messala, in *Ben Hur*. His gruesome screen death in the spectacular Roman chariot race with Charlton Heston in the title role is enshrined in cinema history. Boyd's portrayal of a man driven into the hell of his own spiritual collapse remains a monument today to the art of film acting. The powerful, dark presence of Boyd in *Ben Hur* as the nemesis to Heston's Judah Ben Hur is tribute certainly to his enormous ability as an actor. But Boyd had another, very private reason to be proud. There was no hint of the native Belfast accent that he secretly feared could stereotype him in Hollywood. It wasn't that Boyd was in any way ashamed of his roots or his accent. In fact he wore his Irishness on his sleeve. Boyd's desire to neutralise his accent was simply a matter of survival in Hollywood.

Boyd wrote of his first visit home to Belfast amid the fame that was thrust upon him with the success of *Ben Hur*. His father and mother met him at the airport. "Nice to see you," his father said casually. Then Boyd kissed his mother. "From then on, everything was back to normal, just as if I'd never left home," Boyd told Peer Oppenheimer writing for *Family*

Weekly in 1963. "To an outsider this may seem informal. But it's a characteristic of the Irish. We don't believe in a show of emotion, but affection is there and open to you when you want it and need it. I prefer this kind of attitude to that which I feel is so typical of Hollywood. Putting up a front to impress others can never have any meaning to me. Not the way I was raised," he told Oppenheimer.

He was born William Millar near Belfast on July 4th 1928, the youngest of eight children. His Canadian-born father was a lorry driver. They were a close and loving family, something which Boyd would be for ever thankful for. One of the first things Boyd did when he became successful was to buy a house in Ireland for his parents who had never owned their own home. "My father is sixty-seven and has attained the highest wage he's ever had, about $18 a week. He's brought up eight children, and only since the war (World War II) has his salary gone up to that amount," Boyd recalled.

Boyd joined the Ulster Theatre Group at the age of sixteen, where he trained for two years before heading to Canada to take up with a touring stock company. The training in Canada gave him confidence enough to take on London in the early 1950s with dreams of stardom in his head. Starvation soon made him realise how naïve his dream of West End fame had been. "When I was broke, I used to walk along the queues outside the theatres in London singing folk songs to my own (guitar) accompaniment and then pass around my cap to collect coins." Boyd also took odd jobs earning what money he could to pay for acting classes, voice coaching, and food – in that order. Things were so bad that at one point he became ill from malnutrition.

The utter misery of Boyd's first steps into theatre life in London and eventual stardom in Hollywood are outlined in his own memoirs, recorded by the actor in a diary that is held in the archives of the Academy of Motion Picture Arts & Sciences in Los Angeles.

"I hadn't the remotest idea how to get a job in theatre, so I took a job as a waiter at the Lyon Corner House, Picadilly... " He lived in a flat that was "four feet wide by nine long, had to go into it sidewise (sic) or step from entry right into bed. There were no windows but there was another door which opened out into the garden on the ground floor. Every person who lived in this building went through my room to get into the garden." He was so broke at one time that he confessed to living "on water" for an entire week.

This story continues with Boyd dragging himself from his bed, half-starved and heading for the Empire Cinema at Leicester Square with his guitar. "At the end of a half hour I had collected one pound (and) ninepence... somehow I managed to wobble to my meal, it was like the proverbial nectar of the Gods – I still remember what I had – veal schnitzel, peas and potatoes, which I couldn't finish. God, it was so wonderful, and I had a beer..." That meal, together with the threat of eviction from his humble lodgings, gave him the will to present himself at the Odeon Theatre on Leicester Square where he applied for an usher's job. He was hired on the spot. It seemed to Boyd that the bottom had fallen out of his world and out of his dreams. He could not have known that his new job as a theatre usher would help to realise his ambitions.

Boyd watched with interest one night as an awards ceremony took place across the street from the cinema where he now worked. There was a huge amount of celebrity activity at the Leicester Square cinema. Lauded British actor Sir Michael Redgrave was master of ceremonies at the event. Boyd orchestrated an introduction to Redgrave.

Belfast-born Stephen Boyd in perhaps his most famous Hollywood role as Messala – nemesis to Ben Hur in *Ben Hur*.

"What in the name of Christ are you doing in that uniform?!" Redgrave exclaimed. Boyd explained that he was an out-of-work actor. He told Redgrave, "'I would do anything to act.' Somehow it must have got over to Redgrave how completely I meant it because, bless him, within a fortnight I was working as an actor." Redgrave had arranged an introduction for Boyd to the Windsor Repertory Company. Before the month was out, Boyd was rehearsing the lead role in the company's next production. The Belfast boy finally had his foot in the door and he would not waste the opportunity.

The rep company experience landed him a place with the Midland Theatre Company, a respected government funded theatre group based in Coventry close to Stratford-upon-Avon, William Shakespeare's birthplace and home to the Royal Shakespeare Company. It wasn't the West End, but it was the ideal training ground for Boyd, who built up an impressive collection of glowing reviews. Redgrave continued to take an interest in Boyd's career offering criticisms and advice about his performances. "He has helped me more than anyone else – just with an occasional word and good sound solid intelligent constructive criticism on the subject of acting and particular acting jobs I've done," Boyd would recall.

Boyd returned to London from the Midlands in 1954 and was cast in several small film parts and a handful of television dramas. One of these early British TV productions, *Barnett's Folly*, proved a turning point in his career, a defining moment that set him on the road to stardom. His performance was acclaimed by the critics and led to a screen test and contract with London Films. Shortly afterwards came his first major screen role as the Irish secret agent in *The Man Who Never Was*, released by 20th Century Fox. Boyd's pinpoint characterisation of the spy in this movie won him tremendous critical praise, a contract with Fox and, eventually, a ticket to Hollywood.

His first sight of Hollywood came with his role in *The Bravados*, which reinforced his position as one of the industry's up-and-coming players. Then came the role that finally earned him a place in the ranks of Hollywood's great stars. Boyd was contracted to play Messala in *Ben Hur*. 'It is the fleshy part which will do the trick for Boyd's career in the big way,' wrote Hedda Hopper in her typical gossipy style in 1959 when Boyd was first establishing himself in the film town.

The Hollywood gossip columnist adored the 'tall handsome Irishman' and did more than any journalist, agent or press flack to give Boyd the positive publicity that was such a big part of the success game in Hollywood in the 1950s. If Hopper, or her rival Louella Parsons, took a dislike to an actor, they could put a stop to his or her career through their international syndicated columns. But Hopper in particular raved about this newcomer from Ireland by way of the London stage. 'His personality will hit audiences like a thunder clap,' she said of Boyd when he was cast in *Ben Hur*. 'Mark my words, Boyd will be our next matinée idol. He's thirty, has a wonderful face and a wit to go with it… recently I was discussing him with Mel Ferrer, who said, "This man can be Mr Motion Picture of 1959 – he's got it in the palm of his hand." Baffling, moody and volatile – a typical Celt – he veers from humour to fury in the wink of an eye.'

Later Hopper wrote, 'He's been here a year now and I asked him how he felt about living in Hollywood permanently or if he'd prefer London, New York or Ireland. He admits he's become pretty Americanised, is an avid baseball fan and didn't miss a game at the Coliseum this year, although he'd never seen baseball before coming to America. "We have something called 'rounders' we play in grade school which is much the same game," Boyd said. "I think Los Angeles is the best spot for furthering my career and in view of

Belfast-born Stephen Boyd in the cult science fiction film *Fantastic Voyage* with Raquel Welch.

that, I feel it would be wise to remain here and do film work."' But there would be no more films of the scope of *Ben Hur* to provide the actor with the same breadth of canvas on which to display his talent. It was said that Boyd may have had some difficulty in disguising his Belfast accent – though there was no indication of this challenge in any of the screen roles he played… and there were however numerous other roles in memorable movies that Hollywood liked to refer in those days to as 'superspectaculars'. Not least among these was *The Fall of the Roman Empire* with Sophia Loren, *The Bible* and *Genghis Khan*.

There was to be yet another 'superspectacular,' co-starring with Elizabeth Taylor in *Cleopatra*. But it was not to be. "I waited five months for the picture to get rolling, was fitted for fourteen changes of costume that were never completed, and had my hair dyed every shade of the rainbow from black to light brown to blond and albino for the tests. We started shooting without Liz and a couple of weeks later she was deathly ill… and it was cancelled." During the production 'hiatus,' Boyd moved on to other projects. (The picture was of course eventually made with Richard Burton in the role of Antony). Boyd recounted, "I had other commitments and wanted to get to them… there's still plenty of time." This pronouncement proved tragically unprophetic.

'Stephen Boyd, 48, Irish-born actor, best known for his role as Messala in *Ben Hur*, died suddenly of a heart attack yesterday morning when he collapsed while playing golf at the Porter Valley Country Club,' the announcement read starkly in the daily trades on June 6th 1977.

CHAPTER 18

GENEROUS GENTLEMEN – THE O'HERLIHY BROTHERS

Dan O'Herlihy

Wexford-born Dan O'Herlihy and Marlon Brando were competing for 1954's Best Actor Oscar – O'Herlihy for *The Adventures of Robinson Crusoe* and Brando for *On The Waterfront*. Despite having had some screen success, and certainly plenty of meaty theatre roles back home in Ireland, this was probably the point in O'Herlihy's career that saw him rise from journeyman actor to Hollywood heavyweight. The pair of Oscar contenders dreamt up a delightful prank that would make headlines not just in the Hollywood trades but also in newspapers around the world.

O'Herlihy was producing *Finian's Rainbow* on a shoestring budget at the Hollywood Repertory Theatre, a stage venue in which O'Herlihy was a partner. He recalled this period for the authors at a meeting some years ago at his home in Malibu. "We had no money but it was to be an expensive production with the cast receiving full professional rates. We took ads in the trade papers and announced our opening night for New Year's Eve charging about seven shillings and sixpence per seat, and that was a lot of money then. Fortunately we sold out and raised enough money to keep the show on. Brando was there on opening night. He confided in me after the show that he would love to get back on the stage with the smell of greasepaint and the excitement of feeling one's place in the wings. I jokingly said that I would bear him in mind if there were any vacancies. Well as it happened two students who were playing walk-on parts in the show were injured when they crashed their taxi near the theatre just a couple of hours before curtain. They were only walk-on parts, but were still vital and so quite a flap developed as we searched for replacements. Then a fantastic idea struck me. I grabbed the telephone and managed to get hold of Marlon: 'Get over here quick, you've got twenty minutes, there's a part for you… a walk on. Interested?' To my astonishment Brando accepted immediately and was in the theatre in no time at all and we did a quick run down of his lines in the wings and then, to the audience's complete disbelief two of that year's Best Actor Oscar nominees came on stage in tiny parts. The publicity was sensational and the show ran for eight months. Of course we only played the parts for a couple of nights before being replaced by the now recovered students… but it caused a sensation. It was very sporting of Brando."

The Adventures of Robinson Crusoe, directed by a then largely unknown Luis Buñuel, was one of the highlights of O'Herlihy's long career, which spanned more than six decades in film, television and on stage. He was born in 1919 in Wexford, the son of a senior civil servant at the department of industry and commerce. His mother was the former Ellen Hanton, daughter of the Lord Mayor of Wexford. When he was still a child the family moved to Dun Laoghaire where O'Herlihy attended the local Christian Brothers School. Later he entered the National University of Ireland with a view to studying law. After only twenty-four hours of legal lectures he voted instead to take up with architecture, which he felt would be more to his liking as he was a talented sketch artist. While at college he found himself somewhat reluctantly being headhunted into one of the college's amateur dramatic productions, *The Wind and the Rain* by Merton Hodge. He had been asked to replace a cast member who had left after a row with the director. The production was being presented as part of a local Dublin amateur drama festival and competition. O'Herlihy accepted the part "for the fun of it." He learned the part on Sunday, performed it on Monday and one month later was amazed to learn that he had won a best actor gold medal. In addition, Frank Dermody, one of the judges and also director of the Abbey Theatre, offered him the romantic lead in an upcoming Abbey production of *Three To Go*. From the day of his first professional appearance at the Abbey Theatre, O'Herlihy studied by day at college and acted by night. Over the following four years, while studying for his degree, he played in *Red Roses For Me*, George Bernard Shaw's *St Joan* and some sixty-five other plays. O'Herlihy, who did indeed graduate as an architect, wanted to quit the University at one point to devote himself full-time to acting. His father had other opinions and made his son promise that he would not give up his studies. O'Herlihy was good to his word. Nonetheless he still succeeded in working with all the important theatres in Dublin back then, including the Gate Theatre. Not only that, but he also accepted a job as a news announcer at RTÉ where he could utilise a uniquely rich and silky voice that would be one of the hallmarks of the actor's career. Each night, after a stage performance, he would rush to the station to read the late news then cycle eight miles home.

O'Herlihy's career in Ireland was flourishing at the time that famed British director Sir Carol Reed wanted a cast of leading Irish actor for a J. Arthur Rank production of *Odd Man Out* (1947) which was to star James Mason. Reed flew to Dublin for casting and saw O'Herlihy in a performance at the Gate Theatre and cast him in the important role of Nolan. Also appearing in the film were a host of other well-known Irish actors, several of whom would have more than nodding acquaintance with Hollywood in the course of their careers. These included F.J. McCormack, Denis O'Dea, Cyril Cusack, W.G. Fay, Maureen Delaney and Kathleen Ryan.

In later years O'Herlihy would recount to the authors that in fact his fellow Gate player Kathleen Ryan got the coveted role of Kathleen in part through his intervention. "Ann Todd had been cast for the part but apparently her agent started demanding larger fees and the producers thought it might be a good idea to use an 'unknown' Irish girl. He asked me for advice on the matter and I suggested Kathleen (Ryan). He took my advice. It was this role which led to Ryan making her Hollywood debut four years later, in the Robert Stillman film *The Sound of Fury*. Stillman offered her a pivotal role in his movie after seeing *Odd Man Out*."

In the meantime O'Herlihy's own career was taking a new turn. He was invited to America by Orson Welles to play MacDuff in Welles' movie production of *Macbeth* in 1948. O'Herlihy accepted without hesitation. He explained, "When I graduated as an architect I was faced with the prospect of designing toilets for ten years, too bleak a future to even contemplate so I pursued my first love – acting. It was almost a simultaneous decision to come to Hollywood. For, while I had succeeded in Dublin theatre I felt it

would only be good to me until my youth was gone. The obvious thing was to come to California, to the centre of film-making and where I could prosper."

In his early days in Hollywood O'Herlihy guided the Hollywood Repertory Theatre, scene of the famous walk-on part with Brando. (One of the students in the theatre would one day become the king of Hollywood TV production, the late Aaron Spelling.) "Following 'The Scottish Play' (*Macbeth*) I fiddled around in some RKO pictures and finally got to play Robinson Crusoe for which I got very little money," the actor would remember. His nomination for an Oscar for his role as Crusoe caused a minor sensation in Hollywood. Brando would of course walk off with the trophy, but the fact that an unknown actor in a very low budget film could even get nominated brought O'Herlihy attention from all angles. The powerful Hollywood gossip columnist of the day Hedda Hopper wrote of O'Herlihy soon after the Oscar Awards that year, 'When you discuss Hollywood's top talent these days – the kind of talk that separates the men from the boys – Dan O'Herlihy's name invariably crops up as a big bet for a sensational star future.

'Dan has been around Hollywood for eight years but movieland didn't become conscious of his capacity as artist among actors until *Robinson Crusoe* was shown. He won an Oscar nomination for this role in a bargain-basement production – for that is the head under which a $200,000 picture falls in a town where our top quality material runs into millions. But this young Abbey Theatre actor who was alone on screen for one hour of the picture's ninety-minute turning time, proved he could hold an audience spellbound.'

Dan O'Herlihy as Crusoe – the role that made him in Hollywood.

Hopper asked O'Herlihy in her syndicated column that reached many millions of readers, "How come you were here so long and we didn't know how good you were until *Robinson Crusoe?*" O'Herlihy explained that because he had come here to play MacDuff in Orson Welles' version of *Macbeth*, he was seen by one part of Hollywood as a Shakespearean actor. Another part of Hollywood saw him as a 'middle-aged Abbey Theatre player'. So even after being nominated for an Academy Award the big roles that would seem to have been his right were simply not being offered. "I quit movies for about three years after *Robinson Crusoe*," he told John L. Scott of the *Los Angeles Times*. "I was looking for another great part but I couldn't find it… or it couldn't find me. I see now that this was a mistake, but I kept alive." His return to films was strong, mostly in villain roles. His portrayal of a cold-hearted Boston professor in *Home Before Dark* (1958) with Jean Simmons brought him excellent notices. Of the part O'Herlihy would exclaim: "It's an actor's dream – it's the sort of thing that makes an actor's skin crawl with excitement when he reads it. In other words, this is exactly what I've been holding out for these past three years," he confessed to Kendis Rochlen, columnist with the *Mirror News* in Los Angeles in January 1958. "The first year after my nomination I turned down seventeen pictures, mostly on the basis of the scripts," he went on. "The second year I turned down twelve, and it's only now at the end of the third year that I began to get what I wanted. Eventually I'd like to have a reputation so that if people saw my name on a picture they'd say, 'Well it must be good.'"

A little later he played Lana Turner's lover in *Imitation of Life*, a box office hit. In 1959 he co-starred with Robert Mitchum in *The Knight Fighters* which was made in Ireland. Cyril Cusack co-starred. "I was a kind of Irish Hitler, a very good acting part, but a pretty disagreeable character to portray," he would recall. He also made *One Foot in Hell* with Alan Ladd in the same period.

One of his outstanding roles was the co-lead with Henry Fonda and Walter Matthau in the 1964 anti-nuclear war movie *Fail-Safe* in which he plays Brig. Gen. Warren A. Black (Blackie), an army hawk who realises that nuclear proliferation is out of control. The character, haunted by bad dreams and guilt, is brilliantly portrayed by O'Herlihy. The Sixties were good to O'Herlihy in other ways. Television parts flourished for him, in particular the ABC 1963–64 western series *The Travels of Jamie McPheeters* which co-starred a young Kurt Russell. The series was themed around the adventures of Dr Sardius McPheeters and his son Jamie who travel from the east to the California gold fields. He also had recurring roles in the 1960s in the series *The Long Hot Summer*.

By the 1970s O'Herlihy had established himself as one of America's finest character actors. One of his outstanding roles that decade was as President Franklin D. Roosevelt in the Universal Studios production *MacArthur*. Gregory Peck played MacArthur in a role that spanned the general's famous battles of World War II to his farewell speech at the age of eighty-two to the cadets of West Point. O'Herlihy studied films and old television biographies of Roosevelt to master his mannerisms. While the film met with mixed critical reaction, O'Herlihy's performance was thought brilliant. But, by and large, television was his staple during the Seventies.

'In the Seventies O'Herlihy appeared in so much episodic television that he had time for little else. The money was irresistible to a man putting children through college. But on a Friday afternoon in 1980, as he was removing his make-up at the end of shooting yet another dreary episode, O'Herlihy realised he'd had it. He called his agent and informed him that he would accept no more roles in television,' reported Frances Haines in *The Reader* in December 1987. O'Herlihy of course would take on more TV in future years, including the much-praised role of Joseph Kennedy in the 1998 TV movie *The Rat Pack*.

The Haines article continues, 'It could have been the end of his career, but he soon found much more rewarding work on the stage in London and Dublin, and is still in demand for film roles.' The roles that Haines was referring to included his major part in the hugely successful *Robocop* and then in the John Huston-directed *The Dead*, the lauded screen adaptation of the James Joyce story. O'Herlihy co-starred in the role of the outspoken dinner guest Mr Brown alongside a bevy of great Irish actors. Anjelica Huston played the pivotal role of Gretta alongside Gretta's husband Gabriel, the late Donal McCann.

The *Robocop* role saw him play the sinister CEO of Omni Consumer Products in the 1987 original and in 1990's sequel. From classics such as *Robinson Crusoe* to *The Dead* or from action yarns *Robocop* to his role as a friendly alien lizard in *The Last Starfighter*, from Shakespeare to Shaw on the stage, O'Herlihy was perhaps one of the most versatile actors ever encountered in Hollywood. He was a gentleman with impeccable manners who will be remembered by all who knew him, even briefly, as a ready and willing host and a charming personality. He died at the age of eighty-six of natural causes in February 2005 at his home in Malibu, survived by his wife of fifty-nine years, Elsie, and five children, Olwyn O'Herlihy Dowling, Patricia O'Herlihy Wisda, Gavan O'Herlihy, Cormac O'Herlihy and Lorcan O'Herlihy.

Michael O'Herlihy

A great fondness existed between O'Herlihy and his equally famous and talented younger brother, one of America's most noted television directors, Michael O'Herlihy – who also garnered considerable recognition as a film director. So it was a particularly harrowing experience for Dan O'Herlihy when in 1956 he received word that Michael, who was sailing his yacht from Ireland to Florida with two friends, was reported lost at sea. All shipping in the areas of the Atlantic where Michael was last reported was alerted. Word of the possible tragedy had reached the newspapers and trades. Dan O'Herlihy, close to despair, waited for word of his brother's fate for days – then finally the good news arrived. Michael was safe. His yacht was back in radio contact and he would soon be in Hollywood, determined to become a director. Michael, also an architectural graduate, had been a particularly brilliant and innovative stage designer in Dublin and he was determined to give Hollywood a try. He had set sail from Dun Laoghaire amid a blaze of publicity and a cheerful farewell party thrown for the adventurers by the Dun Laoghaire yacht club. O'Herlihy had just completed his last set design for the Gate Theatre for its production of *The Matchmaker and the Wayward Saint*, which would open when he was two weeks out on the Atlantic. *The Irish Independent* reported, 'To the crash of a starting gun backed by the cheers of hundreds of well-wishers who defied a heavy downpour of rain, Michael O'Herlihy and his companion, Terry Murray, last night set off from Dun Laoghaire on their adventurous yacht journey across the Atlantic.' The reported noted also, 'Dan O'Herlihy, Michael's famous film star brother, was also on the pier and when asked how he would prefer to return to America – sailing or flying – he remarked "21,000 feet up".' The reporter also made it clear that both O'Herlihy and Murray 'have an extensive knowledge of the art of sailing and for many years have taken part in races, particularly in the 21ft class at Dun Laoghaire.'

When Michael O'Herlihy eventually arrived in California he stayed for a time with his brother and his wife, and also visited often with actors Barry Fitzgerald and Arthur ('Boss') Shields who were close friends of the O'Herlihy family. "I gave myself four years to break in," Michael O'Herlihy told the authors during a visit to his house at the foot of the

Hollywood Hills on Kings Road, just above Sunset Boulevard. "I decided that if I had not succeeded after that period I was going back to Dublin."

In his early Hollywood career he worked in any capacity he could and one of his first jobs was as a dialogue coach on Walt Disney's *Darby O'Gill and the Little People* which starred beloved Dublin actor and comedian Jimmy O'Dea and a very young Sean Connery. He got his first directorial assignments in television when MGM hired him to direct an episode of *Dr Kildare*. He went on to direct many episodes of the famous TV series. Over the years he would go on to gain a litany of television credits from *77 Sunset Strip* to *M.A.S.H.* and on to probably his best-known TV assignment *Hawaii Five-0* on which he remained for years. It was while directing *Hawaii Five-0* that he was contacted by a young Irish producer called Morgan O'Sullivan who wanted to come to the islands to interview and film Michael at work. O'Sullivan, who has since gone on to be a true doyen of the Irish film industry, fondly remembers how the director rolled out the red carpet for the green young producer. "Everything was laid on and Michael was an incredible host. He made it all happen." That was typical of O'Herlihy who once told the authors that he was prepared to help anybody in the film and TV business from Ireland who cared to contact him.

Michael O'Herlihy's first film directing job was on Disney's *The Fighting Prince of Donegal* (1966), a colourful account of the story of Red Hugh O'Donnell. As his next directing assignment Disney chose him to helm *The One and Only, Genuine, Original Family Band* (1968). Hollywood columnist Patricia Marlowe wrote of the young director, 'Disney discovered that his young director had a sense of pageantry, and his handling of crowd sequences were reminiscent of King Vidor and Marcel Carné (two great names in the film industry)... he (Michael) would walk through the crowds with that short-stepped gait of the native Dubliner. His direction and involvement with the screen extras so overwhelmed them that they presented him with their own Oscar at the conclusion of filming.'

Michael O'Herlihy would go on to work mainly in television, amassing literally hundreds of hours of primetime dramas to his directorial credit lists – these included the important 1979 nine-hour mini-series *Backstairs In The White House*, an historical account of the early years of the White House and the first black maid to work there. One of the major roles in that series, that of an Irish maid, was played by Helena Carroll, daughter of the famous playwright Paul Vincent Carroll. A witty, talented and personable actress, Carroll carved out a hugely successful stage career in London, Dublin and New York and has appeared in numerous Hollywood films, including John Huston's *The Dead*, with Dan O'Herlihy.

Upon his retirement Michael decided to return to live in Ireland for the remaining years of his life. He died in his sleep at the age of sixty-nine in June 1997. Michael is remembered by those fortunate enough to have known him as a generous host, a gregarious and entertaining story-teller and very genuine gentleman, always ready and willing to give a candidate for the film and TV industries a helping hand.

◀ *The One and Only, Genuine, Original Family Band* (1968) which was directed by Michael O'Herlihy starred Goldie Hawn (as Giggly Girl) and John Davidson (as Joe).

CHAPTER 19

IRISH CONNECTIONS –
PETER O'TOOLE AND ANTHONY QUINN

Hollywood and the studio system was traumatised in the period after World War II, as the film industry took on a distinctly global aspect. Great directors and producers remained at home amid their own burgeoning film industries. Britain was producing its own 'A-list' of brilliant film-makers and films including legendary directors Carol Reed, David Lean, Michael Powell and Emeric Pressburger, who were forging world class films such as *Odd Man Out, The Third Man, Brief Encounter* and *A Matter of Life and Death*. The decline of the studio system was irreversible as more and more films were made on location overseas and storied studios such as Pinewood in the United Kingdom and Cinecitta in Italy appeared on the scene in the post-war years. Hollywood films became more indigenous in their quest to win American audiences, particularly in the face of the very real threat of the increasingly stay-at-home entertainment medium called television. The demise of the studio system resulted in a much-reduced demand for the myriad character roles studios had employed during their heyday. Films were being shot on tighter budgets with an eye to trimming fat. This in turn put a crimp on the flow of acting talent that had come out of Ireland in previous years. Film talent was increasingly required to forge world reputations at home before making the move to Hollywood – which then, as today, continued to represent the financial if not the artistic pinnacle of success. Among the first of these great homegrown movie stars were Peter O'Toole and Richard Harris (*See Chapter 20*). Both of these legendary talents were fortunate in that they emerged in the 1950s at a time when, as Robert Moss observed in the *Saturday Review* in 1981, 'a new guard of English playwrights was introducing a new sort of English play: the working-class drama that would soon dominate the London stage. In these plays, beginning with John Osborne's *Look Back In Anger* lower-class heroes rebelled against the status quo. And so did the performers who appeared in them … those playwrights found their voices in the dialects of O'Toole and his peers. By the early Sixties, Kenneth Tynan, the Zeus of British theatre critics, had pronounced O'Toole, Albert Finney, and Harris as the best actors of their generation.'

Peter O'Toole

"I'm not an actor – I'm a movie star!" bellows the inebriated character of Alan Swann, the larger than life Errol Flynn-like swashbuckler portrayed unforgettably by Peter O'Toole in *My Favourite Year*. There may have been many similarities between the colourful and exuberant Swann and O'Toole, but that isn't one of them. O'Toole is without a doubt the consummate actor.

There's a sad and certain predictability about Hollywood when it comes to the Irish. If there's the slightest whiff of alcoholic drink around out comes the phrase 'bad boy'. It's been applied liberally throughout Hollywood history to male Irish actors in particular. And certainly Peter O'Toole is no exception – despite the fact that many of the infamous O'Toole legends have usually been imported from places far from Hollywood and have been filtered through innumerable tellings of the same tales. Some admittedly are hilarious, some sad, but few actually emanate from Hollywood itself where, by and large, O'Toole has been an exemplary houseguest. The term 'houseguest' may perfectly describe O'Toole's relationship with Hollywood: as Academy Award nominee at eight Oscar galas and resident on and off when working. O'Toole comes into Hollywood and flits out again with such diffidence that he can sometimes thoroughly confuse the local media. A 1980 article in *The Los Angeles Times* quotes actor Omar Sharif (who co-starred with O'Toole in *Lawrence of Arabia*). "I saw him once at a Hollywood party and it was interesting to see how out of place he looked. I've never seen anyone so uncomfortable. As though he just didn't belong there." The piece continues, 'today this striking actor is back in Hollywood starring in the massive eight-hour television series *Masada*. Not many people know he is here. For he is an actor whose capacity for lying low makes even a professional hermit like Steve McQueen seem rather social. He is living in an unpretentious little house in West Hollywood and working a backbreaking day to get the series finished.' The writer of that piece had to be telling the truth because more than a year later the same newspaper would report, '(O'Toole is) working in Hollywood for the first time in his career, making *My Favourite Year*, in which he stars as a hard-drinking, hell-raising, old-time movie star.'

O'Toole was back in Hollywood again in 2007, nominated for the eighth time for an Oscar. This time it was for his touching portrayal of an aged actor in *Venus*. O'Toole was again on his best behaviour as he did the rounds of obligatory pre-Oscar cocktail parties and receptions. Photographs of O'Toole, smiling, happy and jovial peppered the front pages of the local media. Journalists who interviewed him came back with accounts of a serious man who talked about serious things. There were few, if any references to alcohol, other than those that O'Toole himself decided to resurrect in a seemingly self-deprecating manner. He was, as always, the perfect houseguest in Hollywood. He was gentle and nice with the media, mannerly and upstanding and charming at every pre-Oscar event (as the authors can personally confirm). Douglas J. Rowe of the Associated Press reported, 'In a long, rambling conversation, O'Toole displays his lyricism when discussing topics as far-ranging as how delightful he found *Little Miss Sunshine* (a competing film in the Oscar race), his regret over never getting to work with Marlon Brando, the failure of even legendary authors at writing screenplays, and "one of the most noble documents in the world, the American Constitution."'

That may not fit the media image of O'Toole as the hell-raising Irish 'Hollywood' actor, a picture so often embellished by the actor himself, but there's much about O'Toole that doesn't fit that portrait. To the public eye he's all that he appears to be as told by a lifetime

of sensational headlines. But he's also one of the most lauded stars of the screen and stage, a perfectionist whose gruelling hard work and genius has almost entirely been overshadowed by his off-screen adventures. The legendary British actor Sir Alec Guinness commented, "You can believe anything you want about his drinking but Peter is a real professional. He threw no tantrums and hardly missed a single moment of rehearsal time. I can't say a thing beastly about him."

If his peers have lauded his astonishing dedication to his work, then O'Toole himself has seemed always more happy to ham up his drinking adventures in interviews rather than talk about his work methods. But there were exceptions. He said of himself in a 1965 interview in *Playboy* magazine, "Discipline? I've always had that. I'm one of the most frightening disciplinarians who ever drew breath." And in another interview: 'O'Toole is colourful in a contradictory way. Off-camera he fosters an engaging if not altogether true picture of himself as a brash irresponsible sort – a latter-day Errol Flynn. On-camera he changes pitch, seldom sulks, squeezes every shade of meaning from his lines in a furious cast-iron desire to excel. "I'm the hardest-working bloody actor I know," he says,' *The Saturday Evening Post* in New York reported in 1963.

When preparing for yet another great film role as Henry II in producer Joseph E. Levine's *The Lion in Winter*, co-starring Katharine Hepburn (who won an Oscar for her portrayal of Eleanor of Aquitaine), O'Toole, then thirty-five, faced the problem of ageing to a grizzled fifty-year-old and making his lean frame look bulky. '(O'Toole) took lessons from his stand-in, famed Irish stuntman and athlete, Bill Reed . . . for nine hours a day he advised O'Toole on the way a man of fifty would walk, sit, stand and fight,' recounts a biographical note on O'Toole from the Levine company and Avco Embassy Films in 1968. O'Toole is quoted adding, "The speed of reaction was very important. I had to learn a kind of limp or shuffle and took deep breathing exercises to make me relax completely with the part. I wanted to give the part everything." O'Toole's dedication to his craft and to detailed preparation is borne out time and time again throughout his career. Perhaps never more so than when launched to instant stardom in *Lawrence of Arabia* in 1962 playing T.E. Lawrence. A 1966 biography of O'Toole provided by the Motion Picture Academy of Arts & Sciences library reports, 'O'Toole threw himself into his work as he had for Shylock (when he lived for four weeks in a shack on a Welsh mountain reading books of Jewish law and customs, then spent nine weeks on rehearsal without pay). For *Lawrence*, O'Toole nearly memorised the 661 pages of the World War I hero's *Seven Pillars of Wisdom* (on which the Robert Bolt script for the film is based), studied every book written about T.E. Lawrence, then flew to the desert weeks before the camera crew arrived and talked to Arabs who remembered (Lawrence).'

Perhaps the seed of such dedication to his craft can be uncovered in a promise to himself that he wrote and recorded at a particularly trying time in his teenage years. The lines would be his lifelong credo: "I do not choose to be a common man; it is my right to be uncommon, if I can. I want to take the calculated risk, to dream and to build, to fail and to succeed. I prefer the challenges of life and the thrill of fulfillment to the calm, stale, guaranteed existence."

He was born Peter Seamus O'Toole on August 2nd 1932, in Connemara, Ireland, to Irish racetrack bookie Patrick Joseph 'Spats' O'Toole and Scottish-born nurse Constance Jane Eliot Ferguson. When he was about one year old, the O'Tooles moved first to Kerry, then to Dublin and finally to Leeds in the north of England. O'Toole referred to that period as "a happy time," adding as an aside to one interviewer that life for the family swung from one extreme to the other. "It was either a wedding or a wake."

His mother, a nurse, taught him to read and write, but he was obliged to attend a Catholic school, the memory of which lingers still. "I used to be scared stiff of the nuns . . . the black dresses and the shaving of the hair — was so horrible, so terrifying," he later commented. "Of course, that's all been stopped. They're sipping gin and tonic in the Dublin pubs now, and a couple of them flashed their pretty ankles at me just the other day."

O'Toole abandoned school at the age of fifteen and would later explain his early leaving of school, reasoning that he was the only genius in the class. His first job out of school was at the *Yorkshire Evening Post* as a copyboy. He worked through the usual ritual of rising to the post of cub reporter. He hated every minute of it, but took some joy in attending cinema and theatre opening nights. A lifetime later when he played the faux-Flynn character in *My Favourite Year*, he would recall those days spent in local cinemas in Leeds. The plot of the film, for which O'Toole was again nominated for an Oscar (his seventh such), revolves around Swann guesting live on a TV show in New York in the 1950s. The colourful but ageing Swann is totally and hilariously out of control and leads the young man charged with minding him on a merry old dance. In the film some of Swann's old movies are screened and depict the character in better days. Swann's biggest film had been the so-called *Defender of the Crown*: the script called for O'Toole to re-create Swann as the young swashbuckler he had been thirty years before. "So, they glued my face up tight and let me loose with a sword," O'Toole recalled in a *Los Angeles Times* interview in 1981. "I wanted to do it myself since one of the

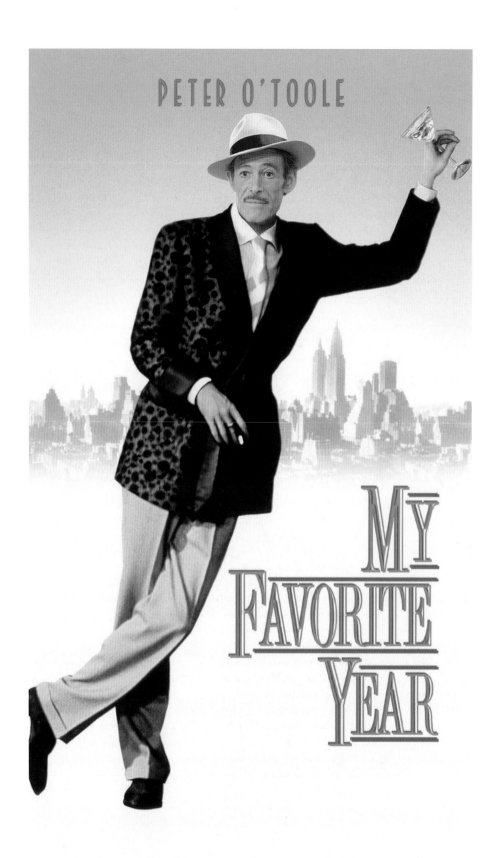

PETER O'TOOLE

MY FAVORITE YEAR

Peter O'Toole as a parody of himself/Errol Flynn in the comic hit and cult classic *My Favorite Year.*

reasons that Flynn and (Basil) Rathbone are held in such regard is that they always did their own fencing. I had learned at the Royal Academy of Dramatic Arts, so it wasn't difficult. In fact, it was great fun. Though when I watched the fight later on screen I thought: 'Listen, I never looked *that* young in my life.' I adore this film. Having watched Rathbone and company battling with each other as a kid, I always wanted to have a go . . ."

The young O'Toole was also captivated by what he saw on the live stage. So much so that he signed up with the Leeds Civic Theatre with which he played in numerous roles. It should be noted that this was not O'Toole's first 'theatrical' experience. As a child he had served as an altar boy in the local Catholic church. "I enjoyed that very much. There was something theatrical about it with Father Leo playing the lead part, I, at least mentally, the understudy."

But his dream of being an actor was rudely cut short by the intervention of military service and his drafting into the Royal Navy. 'Once assigned to a ship, O'Toole began to rebel – as he would rebel later against other authoritarian forces . . . in the Navy he persisted in calling it the "floor," not the "deck," the "windows," not the "portholes," the "chimneys," not the "funnels", ' recounts writer Gay Talese in *Esquire* magazine in August 1963. O'Toole detested every minute of his military service. 'After two years, the Navy was quite pleased to be rid of him, and he of it,' Talese maintains. "It was a bloody nightmare," O'Toole would recall. Some years later, when filming *Lord Jim*, O'Toole became concerned about how much time he would have to spend aboard boats. He warned the director, "I was in the Royal Navy for two years and I was seasick every day we were at sea."

O'Toole used his 'demob' money to fund a tour of the nation's theatres, ending at Stratford-upon-Avon where he spent all but seven of his last shillings to see Michael Redgrave playing King Lear. That night, he would remember, he slept in a manure-scented haystack. But the performance had so inspired him that the next day he took a train to London and literally knocked on the door of the famed Royal Academy of Dramatic Art, and demanded an interview and audition. The reward for such boldness was a scholarship to the Academy.

He was also making new friends in London, some of the era's greatest-actors-to-be, including Limerick-born Richard Harris, Albert Finney and Alan Bates. O'Toole and Harris would remain lifelong friends and provide the British theatre with some of its most memorable tales of thespian shenanigans. "We weren't reckoned for much at the time, perhaps because we were all considered dotty," O'Toole once stated.

His first professional experience came with the Bristol Old Vic Company which O'Toole described as "the best repertory company in the country and the most beautiful theatre in the world." In just over three years with the company O'Toole played seventy-three different roles, from comedy parts in Christmas pantomimes to contemporary dramas such as *Look Back in Anger* and Shakespeare's *Hamlet*, which won him critical praise and first brought him to the attention of national theatre critics, including a major piece in the London *Times* in which the interviewer commented on the 'strange, moody intensity of Mr O'Toole's stage personality.'

Many parts later, and yet more critical attention, and O'Toole won his first West End role in the musical *Oh Mein Papa*, in which he introduced the title song. His second West End role came with *The Long and the Short and the Tall*. He was acclaimed for his extrovert performance as Charlie Bamforth, the uncouth soldier with a passion for humanity. 'More important to his future, Sam Spiegel saw him in the production and expressed interest in him,' records a biography put out for *Lawrence of Arabia* by producer Spiegel and David Lean's company in 1962.

During the run of the play, O'Toole appeared in three half-hour television films and also made his film debut in a small role in *Kidnapped*. He also won the part of a young captain in the Scots Guards in *The Day They Robbed the Bank of England* (1960). That same year director David Lean was searching for an actor for upcoming *Lawrence of Arabia*, after Albert Finney and Marlon Brando had turned down the role. Lean recalled, "One day I went to a film called *The Day They Robbed the Bank of England* and there was Peter O'Toole, playing a sort of silly-ass Englishman in a trout fishing scene." Lean recommended O'Toole to Spiegel who, despite having been impressed with O'Toole's performance as Charlie Bamforth, had serious misgivings – brought on in part when a pint bottle of scotch whisky fell out of O'Toole's coat pocket during their first interview. But a screen test was arranged – for which O'Toole dyed his hair bleach-blond. 'When the test film was screened the next day, both Spiegel and Lean agreed that there was no question about this being the newcomer with the highest promise of any they had encountered,' reads the bio later put out by the director and producer.

Lawrence earned O'Toole his first Best Actor Oscar nomination and launched him as a superstar. He immediately bought a white Rolls Royce and drove down Sunset Boulevard wearing dark specs and a white suit, "waving like the Queen Mum," O'Toole later recalled. "Nobody took any notice, but I thoroughly enjoyed it." Many major roles ensued. Co-starring with Richard Burton he was powerful in the 1964 production of *Becket* for which he gained his second Oscar best actor nomination. O'Toole was also a screen powerhouse opposite Katharine Hepburn in *The Lion in Winter* (1968) – yet another best actor Oscar nomination. His career was soaring in the 1960s and 1970s, despite numerous accounts of youthful cavorting. "We were silly and young and drunken and jumping up and down and making complete clowns of ourselves," he later admitted.

The lifestyle took its revenge on O'Toole who in mid-life suffered a near-fatal haemorrhaging and the removal of part of his stomach and intestines. Asked whether he had regrets about those days O'Toole reflected, "Only French singers don't have regrets." But he came back with yet more best actor nominations for *The Stuntman* (1980) and *My Favourite Year* (1982). These of course came on top of the nominations for *Lion*, *Goodbye Mr Chips* in 1969, *The Ruling Class* in 1972, and *Becket*.

Later, would come the greatest Academy of Motion Picture Arts & Sciences compliment of an Honorary Oscar in 2003. He famously refused at first, saying he was "still in the game" and would like a chance to "win the lovely bugger outright". He later laughed that off as a "miscommunication". He cited cultural differences between the United States and Britain as being to blame for the blow up. "There is such a different way of doing things. We speak the same language, but it's a barrier," he told journalist Hillary Atkin writing in *The Hollywood Reporter*. When he first received the letter from the Academy informing him of its intention to award him the singular honour he didn't realise it was a 'done deal' and so he wrote back suggesting that it wait until he turned eighty. He received a letter back explaining that he had the award and that it would be presented even if he didn't turn up. "I didn't know that. I happily accepted," O'Toole explained. As per usual, O'Toole was a wonderful guest on the night, accepting the honour with grace and wit – the same grace with which, four years later, he would yet again face losing in the Oscar contender race for *Venus*.

In 2004 came O'Toole's unforgettable portrayal of King Priam, the patrician ruler of Troy in the $200 million epic *Troy* in which he co-starred with Brad Pitt. O'Toole, in his charming way, confessed that he would dearly have loved to play the godlike role of Achilles, Pitt's character. "Well, of course, I'd have killed to play Achilles forty years ago. In fact, I asked the producer if I was too old. But Brad does it brilliantly. I mean, he looks like a god, for God's sake. You can see him decorating a Bronze Age vase, can't you?" O'Toole told the *Times* of London in an interview published May 31st 2004.

There had been talk on that film about the need for O'Toole to modify his accent. O'Toole, upon meeting the voice coach, said famously, "This film is in English, I presume . . . well I have been speaking English for an awfully long time, dear boy. I think I'll be all right."

O'Toole has reflected publicly on his past private life many times. But it is perhaps most fitting as a salutation to the artist and the man that he signs off here with his musings about the discipline that he loves so well – acting. He has said, "Oh, it's painful seeing it all there on the screen, solidified, embalmed. I love the theatre, because it's the art of the moment. I'm in love with ephemera and I hate permanence. Acting is making words into flesh. And I love classical acting, because you need the vocal range of an opera singer, the movement of a ballet dancer and the ability to act – as you turn your whole body into the musical instrument on which you play. It's more than behaviourism, which is what you get in the movies. Chrissake, what are movies anyway? Just f***ing moving photographs – that's all. But the theatre! Ah, there you have the impermanence that I love. It's a reflection of life somehow. It's . . . it's like . . . building a statue of snow."

Anthony Quinn

But if O'Toole ended up getting his Academy Award as an Honorary Oscar, Anthony Quinn, his Mexican-Irish co-star in *Lawrence of Arabia* was already a seasoned actor, with two Oscars already under his belt for *Viva Zapata!* and *Lust for Life* when producer Sam Spiegel and director David Lean invited Anthony Quinn to play the role of Auda abu Tayi, "the greatest fighting man in northern Arabia" in *Lawrence*. Quinn was already juggling three other acting assignments. He was still working the title role in *Barabbas* for producer Dino de Laurentiis and he was also due in London to help publicise *The Guns of Navarone* in which he had one of the starring roles. He had also agreed to star in *Requiem for a Heavyweight* to be filmed in New York.

He was so eager to portray Auda, the chief of the Howeitat tribe, that he rearranged his schedule and flew to the *Lawrence* location in Jordan for his exterior scenes. Three weeks later he headed to Rome to complete *Barabbas*. Then it was on to *Requiem for a Heavyweight* and then back to *Lawrence* for more filming. Like O'Toole, Quinn was a stickler for detail and he had spent days trying to master the Arab style of horsemanship when he first arrived on the *Lawrence* set. "You'd think, after all the Westerns I've done, that I'd have no trouble with horses," he remarked. "But this is the first time I've ever tried an Arab saddle." This same eye for detail and authenticity marked all of Quinn's performances, throughout a lifetime that began in dire poverty and hardship in Mexico.

Quinn's journey to the top of the Hollywood hierarchy could hardly have been imagined in fiction. He was born in Chihuahua, Mexico in 1915 at the height of the Mexican Revolution. His father was Irish-born Frank Quinn. His mother was Mexican. At the time of Quinn's birth his father was serving with Mexican revolutionary leader Pancho Villa. To escape the hardships of the war his mother, who was then only seventeen years old, walked with her young son on her back some 500 miles to El Paso, Texas. Quinn would later recount an early memory from that time. He was just three years old, and playing in a mud puddle in El Paso. He recalled a shadow looming over him and looking up to see his father. Frank Quinn remained with the family for just a day before enlisting in the U.S. army. The father would reappear again a few years later and bring his family to Los Angeles, where Frank Quinn found work as a prop man at the old Selig Studios. It was the first home life that young Anthony would know – and the last. His father was killed in a car accident when Quinn was still a boy. For a time he had to take odd jobs to support his mother. But she remarried within a few years of Frank Quinn's death, which left Anthony free to enrol at the Polytechnic High School in Los Angeles to study art and architecture. He was a gifted artist and indeed would continue to paint all his life. When he discovered that he would have to study for seven years to qualify as an architect, he turned his attention to acting and enrolled in the Katherine Hamil School of Acting in Hollywood. Determined to catch up on his missed formal education, he followed a plan for self-education and read one book each week and every page of every newspaper he could lay his hands on. At that time Quinn was paying $10 a month for a humble room and worked as a hauler on vegetable trucks for free food. He also cleaned a butcher's shop for free bones and stewing beef. But he always paid his acting class dues and was eventually repaid when he landed a role working with Mae West at a salary of $30 a week.

Quinn got a break into films playing a Cheyenne Indian in Cecil B. DeMille's *The Plainsman*. At the same time, he met his future wife, DeMille's daughter Katherine. But Quinn would recount many years later that despite being the son-in-law of the legendary Hollywood producer he never really got to know him. "He and I had only seen each other at Christmas, although for twenty years I had been married to his daughter. I think he kind of thought I was an Indian from some reservation and was always terrified that the tribe would gather around his house some night for a war dance."

He continued to work in support roles, mostly in 'bad guy' parts in Hollywood. By 1947 Quinn had amassed credits in more than twenty movies before opening on Broadway in *The Gentleman from Athens* in which he was a major critical success. He moved on to star in *A Streetcar Named Desire* with which he toured for more than two years. Several more major stage roles followed before he returned to Hollywood in 1950, where he began to finally get noticed for more important roles. His break came when he was cast opposite Marlon Brando in Elia Kazan's *Viva Zapata!* (1952) for which he won his first Academy Award for best actor in a supporting role.

After seven more Hollywood movies, Quinn headed for Europe where he was deluged with offers. He remained in Italy for two years where his most successful screen outing was in Federico Fellini's *La Strada* which won the Venice Film Festival Award in 1954. Later Quinn went to Mexico to star with Maureen O'Hara in *The Magnificent Matador*. He returned to Hollywood to win his second Oscar for best supporting actor as the painter Gauguin in Vincente Minnelli's Van Gogh biopic, *Lust for Life* in 1956. Later he went on to play starring roles in big-budget Hollywood films such as *The Guns of Navarone* in 1961 and then *Requiem for a Heavyweight* and *Lawrence of Arabia* both in 1962. One of his greatest screen successes came with the classic *Zorba the Greek* (1964) for which he was nominated for an Oscar.

Quinn, a Method actor, acquired what appears to have been a well-deserved reputation for attention to detail, and was never shy about expressing his opinion to the director. This was to infuriate the famous actor/comedian Jackie Gleason, who co-starred with

Quinn in *Requiem for a Heavyweight*. Quinn spent an entire day of shooting "trying to get the proper feel" for one critical scene. Jackie Gleason, who played his manager, spent the entire session fuming. At the end of the day, Gleason called the producer and director to his trailer and barked, "If that Indian says 'I think' one more time, I walk. Pals, don't make me walk."

"We can't promise," said director Ralph Nelson. "Quinn works from the inside out."

"Tell you what," said Gleason. "I'll give him three more 'I thinks'."

The *Saturday Evening Post* in 1962 recounted the Gleason-Quinn encounter. 'The next morning the scene was set, the camera poised. Then Quinn frowned. "Ralph," he began, "I think . . ." Gleason bolted from the set with (the producer) in pursuit. "But Jackie, you promised us three 'I thinks'." '

On the set, Quinn stared blandly at Nelson. "I think," he continued, "the way we've worked out the scene is now marvellous. But how the hell can I rehearse if Gleason keeps walking off the set?" Afterwards Gleason joked about the experience. "We got along," he said. ". . . I drank."

Quinn would continue to enjoy a highly successful Hollywood career for the rest of his life with numerous screen highlights including *Lion of the Desert* in 1982 with Irene Papas, Oliver Reed, Rod Steiger, and John Gielgud. He began to slow down with age in the

Mexican-Irish actor Anthony Quinn as Zorba the Greek in one of his most famous roles.

1990s, but he did choose roles in some memorable films, most notably *A Walk in the Clouds* (1995) which co-starred Keanu Reeves. He died aged eighty-six in Boston, Massachusetts, from pneumonia and respiratory failure. Remarkably, Quinn had succeeded in not just creating a lifetime of crafted and award-winning screen and stage performances, but at the time of his death had become a lauded artist whose work was in demand for private collections around the world.

CHAPTER 20

'A GIFT OF LAUGHTER' - RICHARD HARRIS

'He was born with a gift of laughter and a sense that the world was mad.'

Upon reading this epigram that had been penned by novelist Rafael Sabatini to describe the fictional daredevil Scaramouche, Harris remarked, "you could put that on my tombstone". This was Jon Borgzinner writing of a young thirty-something Harris in *Life* magazine in 1967. 'He gives the first impression of a great lump with I-beam shoulders, a chin the size of Wales (and) a nose that decides several times which direction to go in.' Harris indeed had a great sense of the world's madness and in his own insatiable instinct for living in the centre of it. Like his friend Peter O'Toole, his career was pockmarked by the very public fracas and controversies to which his volatile passion as an artist inevitably led. But, like O'Toole, his passion for his work was far more consuming than his worldly dramas. His reputation among his peers was that of an actor with a masterful command and love of his craft – a consummate professional who would brook no half-measures from those he was working with, as Marlon Brando would find to his dismay when working with Harris on *Mutiny on the Bounty*.

Harris told an interviewer in the 1970s, "I've always had a label as a rebel. I don't deny it. It's hard to shake off a hell-raiser's shadow when a certain portion of your life has been spent being drunk or getting into fights. But I've also spent an awful lot of my time alone. Around eighty per cent, I'd say. That's the bit that never gets into the headlines. I couldn't have written a volume of poems, short stories and a novel if I'd spent all my time in bars getting beaten up . . . I've always played a double game, a reverse Jekyll and Hyde: the public boozer and womaniser, the private me who is really extremely serious." He added, "You see I take acting very seriously. Like O'Toole and Albert Finney, I prepare every part thoroughly, developing it like a mosaic, grading the texture of the role, colours against colours."

Jim Sheridan, who directed Harris in *The Field*, said of the actor, "Richard was able to tap into a tremendous level of passion and it shows." Ridley Scott, who directed him as Emperor Marcus Aurelius in the Oscar-winning *Gladiator* (2000), said of Harris upon his death that he was "one of the giants of the old school. (He)… came out of a generation that worked hard and played hard." Scott said that Harris and O'Toole were "icons" adding, "There aren't a lot of icons left." Clint Eastwood said in the wake of Harris's death in October 2002, that he found him to be a "slightly mad Irishman and a truly gifted performer. His presence on the set during the filming of *Unforgiven* always gave us a much needed lift during the many hours of difficult work."

Without his own special brand of determination and vision as an actor, Harris may never have won the role of Bull McCabe in *The Field*, the role that earned him his second Oscar-nomination, says his lifelong friend and fellow Limerick man Malachy McCourt, the New York-based actor, author, raconteur, and brother of *Angela's Ashes* author Frank McCourt. Though the story has been told in part prior to this, McCourt has brought a new and ironic twist to the tale of how Harris got the role and came to revive his film career from near ruin. Harris had been offered the role of the local parish priest in *The Field*. Dublin-based stage and screen actor Ray McAnally had been cast by the producer and director Noel Pearson and Jim Sheridan in the pivotal role of Bull McCabe. McAnally had played Christy Brown's father in the Sheridan/Pearson Oscar-winning sensation *My Left Foot*. McCourt, who played the Garda Sergeant in *The Field*, takes up the story. "I was calling Jim Sheridan to find out when they were going to need me because I had a couple of conflicting things going on and he said 'I don't know because you caught me at a bad time. Ray McAnally died this morning. So it's all indeterminate now.' So I said to him that Harris had once told me that he would love to play the part of Bull. And I quoted Dickie verbatim. I told (Sheridan) that I truly believed he had the passion for the part and the passion for the character that would follow. So I rang up Harris who was over here staying in the hotel that he would stay in and I (told him about my conversation with Sheridan). And he said, 'I'll do something I never did for years; I'll audition.' And he flew over and called up Sheridan and Pearson to meet him and he went to a costumers and he got a wig, a white wig, and he auditioned and that's how he got it. But did you know that the wig he was given was the same wig that Ray McAnally had worn in *The Mission*? It had McAnally's name written inside it..." Of course Harris would indeed get the role of 'The Bull' and film history was made. He was triumphant.

The role marked Harris's return to the screen after an eight-year absence. The film was based on the J.B. Keane play of the same title and tells a tale of dark tragedy that has its roots in Famine times. Bull rules over his fellow villagers in Connemara with an iron will – until a stranger comes to the village determined to buy a field that the Bull and his forefathers had coaxed and nursed from rocks to verdant green. For Harris, it was the "second role of a lifetime". The first was his breakthrough performance as a disillusioned rugby player in Lindsay Anderson's *This Sporting Life* (1963). Harris told interviewer Bob Strauss of the *Daily News* in Los Angeles in 1991, "An actor waits thirty years, maybe all his life, and never gets things this good (*The Field*)." When offered the role of the priest in *The Field* Harris, as he recounted, "hadn't done a picture for eight years and I had virtually disappeared. If I say I had disappeared through choice, that would be correct. But the choice was made because I was being offered nothing, really second- and third-rate pictures. So one day I said to myself, 'I'm rich. I don't have to do this anymore.' There was a certain lack of grace to the films I was making. I felt I was better than what I was being offered. But no one seemed to know it – or maybe I'd messed it up myself by some poor choices or whatever. So I told Noel Pearson not to bother sending me the script. But he's a very persistent man. As all producers should be." Pearson eventually convinced Harris to read the script. Harris fell in love with the Bull and begged for the role. Harris picks up the story of how he got the role after arranging a meeting with Sheridan. "As I talked with Sheridan, I started pulling my hair back. I'd leave the room at times, and come back wearing the hairpiece, different clothes, boots. My accent changed until it was perfect. It took forty-five minutes, but finally he said, 'The Bull!' I said 'Yeah.' He said, 'You've got to do it.'"

If it was a mark of Harris's professionalism that he was prepared to go to such lengths to play a part in which he saw such enormous artistic opportunity, it should have come as no surprise to anybody who understood Harris's love of his profession. Three decades before, when still a virtual unknown in Hollywood and with a budding career at stake, he went to war with Marlon Brando on the set of *Mutiny on the Bounty* over what he perceived to be a lack of professionalism on Brando's part. It was a David and Goliath battle of wills.

'… I think it's fair to say the Irish actor will be remembered in our town as the man who stood up to Marlon Brando and told him off,' commented the powerful Hollywood columnist Hedda Hopper in her worldwide syndicated column in 1962. The columnist detailed Harris's anger at Brando at a time when the film had gone two years into shooting and had tallied a $20 million budget, an enormous amount for the time. Hopper wrote, 'Marlon plays Fletcher Christian and his part dominates the Tahiti sequences, in which Harris is a seaman who continuously urges him to mutiny. Harris's part comes to fruition in the Pitcairn scenes but obviously Brando did not want to do them.' She quotes Harris, '"Naturally, I don't feel sympathetic to a man who wants to cut out the Pitcairn sequences… the producer Aaron Rosenberg told him: 'We are going to shoot it and you will perform.' So Brando fouled it up. He came and acted a few days but he was deliberately scuttling it. So I finally told him: 'When you're willing to perform and act as a pro, I'll be in my dressing room.'"'

Harris had yet another encounter with Brando when the final scene was to be shot. "Brando okayed it," Harris told Hopper. "He said, 'this is the final script. I want nothing changed, not a line, not a comma.' On the strength of that I memorised eight pages… we rehearsed it in the morning, went to lunch and the take was supposed to be in the afternoon. We came back and started work, the cameras rolled. Then suddenly I heard 'Cut.' They told me I was wrong. When I asked why, I found out they'd changed the script during lunch. I was astounded. To me it was unbelievable and I demanded the producer be brought on the set. I explained to Mr Rosenberg what had happened – that Brando had guaranteed no further changes were to be made. I told Brando, 'This is utterly inconsistent; changes have been made to your satisfaction.' His answer was: 'Actors are paid to do their jobs without opinion.' I maintained that in England people have the right to say when something is wrong." At this point Harris left the set to go to his dressing room. He recalled that he felt as though he was "radioactive the way everyone backed away from me". But later the director came to him and said, 'Everybody in the whole company wants to applaud. You were great!'

The famous battle is recounted in detail because it serves to illustrate the courage that Harris was prepared to display in pursuit of professionalism throughout his entire life. Harris was born in Limerick, Ireland in 1930, one of eight children who grew up in a relatively well-to-do household. "My family was very big in Ireland, owned great flour mills, gave huge grants of land to the Catholic church, and all that. My grandfather built it all up; by the time my father took it over, it was dwindling," he told one interviewer. The independent flour mills were under siege in Harris's youth from the growing power of conglomerate milling operations. Harris and his brothers were educated at the Jesuit Crescent College in Limerick. While at Crescent College, Harris proved to be a worthy rugby player and was even capped for Munster several times. "They called him Dickie Harris in those days. I came across him when we played rugby together. I played for Bohemians and he played for Old Crescent. He was quite colourful even in those days," recalls his friend McCourt. "I remember we played against each other in the 'under-twenty' championship game and they won. But I found out (years later) that some of the players were over the age limit. So I went to the *Limerick Leader* and told them about this and said that I wanted the medal that was rightfully mine and someone at the *Limerick Leader* said, 'Did you get permission from Mr Harris to come here?' I was astounded." Harris and McCourt would meet up many years later again in New York and became firm friends. They also worked together several times including on *The Molly Maguires* and on *The Field*.

McCourt believes that Harris might have become an internationally renowned rugby player, but his athletic career was cut short when he contracted tuberculosis in his teens. Harris told interviewer Ray Connolly of the London *Times* in 1990, "Just think, if I hadn't got TB I'd probably now be a sixty-year-old ex-international attached to some club, who turns up at dinners and talks about the old days and is a total pain. Instead of which, I'm sitting in the Savoy Hotel in London being roasted by the English press for being irresponsible and temperamental."

Harris recalled how he was confined with TB from the age of nineteen for three years in the family home. "In those days there was a bit of a stigma attached to tuberculosis so I didn't tell my parents at first (after his doctor had diagnosed the illness). But then because I was always sleeping, I became the object of derision in the house. My father thought I was shirking. When they found out the reason for my always being tired there was a complete reversal of attitude to overcrowding affection, which in some ways is worse than derision." His years of confinement were spent reading, studying, writing... and reflecting on the future. By the time he had recovered Harris said he had decided that he wanted to direct in the theatre. He could not find any suitable courses to learn the directing craft and so enrolled in the London Academy of Music and Dramatic Art (LAMDA) to study acting. "While I was there I had fifteen dollars a week from some Guinness breweries shares my grandmother had left me, which I used for school, board, clothes, everything. I put on a Clifford Odets play, *The Country Girl* in a little theatre – it was a disaster, and then I was really down with all my money gone. I ate a boiled egg, a slice of toast and tea once a day. I slept in doorways and was arrested for vagrancy a couple of times." Harris also recalled those days to Dublin journalists Gus Smith and Des Hickey for their book *A Paler Shade of Green*. He confessed, "I had paid my fee (to LAMDA) in advance, but I could no longer afford a room. Some nights I would sleep on a sofa in a friend's room, or a girlfriend would let me stay in her flat until the affair broke up."

It was around this time that he heard that the famous theatre producer Joan Littlewood was casting for Brendan Behan's play, *The Quare Fellow*. He borrowed enough change to make a phone call to the theatre and begged for an audition. He won the role of Mickser in the production and received glowing reviews. He stayed on with Littlewood's work-shop for several years playing a wide variety of roles until he was eventually cast in Pirandello's *Man, Beast and Virtue*. That role brought him to the attention of director Cliff Owen who was readying a TV play *The Iron Harp* by Joseph O'Connor. Owen was looking for an Irish actor for one of the roles. It went to Harris. The TV perform-ance was seen by Bob Evans, an executive of Associated British Film Corporation, who called Harris in and signed him up for seven years. "And that's how it began," Harris told Smith and Hickey. "They put me in a few movies and I was soon getting good featured parts." These included *Mutiny on the Bounty* in which, despite being a relative unknown he insisted upon third billing behind Brando and Trevor Howard. Then came *This Sporting Life*.

"With *This Sporting Life*," Harris commented to Smith and Hickey, "the rest of my career seemed to fall into place." In *This Sporting Life* Harris played an angry young coal miner, Frank Machin, who becomes a locally famous rugby league star. The role won Harris the 1963 award for best actor at the Cannes film festival and an Oscar nomination.

Richard Harris shot to worldwide fame as a result of his first starring role in the 1963 film, *This Sporting Life*. He played a young coal miner who seeks freedom from poverty and obscurity through playing rugby. Harris won an award for best actor at the Cannes film festival for his performance.

Following the launch to stardom in *This Sporting Life* Harris decided he wanted to return to his stage roots. His production of Gogol's one-man show *The Diary of a Madman* was highly praised, and his performance in London was hailed almost universally. More films followed, including *Major Dundee* for Columbia, *The Red Desert* and *The Heroes of Telemark*. His arrival in Los Angeles from Italy for *Major Dundee*, his second Hollywood movie following *Bounty*, was cause for much Hollywood hilarity at the time. A 'hulking, thatch-haired' Harris "began jabbering the moment he cleared the passenger exit… he was exhausted completely, he said. It was a wonder he was alive. He hated aircraft, he said. He had just come from Ravenna, Italy, filming *The Red Desert* for Michelangelo Antonioni. "He's a genius. But mad, mad. He almost killed me,"' so goes the breathless account published in August 1964 in the gossip sheet of the day, *The Bugle*.

Describing Harris's auspicious one-man invasion, *The Bugle* continues, 'Reaching the lobby (of the Beverly Wilshire) hotel, he signed in as 'Richard Harris, Limerick, Ireland.' Not London, his home. Then he dug into his flight bag and said, "I have a gift." He didn't say for who. He extracted a bottle of strong Italian brandy. Grappa by name. It was now 5.30 am. Harris… broke the seal and pried off the cap. One greeter said, "It's a little early, Dick." Another said, "It's a little late." Harris wasn't to be put off. He said, "We'll drink to my safe arrival."'

Hollywood's early impression of Harris – compounded by some renowned partying over the years – would last for decades, despite the obvious and total professionalism that he consistently brought to his work on a movie set or on stage. A shining example of that came when he was doing post-production work for one of his career's most outstanding and praised roles, King Arthur in the 1967 production of *Camelot* with Vanessa Redgrave. The story goes that he was in the dubbing studio doing what the industry calls 'looping'. According to *Life* magazine on one loop Harris is ordering a young boy, who has been proven a hero, off the battlefield and to safety. The line requires Harris to shout at the top of his lungs, "Run, boy, run! Run! Run!" For a full fifteen seconds. The take is not to his satisfaction. "Bollix!" he exclaims and begins again. Twelve tries later, his voice sounds like a gravel truck going up a long, steep grade. "That's good," says (director) Josh Logan. "Good isn't good enough," rasps Harris. "It's got to be great." The next try is. His performance in the Lerner and Loewe production earned him a coveted Golden Globe in Hollywood. He would later reprise the role in 1982 for the hugely successful stage version of the classic knights' tale. Harris recounted how he got a call from his friend Richard Burton in 1982. "He asked me to take over his part in *Camelot* because he was so ill." Harris was reluctant to be seen to take advantage of his friend's predicament. But Burton pleaded, "'What's eight weeks out of your life? Just finish the tour.' So I agreed to do eight weeks – and stayed on for five years. Ultimately I bought the show from the producers. It was mine. I loved every single performance. *Camelot* grossed $92 million after I took over the part. Now, do you know why I don't ever need to work again?" he said to an interviewer.

Harris's movie credits continued to build in the 1960s and 1970s with such meaty films as *The Molly Maguires* with Sean Connery, *A Man Called Horse*, and *Man in the Wilderness*. Harris's performance in *A Man Called Horse* in 1970 was particularly significant in his career. Starring as an English aristocrat in the late 1800s who is captured and tortured by a tribe of Native Americans, the film became a surprise hit that led to two sequels. His portrayal of *Cromwell* co-starring with Sir Alec Guinness, won him top honours in the Russian Film Festival. He received an Emmy nomination for his U.S. television performance in *The Snow Goose* in 1968 and later received a Golden Globe nomination for the film *Bloomfield* which he co-wrote, directed and starred in. Harris developed a parallel career as a singer when in the early 1970s he received three Grammy nominations for his album *A Tramp Shining* and scored a huge hit with composer Jimmy Webb's 'MacArthur Park.' In all, he received five gold records and a platinum during his recording career. Additionally, his book of poetry *I, in the Membership of My Days* was a bestseller.

The following decade brought some forgettable roles and a dark time career-wise for Harris. The low point was as Bo Derek's father in *Tarzan the Ape Man* (1981). Then in 1982 he decided to give up drinking. "My doctor told me I had hypoglycaemia and that soon I'd be going into insulin shock and die if I didn't stop drinking... I was in the Jockey Club one night (in Washington DC) and I had them serve us two bottles of Château Margaux at $370 a bottle." He drank the last sip of wine and announced that he would never drink again. He also made another life-changing decision at around this time. He announced that he was retiring from films. "When Brando, Redford and Sinatra announced their retirements, the industry shook [their heads] in disbelief. When I retired, there was a sort of invisible collective shrug," he is quoted in a press bio that was put out with *The Field*. He decided that he was going to do one more stage play and chose as his farewell performance his own interpretation of Pirandello's *Henry IV*. After a none-too-successful provincial tour in England he brought the production to London where his performance prompted Irving Wardell of the *Sunday Independent* to write, 'Harris joined the ranks of Sir Laurence Olivier, Sir Ralph Richardson, Sir Michael Redgrave, Sir John Gielgud, Rex Harrison, Paul Scofield, Albert Finney and Richard Burton in winning the prestigious *Evening Standard* Award for Best Performance.' It was directly in the wake of this triumph that Harris was contacted by Noel Pearson about *The Field*. His retirement never did happen.

Late in his career, he acted in the Oscar-winning film *Unforgiven* co-starring and directed by Clint Eastwood. Harris plays English Bob in the movie, a self-styled gunslinger from England with some inflated ideas about his status in life. He falls foul of Gene Hackman's brutal town sheriff in what was a widely lauded, colourful and personalised performance. Then there was Ridley Scott's *Gladiator...* followed by the role that earned him a whole new generation of fans – Albus Dumbledore in the first two *Harry Potter* films. Harris

Richard Harris as Bull McCabe in Jim Sheridan's acclaimed movie *The Field*.

initially turned down the offer to play Dumbledore until his granddaughter threatened never to speak to him again if he didn't take the role. "I can't afford that," Harris said, and immediately agreed to take the part. It turned out to be his last on-screen character and easily one of his most loved on-screen performances.

Upon his death the Taoiseach Bertie Ahern described Harris as "one of Ireland's most outstanding artists. Richard Harris made a tremendous contribution to the arts and to the entertainment world." It was one of Harris's final requests that he be buried in his beloved red Munster rugby shirt. Harris, according to his friend McCourt, had in older age taken to indulging in the odd glass of red wine mixed with soda. Or a very occasional Guinness. Harris confessed that upon visiting the family plot in Limerick cemetery that he had once wondered, "What wouldn't they all give to come up for five minutes and have a Guinness?"

CHAPTER 21

A NEW AGE IN IRISH FILM

For generations of Irish directors, producers and actors the only possible way to forge an international career was to emigrate – either to London, New York or Hollywood. While Irish theatre provided a living for some, the film and television work available was outside the country for all the Irish legends of Hollywood going back to the days of the silent screen and to the great names of the 1940s and 1950s; Maureen O'Hara, Barry Fitzgerald, Arthur Shields, Stephen Boyd, Greer Garson – their only choice was to set up home in Hollywood. Staying home in Ireland simply was not possible physically (travel was long and often arduous) or culturally (there were simply no film or TV production facilities at home worth speaking of). All that was about to change with two important developments at home in the late 1950s and early 1960s – the building of Ardmore Studios in County Wicklow, and the founding of RTÉ in 1961.

Many years later other developments would take place that would help establish a working environment at home to nurture Ireland's screen talent both in front of and behind the camera: the formation of the Irish Film Board and a government tax incentive scheme for investment in film, now known as Section 481. Most of Ireland's industry leaders interviewed for this book wholeheartedly agreed that the climate for film has changed dramatically over the past two decades. Today acclaimed directors such as Jim Sheridan, Neil Jordan and Pat O'Connor can live and work in Ireland. Three of Sheridan's most important films, *My Left Foot*, *The Field*, and *In The Name of the Father* were produced and filmed in Ireland. Neil Jordan's acclaimed *Michael Collins* was of course lensed at home with a cast of Irish actors who had exploded onto the world scene, most notably Liam Neeson and Aidan Quinn. Though we glance briefly here at the founding of an Irish film studio and of RTÉ and what this meant to Irish talent, this transitional chapter is by no means intended as an in-depth study of that period. We would much rather leave that task to such worthy intellects as Dr Helena Sheehan, whose DCU (Dublin City University) course in the social history and TV drama provides the reader with a provocative and studied account of RTÉ's history in terms of drama production:

"The really outstanding historical drama of this time, indeed of RTÉ's whole history, was *Strumpet City*. It was a seven-part adaptation of James Plunkett's epic novel, an international bestseller first published in 1969, giving a panoramic view of Dublin life during the years 1907 to 1914, years of direct and bitter confrontation between capital and labour. The epic scale and penetrating truthfulness of Plunkett's novel were skillfully reproduced and even enhanced by the quality of virtually every aspect of the RTÉ production: the script by Hugh Leonard, the direction by Tony Barry, the performances by Irish actors,

Historic Ardmore Studios seen from the air. The studio has been responsible for over one hundred films including many classics.

the use of film and authentic locations. It was RTÉ's most expensive production to that date. It functioned as a showcase product, marking RTÉ's biggest breakthrough on the international market and establishing RTÉ's credentials as a producer of high quality television drama," she writes.

While RTÉ was making inroads as the major producer of indigenous filmed Irish drama in the Seventies and Eighties the future of Ardmore Studios was in serious doubt. The studios were built in the late 1950s by impresario Louis Elliman and Major General Emmet Dalton who had experience working in the British film industry. The original idea was to film Abbey Theatre plays with Abbey actors and to distribute them to an international market. Though a noble plan in itself, it failed to materialise and their company collapsed. The studio continued to operate however and served as home base to several notable films in the 1960s, not least of which were *The Blue Max*, *The Spy Who Came in from the Cold* and *The Lion in Winter*.

The studio changed ownership often during the following decade and was frequently operated by liquidation companies. Finally, faced with ultimate closure, the government in 1973 purchased the facility and placed it under the direction of RTÉ. Two years later the National Film Studio of Ireland was formed by the government with a board of directors operating under the chairmanship of noted film director John Boorman.

Sheamus Smith, a veteran of RTÉ and a film-maker himself was charged with running the day-to-day operations as chief executive. Smith today recalls that it was to prove an almost impossible task because of "government neglect". The operation continuously suffered, he recalls, from a lack of promised capital. "I think it was very successful under the circumstances. But it could have been much more vital had we been given money to invest in movies. The whole idea of the government buying Ardmore was that there would be a fund for making films," Smith told the authors in an interview. But the investment plan simply did not materialise. "There were all sorts of proposals being put forward. The bottom line is that we did a lot of work and it was all a waste of time and energy. The problem we faced of course was that when trying to set up a film, and when you went from Ireland you would talk up the facilities and they would say, 'that's all very well but how much does Ireland put into it?' We were competing with some Eastern European countries at the time that were offering so much more than we could." Smith adds, "Considering that we had no incentives and were trying to get people to come to Ireland to make films I think we had great success. We did actually succeed in putting money into two films; one was *Taxi Mauve* starring Charlotte Rampling and Fred Astaire. We also put money in to guarantee the budget for *The First Great Train Robbery*. Then, of course, there was *Excalibur* which was the creation of John Boorman. It was a relatively low-budgeted film at the time, $11 million... That film, it's fair to say, launched the [film] careers of Gabriel Byrne, whom John had seen in [the RTÉ series] *Bracken* and also of Liam Neeson whom John had seen at the Abbey. I believe that this was an important time for an Irish film industry...it's totally different today. There are real incentives and people have been investing in movies now for twenty years, it's a regular thing and no big mystery anymore. Film is now part of the Irish economy. I recall travelling to Australia, Sweden and Denmark (to research tax incentive schemes) and the proposal that I submitted in 1976 was the basis for the present incentives and opportunities."

Excalibur (1981) directed by British director John Boorman helped launch the careers of Gabriel Byrne, Liam Neeson and director Neil Jordan. Boorman, who has made his home in County Wicklow, would also play a pivotal role in the overall Irish film scene. Shown from left: Nicol Williamson (as Merlin), Helen Mirren (as Morgana).

The facility was eventually closed by the government and put into liquidation. In 1986, producer Morgan O'Sullivan brought MTM Enterprises to Ireland. He put a consortium together, led by MTM, that purchased Ardmore Studios. O'Sullivan acted as managing director of MTM Ardmore Studios from 1986 to 1990. In that capacity, he supervised the refurbishment of the facility, the establishment and marketing of the studio complex world-wide, and worked on the production of MTM series in Europe. During his period at the studio, such productions as *My Left Foot* and *The Field* were completed. O'Sullivan has been credited as being among the most influential individuals in reversing the interchange between Ireland and Hollywood and a separate chapter on his life and remarkable career follows.

Jonathan Rhys-Meyers as Henry VIII and Sam Neill as Wolsey in *The Tudors,* another hit filmed at Ardmore Studios

Over the course of its history Ardmore Studios has been home to more than a hundred films, many of them classics. Ardmore's most recent marketing campaign could boast that Julie Andrews, Fred Astaire, Richard Burton, Katharine Hepburn, John Mills, Robert Mitchum, Peter O'Toole and Peter Ustinov were among the famous names who worked in Ardmore during its early years. In more recent times, the studios have hosted stars like Pierce Brosnan, Gabriel Byrne, Sean Connery, Tom Cruise, Richard Dreyfuss, Morgan Freeman, Mel Gibson, Richard Harris, Dennis Hopper, Nicole Kidman, Ben Kingsley, Daniel Day-Lewis, Matthew McConaughey, Colm Meaney, Liam Neeson, Meryl Streep and many more. Top directors working in Ardmore have included John Boorman, Francis Ford Coppola, Michael Crichton, Stephen Frears, Mel Gibson, Ron Howard, John Huston, Neil Jordan, Stanley Kubrick, David Lean, Pat O'Connor, Alan Parker, Kevin Reynolds, John Schlesinger and Jim Sheridan.

Ardmore Studios has always been associated with award-winning excellence, from Katharine Hepburn's Oscar for Best Actress in *The Lion in Winter* (1968) to the five awarded to Mel Gibson's *Braveheart* in 1995, including Best Picture and Best Director. *My Left Foot* was another big winner in 1989, taking Oscars in two categories for Best Actor (Daniel Day-Lewis) and Best Supporting Actress (Brenda Fricker), and nominations in another three for Best Director (Jim Sheridan), Best Adapted Screenplay (Shane Connaughton and Jim Sheridan) and Best Picture. Several other Ardmore-based films have been nominated for Academy Awards over the years. Richard Burton in *The Spy Who Came in from the Cold* (1965), Peter O'Toole in *The Lion in Winter* (1968) and Richard Harris in *The Field* (1990) were all nominated for Best Actor in their respective years. Many more have been nominated for Oscars or won awards at various film festivals around the world including *The Boxer*, *The Butcher Boy*, *The Commitments*, *Da*, *Dancing at Lughnasa*, *Excalibur*, *In the Name of the Father* and *The Snapper*. Showtime drama *The Tudors* about a surprisingly virile and handsome Henry VIII, starring Jonathan Rhys-Meyers as the king and Irish-born Sam Neill co-starring as Cardinal Wolsey entered its second season of production in 2007.

CHAPTER 22

BRINGING IT BACK HOME - MORGAN O'SULLIVAN

Producer Morgan O'Sullivan is justly credited as one of the most significant architects of today's Irish film industry. Dublin-born O'Sullivan began his remarkable career as a child actor with RTÉ radio. Later he worked with various small production outfits in Dublin making commercials and documentaries. There followed a stint as a broadcaster with RTÉ before emigrating to Australia in 1966 with his wife Liz. There he gained invaluable experience working with some of the major broadcasters as a producer, including the Australian Broadcasting Company.

Upon his return to Ireland some years later he went back to RTÉ and established himself as one of the country's leading broadcasters. His fascination with the entertainment industry prompted him to conduct a series of highly successful interviews with leading Hollywood players. It was this venture that would lead directly to a chapter in his life that would launch him into the leadership role that Ireland's nascent film industry so badly needed in the 1980s.

He knew that famous Irish director Michael O'Herlihy was directing the hit U.S. cop TV series *Hawaii Five-0* in Hawaii (episodes from 1969–76) and set out to make a documentary about O'Herlihy and the series. O'Sullivan recounts, "Leonard Freeman (executive producer on the series) and Michael O'Herlihy were incredibly helpful and I did a radio interview with Lennie. That was the start of it really." O'Sullivan went on to make a memorable documentary for RTÉ television in Hawaii with O'Herlihy's full cooperation and unstinting help. O'Sullivan and O'Herlihy would become lifelong friends as a result of the experience. "Lennie said, 'if you want to learn the business you should come to my offices at the Studio Centre (in Hollywood).'" O'Sullivan took Freeman up on the invitation and he undertook a study course in Los Angeles with the assistance of Leonard Freeman Productions.

"It was there that I met Bernie Oseransky who eventually ended up as head of production at MTM Enterprises. He called me in 1984 to talk about bringing the series *Remington Steele* to Europe." That series of course starred Pierce Brosnan. O'Sullivan by now could bring years of production experience to the table. In 1979, with author Frederick Forsyth (*Day of the Jackal*) he had formed Tara Productions to make drama for the Mobil Oil Corporation and a movie of the week for the NBC Television Network. In addition, he provided producers' services in Europe to many major U.S. series. "We crewed [*Remington Steele*] here [Ireland] and shot it all over Europe. It was through that production that I met [MTM chief] Tom Palmieri. I said to Tom that they should look at the idea of making American prime-time television shows [in Europe]." O'Sullivan

Producer, Morgan O'Sullivan

pitched Palmieri on the idea of Ireland as a European production base for the giant production group.

The U.S. television industry was facing economic challenges at a time when deficit financing for primetime series being produced in America would often outstrip the licensing income. Realising that the economics made sense at the time, Palmieri said he wanted to buy Ardmore Studios and make O'Sullivan its chief executive. "Tom put the money together and we bought the studios from the liquidator," O'Sullivan recounts. [The government-owned National Film Studios of Ireland had been put into liquidation and was for sale.] O'Sullivan worked closely with Irish production executive Kevin Moriarty in refurbishing Ardmore. "We put up a new stage that is the one that *The Tudors* is now being shot on." [*The Tudors* is an enormously successful period drama for Showtime cable television in the U.S., made with financial assistance from the Irish Film Board.]

O'Sullivan recounts that the dream was to encourage local production because "MTM was a very giving company to local media concerns… when Noel [legendary Irish film and theatre producer Noel Pearson] came to me with *My Left Foot* it was an attractive deal to them." That Oscar-winning film, directed by Jim Sheridan, would of course prove the forerunner to numerous landmark Irish films, including *The Field*, Pearson and Sheridan's next collaboration that starred Richard Harris. Brenda Fricker won a best supporting actor Oscar for her role in *My Left Foot*, and Daniel Day-Lewis won a best actor Oscar. "Jim and Noel went on to gain huge recognition at the Oscars. The studio gave a focal point for that and I like to think helped in some small way," O'Sullivan says. "I'll never forget that. We got a live feed at three or four in the morning into the studio and there were three or four hundred people crowded into the studio bar watching this little television screen, and when Brenda went up to collect the Oscar and Daniel went up it was bedlam. It was an extraordinary moment and the moment that everybody had worked so hard to make happen."

The MTM-Ardmore chapter in O'Sullivan's career came to a close with the acquisition of MTM by a British media group. TVS had its own studio in England and so decided that it did not need the Irish production operation. O'Sullivan headed back to the U.S. in the early 1990s and established development deals with some major U.S. television groups including NBC and HBO.

He was competing successfully in one of the toughest industries in the world, and the most ruthless city in the world in terms of movie and TV production when he received a call from Dublin from a friend. 'What are you doing in America? Ireland is the place to be now.' The caller referred to the fact that Michael D. Higgins, Minister for Arts, Culture and the Gaeltacht had crafted the Section 35 tax incentive scheme to stimulate film production in Ireland. O'Sullivan immediately recognised this as a way of revisiting his dream of bringing American productions to Ireland. He intended to utilise his now unparalleled (in Irish terms) worldwide production experience and a telephone book of important contacts to set up back in Ireland all over again. "I think it was Tiernan MacBride (the late Irish film-maker) who suggested to Michael that tax incentives would be a great catalyst in developing the industry. I had spent a lot of years in Australia and saw how the tax incentive schemes there worked. I always used to say that if the political will was there that we could do it."

O'Sullivan had barely begun to get the new enterprise off the ground when he was contacted by Steve McEveety who was working for Mel Gibson in preparing *Braveheart* for the screen. Gibson and his producers were exploring the idea of shooting it in Ireland rather than Scotland where the story is set. "*Braveheart* was great. I went to London and met with Steve McEveety [as well as Gibson and other producers on the film] and on the way home I read the script. Then I met with Michael D. Higgins and said that we absolutely must go for this. He called the Minister for Defence David Andrews and asked him if we could have the army (for battle scenes in the movie), and he said 'of course'. The enthusiasm all around was phenomenal and we were able to put together a

The Oscar-winning *Braveheart* proved that Irish policy on film investment and support was building much more than castles in the air. The film benefited from Irish investment as well as the Irish army for battle scenes and local castles.

package that included tax incentives but also the Irish army and castles. It was a breakthrough because it proved we could deliver what we promised in terms of production value. It gave them a production platform and it gave us something we could hang our hats on."

It was also the beginning of many years of outstanding success for the studios and for O'Sullivan personally. The production facility was constantly in use and Irish crews were receiving the best training and experience in the world. "We were able to phase out the American [crews] and bring in Irish professionals into key positions and that helped the whole indigenous industry. Michael O'Herlihy had a very simple theory: There are very few traditions in the U.S. and film-making is one of them. If you learn from them then you learn from the best in the world. And I think we have benefited from that experience and now this is pretty good place from an American [producer's] point of view. Previously when American companies came to Europe they would crew up in London and then pick it up here. We formed a direct link with the U.S."

As head of his own Ardmore Studios-based company World 2000 O'Sullivan has been responsible for securing finance and providing production services to productions such as *Moll Flanders, Scarlett, The Old Curiosity Shop, The Informant, Kidnapped, Sweeney Todd, Oliver Twist, Miracle at Midnight, The Unexpected Mrs Pollifax* and other Irish co-produced projects. In 2000 O'Sullivan met with Ned Dowd, head of Spyglass Entertainment, and found that his grandfather had been born in County Kerry. Dowd was anxious to produce in Ireland and worked with O'Sullivan to make *The Count of Monte Cristo."* Later Dowd, who today is an integral part of the Irish production scene, brought *Reign of Fire* to Ireland.

O'Sullivan, a personable and unassuming man who has dedicated a life and a career to the dream of an Irish film industry typically refuses to take credit for the enormous contribution he has made to creating a new age for Irish film. "There were many, many people: James Hickey (leading Irish entertainment attorney who has been a key advisor and participant in scores of Irish films and who has worked unsparingly with Irish film-makers and the government in helping to create the current climate for film at home), Tiernan MacBride, Neil Jordan, Jim Sheridan, Noel Pearson, John Boorman. There wasn't just one person but a whole panoply of people who helped it flourish."

CHAPTER 23

THE DIRECTORS – SHERIDAN AND JORDAN

Ireland's century-long relationship with Hollywood was altered irrevocably in 1989 with the Oscar success of Jim Sheridan's film *My Left Foot*. Until then, it had been essentially a one-way relationship, with great Irish stars and directors coming to world renown in America rather than at home where traditionally there was little or no history of film-making. Actors were snatched from the Irish theatre by directors such as John Ford and John Huston and thrust into the Hollywood limelight, or they made their names on the British stage and film before making the transition to Hollywood. Many, in the early days, had emigrated to America seeking their fortunes and found both fame and fortune in the movies. So-called 'Irish' films had largely been the result of American film-makers, Ford in particular, making production forays into Ireland for projects such as *The Quiet Man* or *The Informer*. Ireland had been seen until *My Left Foot* more as a place for Hollywood film-makers to utilise for the grandeur and beauty of its scenery.

Sheridan, the doyen of the Irish film renaissance, accepts that *My Left Foot* and *The Field* (his subsequent film with producer Noel Pearson), "were the beginning of some kind of revitalisation." Sheridan rightly credits Dublin-born and world-renowned producer Pearson as the brains behind the business end, putting the financing together for both landmark films at a time when Ireland was just beginning to see a more enlightened attitude to film investment. "That was all Noel, I only got into the production side of things with *In The Name of the Father*. But at that time we had the benefit of ignorance and not knowing anything (about making big movies)." But Sheridan says that as a first-time director with *My Left Foot* and on his second outing with *The Field* he had the benefit of having spent "seven or eight years in America," where as artistic director of the Irish Arts Centre in New York he had come to "understand American audiences and the limitations of what would work" in the U.S. "I looked at what they liked and realised that you couldn't do theatre at the Irish Centre that was experimental, because the audiences were so conservative as to be on the right of right. I realised that there is not really an Irish-American audience, not an ethnic Irish audience (for Irish films), but I think I also knew how to position a film instinctively with an American audience relating to the underdog."

My Left Foot was the biopic of disabled Irish artist Christy Brown, who from childhood displayed astounding courage in overcoming his handicap to become a lauded writer and social commentator. The role won Daniel Day-Lewis a Best Actor Oscar and gave Brenda Fricker a Best Supporting Actor Academy statuette for her role as the patient, loving mother struggling to raise Christy amid grinding Dublin poverty. Cyril Cusack, Ray McAnally, and Fiona Shaw also provided sterling performances.

Daniel Day-Lewis as Christy Brown in Jim Sheridan's cinematic triumph *My Left Foot*, for which Day-Lewis won an Oscar.

The co-author of this book Steve Brennan wrote about the enormous impact of the film in America in an article for Ardmore Studios' in-house magazine. Both authors were on hand for that historic Oscar event in 1990: 'The Hollywood trade press tracks the box office progress of the $3 million-budgeted film, counting the take in growing millions and reporting it with an almost wicked glee – almost as though it were cheering a last-placed but popular college team to victory… Every day some new snippet appears about *My Left Foot* – or about its producer Noel Pearson's latest plans. The Irish are the latest fad in Hollywood with the entire town cheering the 'Emeralds of Tinseltown,' as they have become affectionately known… For days, Noel Pearson and Jim Sheridan had been fortified in their West Hollywood hotel taking as many as twenty press and television interviews a day. Brenda Fricker, Daniel Day-Lewis and Shane Connaughton, who co-wrote the *Foot* screenplay with Jim Sheridan, were nervously waiting on the sidelines.

'The night before the Big One, (we) joined Noel and Jim in Molly Malone's Irish pub in Los Angeles as they hosted family and friends in a typically unglitzy, Dublin evening away from the camera lights and the phone calls.… with an almost trademark reserve and modesty which made him popular with the press in Hollywood, (Noel) told me quietly; "It amazes me that everybody seems to know what we will win, what we won't win, what we should win, what we shouldn't win and why we should. And nobody seems to agree. All I know is that by tomorrow night it'll all be over and Jim and myself can get on with our plans, no matter what."'

The big night came on fast and the limousines carrying the Irish team pulled up fittingly enough on Hope Street to allow them disembark for the red carpet trek to the Oscars. 'If Noel Pearson had wanted the tense evening to be over quickly, then some director in the sky was toying with him. It was one of the longest Oscar ceremonies in recent years. And the minutes lay on the Irish like hours as we waited in turn for each of the *Left Foot* nomination categories to come around: Best Picture, Best Actor, Best Director, Best Supporting Actress, Best Screenplay Based on Material from Another Medium. Brenda Fricker was the first into the volcano. The best actress nominees were listed. Anjelica Huston, Lena Olin, Julia Roberts, Brenda Fricker... 'and the winner is – Brenda Fricker.' The place exploded... Brenda Fricker, a sincere look of disbelief on her face holds her Oscar high and thanks Christy Brown, who died in 1977. Of Christy's mother – whom she portrayed – she says, "Anyone who gave birth twenty-two times deserves one of these.'"

Dublin-born Fricker began her acting career with RTÉ before joining the National Theatre in London and later The Royal Shakespeare Company and the Royal Court Theatre Company in England. She amassed a glowing list of theatre and television credits and critical praise with roles in such TV features as *High Kampf* in 1973 and *Your Man from 6 Counties* in 1976 as well as her highly visible role of Nurse Roach in the drama series *Casualty*. Her Oscar win would gain considerable attention from Hollywood and lead to such high-profile productions as the mini-series *Relative Strangers* in 1999, and films as varied as *Home Alone 2: Lost in New York* in 1992, *So I Married an Axe Murderer* in 1993, *Masterminds* in 1997 and *Veronica Guerin* in 2003. She would work with Sheridan again in *The Field* in the hugely lauded role of Bull McCabe's silent and suffering wife.

As for that triumphant Oscar night for the Irish, the evening trundles on, not without its share of disappointments. Jim Sheridan is beaten out for the award as best director. He also misses out on the screenplay wreath with Shane Connaughton. But his victory is already secured. As one famous Hollywood columnist put it: 'Sheridan has overcome all the odds by just being nominated.' ...Then it's 'Best Actor' time. Again the long drawn-out introduction. Again the camera pans the nominees. Again the tension mounts. And those familiar words... 'And the winner is... Daniel Day-Lewis.' "...Oh my God we did it. We bloody did it."

The atmosphere was electric as well-wishers including Bono, Bob Geldof, Kenneth Branagh (who was nominated for two Oscars the same night for *Henry V*), Ted Turner, Jane Fonda, Robin Williams, Warren Beatty, Billy Crystal (who hosted the Oscars that evening), Beau Bridges, and a host of other Hollywood royalty back-slapped and congratulated the victorious *My Left Foot* team. Daniel Day-Lewis was awe-struck to hear that a civic reception for them had been organised in Dublin upon their return. On a humorous note the lone barman on duty at the subsequent Hollywood reception was struggling to keep pace with the orders. "You'd better get some back-up. One barman into two Irish Oscars won't go," one of the guests wisely advised him.

For Sheridan it was the culmination of what had already been an outstanding career as a theatre director, writer and actor. He had certainly come a long way from earlier days at the Project Theatre, an adventurous Dublin group that he moulded with his brother Peter into a dynamic, sometimes controversial theatre centre. The Sheridans' work in theatre was cutting edge and the centre served as a training ground for a host of rising new theatre talent.

Jim was intrigued with the idea of working in America and eventually decided to take up the post of Artistic Director at the vibrant new Irish theatre centre in New York. Director Neil Jordan was also emerging at this time in the film world, having achieved international renown as an award-winning and best-selling author. Sheridan told the authors, "John Boorman offered me and Neil the chance to do movies when I was at the Project.

He (Boorman) was doing *Excalibur* and Neil took up the opportunity and I just thought I would go to America and break into film through theatre."

Sheridan moved to New York in the early Eighties with his young family to begin work at the Irish Arts Centre. The family set up home in a part of New York fondly referred to as Hell's Kitchen, once a bastion of the Irish immigrant community. Sheridan would later name his Irish production company 'Hell's Kitchen'. The authors were welcomed once by the Sheridan family for a visit and given a personal tour by Sheridan of the Arts Centre that at the time was staging a production of Beckett's *Waiting for Godot*. Years later of course, these early New York adventures would serve as the backdrop for his triumphant Oscar contender *In America* which Sheridan co-wrote with daughters Naomi and Kirsten. All three were nominated for Oscars in the Best Screenplay category. The 2004 film also brought nominations in the Best (leading) Actress and Best (supporting) Actor categories for Samantha Morton and Djimon Hounsou.

Sheridan believes that to some extent at least his years of directing theatre in such intimate spaces as The Project and the Irish Arts Centre were key in his development as a film director and helped forge his reputation as 'an actors' director'. "The thing about the Project and the Irish Centre is that they were little spaces where you were up close with the actors. I was more used to theatre in-the-round than with the proscenium arch and I think it was much more cinematic. You felt you were up there with the actor but when you went into the Abbey and looked up at the stage it might as well have been in Texas."

Sheridan attended the New York Film School while directing and producing at the Irish Arts Centre and raising his young family. He moved back to Dublin in the late Eighties with the idea of making a film about Christy Brown's life. He was welcomed back to Dublin by the theatre community like a long-lost hero. On one particularly rainy day he and Noel Pearson were to be seen lunching together in Neary's Bar on Chatham Street, and

Director Jim Sheridan on the set of *Get Rich or Die Tryin'*, a rare journey into an all-American Hollywood movie for the artist.

word quickly spread that something big was happening. Various actors came on the scene and stayed, trying to figure out what was in the air. It was *My Left Foot*.

Following the Oscar triumph both Sheridan and Pearson were the recipients of a slew of multi-million dollar Hollywood offers, including one for an eight-picture deal from the then mighty Guber-Peters Productions. That could have been a critical moment for the future of Irish film. As it was Sheridan and Pearson decided that their future lay in Ireland and with Irish films, and they went on to make the landmark Irish drama *The Field*, which gained an Oscar nomination for Richard Harris.

Sheridan followed this with *In The Name of the Father* in 1993, in which he teamed up again with Daniel Day-Lewis to make the screen adaptation of the story of Gerry Conlon, an Irishman wrongfully convicted (along with his father) by the British for crimes perpetrated by the IRA. The screenplay was an adaptation by Sheridan and Terry George from Conlon's autobiography, *Proved Innocent*. The film – produced under the banner of Hell's Kitchen which he founded in 1993 with Arthur Lappin – garnered an Oscar nomination for Day-Lewis in the Best Actor category. It also earned nominations for Best Picture, Screenplay Adaptation, Supporting Actress (Emma Thompson), Supporting Actor (Pete Postlethwaite), and Film Editing.

He teamed up yet again with Day-Lewis for *The Boxer* in 1997, which was also set against the backdrop of 'The Troubles' in Northern Ireland. Following the same theme Sheridan then went on to make the powerful *Some Mother's Son*, which centred on the nightmare facing two mothers whose sons were part of the 1981 IRA hunger strike, and starred Fionnula Flanagan and Helen Mirren. Terry George directed and co-wrote with Sheridan (*see Chapter 24*).

In 2003 Sheridan made *In America* and in 2005 he directed *Get Rich or Die Tryin'*, starring rap star 50 Cent. Under his Hell's Kitchen banner he has also made *Borstal Boy*, based on the Brendan Behan story and directed by Peter Sheridan; *Agnes Browne* (starring Anjelica Huston as a Moore Street fruit and vegetable seller); *On the Edge* as well as the docudrama *Bloody Sunday*.

Referring to John Boorman's offer to segue to film directing, Sheridan mentioned that both he and acclaimed director and author Neil Jordan had received the same offer. Jordan's decision to work with Boorman on *Excalibur* would prove his stepping-stone to the heights of renown as a director and he made a much-praised documentary about the making of that epic film.

Born in Sligo in 1950 Jordan went to University College Dublin before embarking on a successful writing career and founding the Irish Writers' Co-Op. His literary works include the short story collection *Night in Tunisia* which won the Guardian Fiction Award in 1978, the novels *The Past* (1980), *The Dream of a Beast* (1983), *Sunrise with Sea Monster* (1994) and *Shade* (2005). Neil Jordan's film credits also include *High Spirits* (1988); *The Miracle* (1990); *The Butcher Boy* (1997); *The End of the Affair* (1999); *In Dreams* (1999); *The Good Thief* (2002); *Breakfast on Pluto* (2005) and *The Brave One* (2007).

Jordan's first feature, *Angel* in 1982, was a haunting thriller that drew from his own earlier experiences as a musician and was hailed as a 'formidable' debut. It was also the first time that Jordan and Belfast-born actor Stephen Rea teamed up for a movie.

Neil Jordan on the set of *Michael Collins* in 1993.

Stephen Rea originally trained at the Abbey Theatre in Dublin and later joined the Focus Company where he worked with Gabriel Byrne and Colm Meaney. He went on to achieve acclaimed performances in some of England's most important theatres, including the famed Royal Court before famously forming the Field Day Theatre Company with playwright Brian Friel. His move to television and film began in the 1970s when he was cast in numerous television roles in England. But his first big break on the big screen came when he was cast by Jordan in the director's debut feature, *Angel* in 1982. The dark mood-driven film saw him play an introverted musician who gets caught up in the violence of Northern Ireland in the 1970s. Rea proved himself an immense screen presence and garnered enormous critical acclaim for that remarkable debut Jordan film. They have gone on to make a further six notable films together.

Rea worked on number of English films before he again worked with Jordan to great effect on *The Company of Wolves* in 1984. Taken from the writings of Angela Carter, the film was an eerie take on the Red Riding Hood fairytale with a werewolf twist. Rea was a commanding force in the film. Jordan followed this success by the film now considered to be a modern classic by many critics. *Mona Lisa* (1986) starring Bob Hoskins was set at the heart of London's gangland.

Jordan continued his triumphant ascent in the international film arena with *The Crying Game* in 1992 that brought the Northern Ireland Troubles into play as its dramatic backdrop. Stephen Rea starred again and his memorable performance as an IRA man who falls in love with the girlfriend of a man in whose death he was involved made Hollywood sit up and take notice. The performance won him an Oscar nomination as Best Actor. Offers for Hollywood roles poured in and Rea found himself playing a variety of characters from the happy-go-lucky Irishman in *Angie* to the off-the-rails egomaniac photographer in Robert Altman's hilarious *Ready-to-Wear (Prêt-á-Porter)*.

Stephen Rea (as Fergus) and Jaye Davidson (as Dil) in *The Crying Game.*

Jordan went on to make a number of major Hollywood studio releases, including the adaptation of the Anne Rice novel *Interview with the Vampire* starring Tom Cruise, Brad Pitt and a young Kirsten Dunst. Rea played the role of the vampire Santiago and demonstrated a world-weary style of understatement to perfection. Jordan would follow this with *We're No Angels* starring Robert De Niro, and of course *Michael Collins* which once again featured Rea.

Of the many years of work that he dedicated to the writing and production of *Michael Collins* (*see Chapter 25*) Jordan would comment, "I have never lost more sleep over the making of a film than I have over *Michael Collins*, but I'll never make a more important one. In the life of one person you can tell the events that formed the north and south of Ireland as they are today."

Jordan's place among world film-makers as an enigmatic, daring, explorative director and writer is secure. Like his friend and regular collaborator Stephen Rea, his career has been influenced by a spirit of independence that has constantly set him above the typical Tinseltown fray. Rea has established his name as an actor's actor in film, television and stage and his career continues to unfold. The annals of cinematic history will record Jordan's pivotal role in the Irish film renaissance.

CHAPTER 24

'AS GAEILGE' - FIONNULA FLANAGAN

She has a litany of award-winning and critically lauded starring roles to her credit, but for the moment Fionnula Flanagan seems happiest talking about her latest part in a little-known TV series shot in Ireland and all in Gaelic called *Paddywhackery*. Flanagan is a rarity among Hollywood A-list actors in that she's just as likely to be found down at the local market as at some celebrity-filled Hollywood awards event. So it's no surprise to find her talking passionately from the set of one of the most acclaimed TV series in America in 2007 – *Brotherhood* – not about this latest U.S. hit, but about her portrayal of Peig Sayers, legendary Irish writer and *seanachaí* in the Irish-language production.

Her career has brought her from the Abbey Theatre in Dublin to the most important theatre companies in London, to Broadway and Hollywood, yet she is most excited during our interview about the Irish project that she has just recently completed with director Daniel O'Hara. The comedy centres on a man who wakes up only able to speak and understand Gaelic. "And I get to play Peig Sayers all 'as Gaeilge' [in Irish]. I had the advantage of having gone to an all-Irish school and of course had to do Peig Sayers." Flanagan, a fluent Irish speaker, describes the job of working in her native language alongside a cast of Irish-speaking actors in such a "charming and clever" mini-series as one of the "happiest" film-making experiences of her life.

The journey back to play Peig Sayers was a happy return to her roots for Flanagan, who has starred in an array of award-winning and box office hit movies such as *The Others* (alongside Nicole Kidman) and *The Divine Secrets of the Ya-Ya Sisterhood* (with Sandra Bullock, Ellen Burstyn and Maggie Smith), *Waking Ned* [*Devine*], and *Transamerica*. *Some Mother's Son* (1996) co-starring Helen Mirren, written by Jim Sheridan and Terry George and directed by the latter, was another role close to Flanagan's heart.

"That was a story that many people had wanted to make and many scripts had floated around about the hunger strike, but nobody had reached out and attempted it from the point of view of the families and the mothers who brought world attention to the men on the blanket, and I was thrilled to do it. This was a watershed in our history and something from which we are still feeling the fallout. I thought the script that Terry and Jim wrote together was wonderful. I also got to meet a lot of the families of the hunger strikers and they were very generous with their time and in sharing their intimate feelings. That was something that I could not get elsewhere. I wanted to do my part to give them a voice and the dignity they deserved." Flanagan recalls that she was very determined to play the role of the hunger striker's mother. "I just knew it was my part and that nobody else would

Former Abbey
actress Fionnula
Flanagan as Rose
Caffee in the
acclaimed Showtime
series *Brotherhood*.

serve it as I could, and I believe that without being vain. I also felt it was also important not to play it as a victim though all involved were victims." The film was George's first time out directing a full feature. Flanagan recalls, "He had written it with Jim. They both had difficult roles to play because Jim was not directing and that must have been extraordinarily difficult, but he was so supportive of Terry in so many ways and the whole experience was a real journey for all involved."

Some Mother's Son was also a way of pursuing her passionate support for the film industry at home, much in the same way that Sheridan, Byrne, Jordan, Brosnan and other leading lights in the industry have done. Though much has changed in the past two decades for Irish film-making, more government support is still needed, she believes. "Film-making is like playing polo; you have to feed the horses even when they are not out playing. There's so much that goes on behind the scenes all the time that needs to be supported and needs seed money. There's so much writing and re-writing and development long before you see it on the screen." She reflects, "We suffered through the economy of the grey Fifties when there was no money available in the country and we were building up after the war. The money was going into electrical plants and Bord na Móna and people weren't thinking 'let's make movies'." The thinking then was that movies don't bring employment. But Flanagan sees that changing now, with new film talent emerging in an industry that is now on a solid footing. "But the government needs to understand that bringing young film-makers along takes time and effort and underwriting and I think they are waking up to that now. I think the very best short films in the world are coming out of Ireland and that may have something to do with our history as short story writers. I see that translating into film and it's interesting to me that (makers of short Irish films) have shot up like sprouts."

Some Mother's Son was followed a few years later in 2001 with her co-starring performance with Nicole Kidman in the surprise box-office smash *The Others*, which brought a Saturn Award and critical accolades for Flanagan. The ghost suspense thriller threw a new focus on

Flanagan as one of the modern screen's most versatile actresses. "*The Others* was marvellous to work on and that came out of some *Some Mother's Son* because (Spanish/Chilean director) Alejandro Amenábar had seen *Some Mother's* and had got in touch with me. I met him in London where we had an extraordinary meeting because I don't have great Spanish and he didn't have great English. I knew he wanted me for the film and I thought if he can bring this off it will be brilliant, because the concept and the twists were just so complex."

The film is set on an island in the English Channel near the end of World War II, where Grace, played by Nicole Kidman cares for her children Ann and Nicholas in a cold, empty country mansion. Grace has been told that her husband (Christopher Eccleston), who's fighting, is missing in action. The house's staff have vanished. The daughter starts seeing visions of another family who she says used to live in the manor house. Doors fly open and screams and sobs echo through the empty rooms. Meanwhile, the new housekeeping staff led by the friendly but quite scary Mrs Mills (Flanagan) slowly begin to take control of events. The film was a huge success both at the box office and critically.

'*The Others* is a throwback to those older (and wiser) horror films that would build a foundation of terror and dread slowly and thoughtfully, and then scare the audience out of their skin,' commented one reviewer. Others compared the film to classics such as *Rosemary's Baby* and *The Shining*, as well as *The Cat and the Canary* and even *The Spiral Staircase*. The film cast Flanagan more definitively than ever into the world spotlight.

Born in Dublin and trained at the Abbey Theatre, Flanagan first came to prominence in the leading role in Tomas MacAnna's Irish language production *An Trial* (*The Trial*) in the 1966 Dublin Theatre Festival. The following year she received the Jacobs Award for most outstanding performance of the year for her re-creation of the role on RTÉ. She went on to play Katherine in *The Taming of the Shrew* and later played Pegeen Mike in *The Playboy of the Western World* with the Old Vic Company in Bristol. She starred with Malcolm McDowell in *Twelfth Night* at the Royal Court Theatre in London and in numerous BBC and RTÉ television dramas including the title role in W.B. Yeats' *Deirdre* and Sean O'Casey's *The Shadow of a Gunman*. Flanagan adapted her stage skills effortlessly to the medium of television, so much so that later in her career in the U.S. she would amass a string of credits in major series including *The Legend of Lizzie Borden, Murder She Wrote, Star Trek: The Next Generation, How the West Was Won* (for which she received an Emmy Nomination as Best Actress) and *Rich Man, Poor Man* (1976) for which she received an Emmy Award.

Flanagan made her Broadway debut with the 1968 production of *Lovers*, directed by Hilton Edwards and starring Art Carney. Following its national tour, she spent a season at the Goodman Theatre in Chicago. Other Broadway roles included *The Incomparable Max* with Clive Reville, Mrs Alving in Ibsen's *Ghosts* and Molly Bloom with Zero Mostel in the 1974 production of *Ulysses in Nighttown* directed by Burgess Meredith, for which she won a Tony Award nomination.

"I played four other roles in that production as well as Molly," Flanagan recalls. But it was the role of Molly that drew the critics' attention to Flanagan, who credits Meredith as "knowing how to stage Joyce more than anybody". She adds, "He and I became very close." When the acclaimed production was over "Tommy Lee Jones (who was playing Stephen Dedalus) went off to do pictures for Roger Corman and Zero went off to do something else, and I was out there very unhappily doing a lot of TV work. I began to look at the other women in Joyce's life and that's when I sat down and wrote *James*

Fionnula Flanagan with director Alejandro Amenábar on the set of *The Others.*

Joyce's Women." I found that all of the people who were allowed to have a voice about Joyce and to have a say were all male. I wanted to collectively look at the women in Joyce's life such as Harriet Shaw Weaver (his patron) and Sylvia Beech (his publisher), his wife Nora."

That was how Flanagan's triumphant Universal release *Joyce's Women* emerged. "I brought it to Burgess and asked him would he direct. It was a mentor and tutor relationship and we took the play around the world before sitting down to do it as a film." It premiered at the South Coast Repertory Theatre in Costa Mesa, California in August 1977, produced by Flanagan and her husband Garrett O'Connor and directed by Meredith. Later came a U.S. tour, a British tour, a tour of Australia and, much to Flanagan's delight, a run at Dublin's Gate Theatre as part of the James Joyce Centenary celebrations in 1982. "I didn't know anything about films but Universal gave me the money to do it while saying they would feel better about it if I had some other entity involved." The film was made with RTÉ in Ireland. But Flanagan was unhappy with the finished result and the situation ended up in the Dublin courts. Flanagan hired a new director and crew and essentially shot the film again, she says. That second version is the one that went out on release with Flanagan's stamp of approval. She does not regret the experience. "It was of great value to me and an incredible learning experience… *Joyce's Women*, which was a long period in my life, was superbly important to me because what it did was to liberate from fear, the fear that permeates the industry. It took away any fear of anybody in the industry whether in places of power or not – it did something extraordinary for me and I am so grateful to all concerned for that. It was a wonderful adventure." Today, Flanagan and her husband Garrett currently divide their time between Los Angeles and Ireland where they maintain homes. Her fervent hope is to be able to make more films and television at home, and particularly in her native Gaelic. "After all, you will find nowhere more beautiful than the Irish landscape."

CHAPTER 25

A MODERN MATINÉE IDOL – LIAM NEESON

'Liam Neeson has been making movies since 1979 and through his work on films like *Schindler's List, Michael Collins* and *Rob Roy* has become a key figure in the film world, cornering the market in troubled, sensitive, noble types with forearms like hams.'

That's how Harriet Lane described the actor back in May 1999 upon the release of Hollywood blockbuster *Star Wars: Episode I – The Phantom Menace*, in which Neeson played Qui-Gon Jinn, the Master Jedi Knight who bestows his wisdom upon the young Skywalker.

'Liam Neeson is the matinée idol who stepped on a rake,' guffawed the *Times* in October 2002 in a profile of the Ballymena-born Neeson. The piece was referring to a nose that Neeson can credit to a keen interest in boxing in earlier days. Neeson's hulking six foot-four inch stature and striking visage seem to dominate just about every magazine and newspaper piece ever written about this most serious of actors. Handsome though he may be it seems unfair to label Neeson as a matinée idol. It's impossible to imagine a matinée idol with the seemingly limitless range that Neeson continues to display in one challenging role after another – both in film and the theatre. Whether it is his Academy Award-nominated role of Oskar Schindler in Steven Spielberg's acclaimed *Schindler's List*, his award-winning portrayal of the title role in *Michael Collins* or his role as controversial sex therapist Alfred Kinsey in the critically lauded *Kinsey* (2004), which garnered him a best actor award from the Los Angeles Film Critics Association, Neeson continually brings extraordinary depths to myriad and varied characters.

Neeson's big break to international stardom came in 1990 through his passion for theatre. Natasha Richardson asked him to join her in *Anna Christie* on Broadway. 'It was an auspicious move,' wrote Jane Brown in *The Observer*. 'He ended up falling for his leading lady, (they are now married, with two children), winning a Tony and being spotted by Steven Spielberg, who cast him as Oskar Schindler. His starring role in the Academy Award-winning film *Schindler's List* won him an Academy Award nomination for Best Actor, as well as nominations for a Golden Globe and BAFTA Awards.' It should be remembered that Neeson had in fact also impressed Spielberg in an earlier screen test for the role, which Neeson himself actually accounts for his being hired for the part that would launch him to stardom.

He had come a long way from his native Ballymena where he was born in 1952. Both his parents worked in the local school system. Neeson himself attended a teacher-training course in Newcastle in England that also offered education in theatre. It was here that his interest in acting was piqued and upon returning home after two years at the college he

was determined to become a professional actor. One day in 1976 he telephoned the Lyric
Theatre in Belfast, and was fortunate enough to be put directly through to the head of
the theatre Mary O'Malley who invited him in for a reading. She was casting for a stage
version of Joseph Plunkett's *The Risen People* and at six foot-four Neeson would make a
perfect 'Big' Jim Larkin, the union leader. On hearing Neeson read for the role O'Malley
offered him a spot with the theatre, and even signed him up with a professional Actors
Equity contract. "It was the best training any actor could have," he would later comment
of his two years with the Lyric. Following his time at the Lyric Neeson moved to Dublin
to pursue a freelance career, during which he stunned Dublin audiences with a harrowing
portrayal of Gypo Nolan, the simple giant who is misled into betraying his best friend in
Liam O'Flaherty's *The Informer* at the Olympia Theatre. The role seemed to have been written for Neeson who drew enormous critical praise for his portrayal. His freelance work in
Dublin in various theatres, including the Focus and the Project, led to a stint at The Abbey
Theatre where in 1980 film director John Boorman spotted him playing Lennie in John
Steinbeck's *Of Mice and Men* and cast him in his epic saga of the Arthurian legend *Excalibur*
in the role of Sir Gawain.

"I don't think I've ever been as happy acting as I was back in those days," Neeson would
recall in an interview with American *Premiere* magazine some years later. "John Boorman
cast me in my first film, *Excalibur*. He was such a wonderful teacher. He'd take us round back
of the camera and show us what he was doing. Besides being a great director, he was also
a great editor. While shooting he would explain how he was going to cut it. We were on
that film for four months and he gave me a great grounding in film-making. At this point
I'd done eleven years of stage work and here was this other avenue presenting itself, which
I was very attracted to. But one couldn't stay in Ireland and make movies. There was no
industry there. So I moved to London and started doing bits and pieces here and there," he
told interviewer Susan Royal in that 1992 article. In 1980 he had joined Field Day, the Irish

theatre company that had been founded by actor Stephen Rea and playwright Brian Friel. He moved to London to start production on Friel's *Translations* at the National Theatre.

Neil Jordan was also settled in London and had completed filming on *The Company of Wolves*. Jordan contacted Neeson and told him that he had a project that he wanted Neeson to star in. That project was *Michael Collins*. Neeson recalled in an interview in the *Los Angeles Times* in 1996: "As we talked, he kept saying, 'He is one of the unsung heroes of Ireland, isn't he?'" Neeson and Jordan would continue to discuss the project for years to come. But in the meantime Neeson needed to pursue other parts, which he did with a modicum of success for a number of years in London.

His work on *Excalibur* led to a succession of television roles in England and more movie work including *The Bounty* directed by Roger Donaldson and co-starring Mel Gibson and Anthony Hopkins. Neeson played essentially the same role that Richard Harris had in the previous version starring Marlon Brando. He also landed a serious role in *The Mission*, on which he worked with the late Ray McAnally and Robert De Niro. There was also a brief encounter at the time with Steven Spielberg who was in London preparing for his film *Empire of the Sun*. A casting director said Spielberg wanted someone to read with a group of boy actors from whom the lead in the movie would be chosen. Neeson spent an entire day reading with the young actors. "At the end of the day he said to me, 'We'll do something special someday.'" Neeson told the *Los Angeles Times*. But television work was a staple. "American production companies were coming into England then. They were shooting lots of mini-series and I did a few of those. But then it just started to dry up," Neeson recalled in an interview in the *Sunday Times*. He felt he needed to be in Hollywood in order to realise his ambitions to become a force in the movies. He arrived in Los Angeles in January 1986, with severely limited funds. "I literally was able to stay five or six weeks tops. I was at this little hotel on Hollywood Boulevard." But Neeson's Los Angeles agents were on his side. "The first two weeks I was just out on casting calls. I was a stranger in town and I was really surprised by the welcoming attitude. I was called in on an ABC movie-of-the-week. It was a very good part, a serial killer, a case that actually happened in the 1970s. I got it! So I was able to stay on in LA for a few more months. It's funny how work breeds work, because Peter Yates got in touch with me." Author of that interview, Anthony Haden-Guest, takes up the story: 'Yates, the veteran British director (*Bullitt, Breaking Away, The Dresser*) gave Neeson a part in a movie called *Suspect*. The female lead was Cher, and Yates told Neeson he wanted him for one of the male leads. It was a challenge: a deaf-mute wildman of the streets. [The role was a homeless mute unjustly accused of murder.] "Peter said, 'it's going to be a battle getting you into it'" [said Neeson]. But there he was in Los Angeles, and he was called to a meeting in the thirtieth floor office of an executive of the production company Tri-Star. "I met this man and he said, 'Peter really wants you in. Do you like the part?' I said 'Yeah, I love it. I'd love to be able to do it.' He said 'Okay, good, thanks!'"

Yates later told Neeson, "That's the greatest thing that could have happened – the fact that you were in L.A., so this guy could just see your face. If you had been living in Ireland or London there's no way they would have flown over to meet you." Neeson said in another interview, "They had wanted a star. Peter, God bless his socks, held out for me. It was a huge break."

Neeson settled into a home in the Hollywood Hills and proceeded to work in a series of films in which he gave lauded performances but never quite managed to achieve the A-list status that many critics clearly felt he deserved. Demetrios Matheou writing in the London

Observer of Neeson in 2002 commented, 'In the Eighties and early Nineties, before he became famous, he strung together a series of beautiful characterisations, mostly in small-scale movies: as the Catholic priest struggling to care for a sickly boy in *Lamb*; the mute vagrant wrongly on trial for murder in *Suspect*; the scam artist out of his depth in *Under Suspicion*; the unemployed miner turned bare-knuckle boxer in *The Big Man*; as Edith Wharton's tragic New England farmer in *Ethan Frome*. For the most part these are characters struggling to do the right thing, despite their predispositions, usually in the face of strict societal constraints. From *Schindler's List*, which made him a star... he has continued in the same vein, only on a larger canvas. Neeson's best roles have been historical and eponymous. Oskar Schindler, Rob Roy, Michael Collins; flesh and blood characters, men of the people, heroic in differing ways.'

Other memorable screen characterisations created by Neeson to wide acclaim included the passionate Irish sculptor opposite Diane Keaton in *The Good Mother*; and as scientist Peyton Westlake, whose disfiguring accident forces him into hiding in Sam Raimi's fantasy-thriller *Darkman*. He starred as a Nazi engineer in David Seltzer's adaptation of Susan Isaac's best-selling novel *Shining Through* opposite Michael Douglas and as a disgraced policeman accused of murder in the erotic thriller *Under Suspicion*. Neeson pushed himself hard and gained a reputation as a thorough professional who was willing to throw himself heart and soul into a role. Typical of his work schedule at that time was when making *Darkman*. The role as the horribly scarred Westlake required hours of make-up. At the same time he was also preparing for the muscle-bound role of a bare-knuckle fighter in *The Big Man* which required hours of workouts each day. He would get up at two in the morning, work out and then be in a make-up chair by five. "I was a monk, just *Darkman* and doing these solitary workouts. It was a fairly solitary existence, but I liked it for that, because I tend to be fairly solitary. I was there on a quest, to be in the centre of English-speaking cinema and to get a chance to work which I did," he confided in a 1996 interview in the *Los Angeles Times*.

It seems to have been his preference for the solitary life that led to Neeson's gradual discomfort with Hollywood. He began to speak in interviews about his disenchantment with the film town, after seven years of chasing down roles in films that always seemed to hold more promise than they delivered. Part of his problem, he once confessed, was his dislike of the networking circuit that is such a central part of life in Hollywood. Rather than glad-hand at the endless round of cocktail parties and dinners he often simply preferred to sit at home and watch television. "I was stabbing myself," he once confessed.

It was then that Natasha Richardson, now Neeson's wife and mother of their two children, persuaded Neeson to take to the boards again in her Broadway production of *Anna Christie*. The offer came at a crucial time for Neeson who relished a return to the stage in a production that earned him the attention and professional fulfillment that seemed to be eluding him in Hollywood. Neeson was outstanding in the production, which Steven Spielberg attended one night with his wife Kate Capshaw, whose mother was moved to tears by Neeson's performance. Afterwards Neeson, seeing that Capshaw's mother was visibly upset, took her in his arms. "Oskar Schindler would have done that," commented Capshaw. Spielberg was at that very moment seeking a male lead to take the role of Schindler in his film *Schindler's List*. Neeson had already done a screen test for this most coveted of roles. It seems highly likely that his kind gesture on the night secured the role for him. Spielberg later phoned Neeson to tell him the part was his.

Neeson and
Spielberg on the set
of *Schindler's List*.

Schindler was a great role for any actor. But Neeson gobbled it up and gobbled up the
screen in the process. The story is taken from the fact-based novel *Schindler's Ark* by
Thomas Keneally. Schindler is a German entrepreneur with an eye for a pretty lady and a
hunger for the good life. He arrives in Krakow intent on making his fortune during World
War II. He endears himself to the Nazis by bribing them with black-market goodies and
in the process secures big manufacturing contracts, which he fulfills at a factory manned
by Jewish forced labour. Schindler is horrified by the atrocities of the Nazis however and
succeeds in rescuing 1,100 of his factory workers from the gas chamber by smuggling
them out of harm's way. The role earned Neeson an Oscar nomination and launched him
to instant A-list stardom. On the final day of filming on *Schindler's List* Spielberg turned
to Neeson and said, "Remember the day you read for me with all those boys?" Neeson
said he remembered it well. Spielberg reminded him what he had said that day to Neeson:
"Someday we'll work together on something special."

This wasn't the only occasion that things would turn full circle in that period of his life.
The role that had held such promise in so many conversations with Neil Jordan over the
years, that of Michael Collins, now began to materialise for real. With *Schindler's List* having
made him one of the screen's most influential leading men and with Jordan basking in such
international critical and box office success as *The Crying Game* and *Interview With the
Vampire* the pair finally had the clout to get the epic Irish drama made. But they now had
competition. Film star and producer Kevin Costner had become intrigued with the story
of Collins and his almost mythical exploits during Ireland's War of Independence. Costner
was actively developing a project similar to the one that Jordan had dreamed of making
for most of his adult life. Jordan approached *Vampire* producer David Geffen, while Neeson
undertook to speak with Warner Bros. co-head Terry Semel. Neeson said, "Terry, I know
you guys are holding Jordan's script. I know you have a relationship with Kevin Costner
and Kevin is very keen to do this. Can you give us any hope at all? We're just a bunch of

Paddies, and we want to make a film of our own guy. And Terry listened. He kept saying, 'I hear you, I hear you,'" Neeson recounted in the *Los Angeles Times* some years later. Geffen agreed to put up a reported $28 million to make the film and Warner Bros. rowed in behind. The film, co-starring fellow-Irish actor Aidan Quinn and Julia Roberts was an enormous critical success for both Jordan and Neeson who portrayed a striding, confident, charming, cunning and often ruthless Collins. Critics said that Neeson had been born to play the role of the 'big fella' Michael Collins. It was the role that would further secure his place at the pinnacle of the international film industry.

Neeson, his actress wife Natasha Richardson and their sons live today in New York. Though he has often confessed to have become disillusioned with the Hollywood film business and with Hollywood itself, he confessed in an interview with *Playboy* magazine that he might indeed have enjoyed working in the Hollywood of by-gone years – in the studio system and the so-called 'golden age' of Hollywood when so many Irish plied their trade in Tinseltown. Neeson mused, "It would have been wonderful to be part of that, clock in every day at six like an honest tradesman. Then someone would say to you, 'today you're Lord Ponseroy and you're defending the castle.' And four weeks later you would put on a gun belt and go to Dodge City. But God, it must have been exhausting."

CHAPTER 26

HOLLYWOOD'S NEW IRISH LEADING MEN

From Pierce Brosnan to Colm Meaney, Aidan Quinn, Kenneth Branagh and Brendan Gleeson

Producer Morgan O'Sullivan has vivid memories of making *The Manions of America* in 1981 for ABC Television in the U.S. The mini-series was filmed around a Dublin that doubled for 1800s Philadelphia. A future Irish screen star had been cast in the dashing and romantic lead role of Rory O'Manion, who fights his way up from downtrodden Irish immigrant to wealthy Philadelphian businessman. It was a star-making part for Pierce Brosnan. "It really was *The Manions* that discovered Pierce and took him to America," recalls O'Sullivan. "I took part in some of those discussions about them (Brosnan and his wife Cassandra Harris, who has since passed away) going to Los Angeles, because the fact was that with *Manions* Pierce was being seen by some sixty million people in America. And then of course there's the famous story of Cassie going to the bank and borrowing money against the fact that they were doing house improvements, and them going to Los Angeles on the money instead." Less than a decade later O'Sullivan's Ardmore Studios-based production company, World 2000, would be co-producing Irish movie *The Nephew* with Brosnan's Irish DreamTime production venture. Everything had come full circle for Brosnan who now finds that he can use his enormous Hollywood clout to bring movies back to Ireland.

"Irish DreamTime has the strongest intention to keep going back to Ireland and to work with young filmmakers," Brosnan said in an interview with the authors. The approach to Ireland is to favour filming there as with *Evelyn* and *The Nephew*. "When Beau St Clair (his partner in Irish DreamTime) and I got together as producers we set out to find an Irish story, and the story (that we found) went straight to the roots of who I am and we did: *The Nephew*."

This was to be Irish DreamTime's first production, and was set in Ireland. The film focuses on star-crossed lovers and starred veteran Irish actors Donal McCann, Sinead Cusack and Niall Toibin alongside Brosnan and American newcomer Hill Harper.

"We were fortunate enough to know people there whom I had worked with like Morgan O'Sullivan from the days of *Remington Steele* and *The Manions*, which gave me my break. So the stepping stones have always been there, it was just a matter of stringing them together and hopefully having a bit of luck to go with it." The next project was as executive producer on *The Match*, a Scottish comedy starring Max Beesley, Richard E. Grant, Tom Sizemore and Ian Holm. Brosnan and St Clair's third project in as many years was MGM's 1999

Star Pierce Brosnan
in *Evelyn* which he
produced at home
in Ireland.

remake of *The Thomas Crown Affair*, directed by John McTiernan, which starred Brosnan, Rene Russo and Denis Leary.

Irish DreamTime's subsequent projects saw them return to Ireland for filming. They were *Evelyn*, with Brosnan playing a single father fighting to keep his family together and *Laws of Attraction*, a romantic comedy, starring Julianne Moore opposite Brosnan. "*Evelyn* came about in a fairly straightforward way, in that Paul Pender (writer of the film) sent us the story and it was just a beautiful ensemble piece and based in reality, and it had huge significance for the (Irish) society of the day back in 1953 when a working man is going up against church and state, and it also touched a lot on my own childhood memories in terms of the power of the church in small rural communities.

"Hopefully we'll get to do more Irish films under DreamTime but we are kind of stuck in the trenches of *Thomas Crown* now, and there is only Beau and myself and so we are a slow-moving animal. We have a story that we would like to go back to Ireland with, Sir Walter Scott's *Lochinvar* that we talked about… There are great stories to be done but I haven't got anything up my sleeve."

Brosnan credits *The Manions of America* with having fast tracked his career. At the time, Brosnan and his wife had bought a house in Wimbledon on the proceeds of his salary from *Manions* as well as her savings from a role in the Bond movie *For Your Eyes Only*. The couple believed it would be folly not to at least give Hollywood a shot on the basis of the enormous popularity of *Manions*. With about two thousand pounds in his pocket Brosnan found himself doing the interview rounds in Hollywood the next week. One of the first roles he went up for was in a romantic detective series called *Remington Steele*. He clinched the part. Out of *Remington Steele* would come Brosnan's shot at superstardom as the screen's most famous spy – 007 – James Bond. Of course the story is much more complex than that – and begins very much further back in time.

Born an only child in Drogheda, County Louth, Brosnan was educated in the local Christian Brothers school. He has spoken extensively in interviews about his childhood in Ireland. It was clearly not an entirely happy time for the child, whose father had left him and his mother when Pierce was very young. His mother brought him to live in London. Brosnan, by his own accounts, had it fairly tough at first as an Irish kid in school, and fistfights were not an uncommon part of his day. But he pulled through and set his sights on a career as a commercial artist. He studied commercial illustration at Central St Martin's College of Art and Design. He even held down a job for about two years at an art studio in London before the acting bug hit. He had been chatting with colleagues at work one day about the theatre and movies, when one of them suggested he check out a fringe theatre establishment called the Oval House. Not certain what to expect, but curious, Brosnan took his friend up on the invitation. The Oval House would become almost a second home to him for years to come. He took acting classes there and participated in workshops and numerous plays before enrolling in the Drama Centre in London.

After graduating, Brosnan got a job in 1975 as acting assistant stage manager at York Theatre Royal where, just six months later world-famous American playwright Tennessee Williams selected him to create the role of McCabe in the British premier of *The Red Devil Battery Sign*. Brosnan went on to work in other prestigious London stage productions such as Zeffirelli's *Filumena* and *Wait Until Dark* at the York. After cutting his professional acting teeth in many more stage productions he was offered his first television role in a docudrama called *Murphy's Stroke*, set around the true story of a horse racing betting sting by a group of Irishmen. It co-starred Niall Toibin.

He also had a brief but memorable appearance in the London gangster movie with Bob Hoskins, *The Long Good Friday* (1980) playing a particularly sadistic assassin, and in television series such as *The Professionals* and *Play for Today*. Then came the big break with *The Manions*. "That was my ticket to the California way of life. If it weren't for *The Manions* I wouldn't be here," he would remark years later in an interview. And so it was off to Los Angeles with about two thousand pounds and an arrangement to stay with his Hollywood agent upon arrival. "I had about thirty interviews lined up, and MTM Enterprises was the first place I went," he would recall. "They were looking for somebody to play Remington Steele." He admitted that "it was a gamble to come (to Hollywood) but it was a prestigious role in an American mini-series (*Manions*) and I thought I should take advantage of it... Originally Remington Steele was to be a man in his forties, American. One of the producers said, 'let's deviate from that, make him younger.' Then they decided to make him European to give him extra dimension. We were optimistic. We thought something would come of it. But I hadn't thought until then of doing a TV series. We went back home. At Christmas time I got a call to come back. They were still casting for Laura (the female co-lead in the series) and I did all the readings with the actresses. In the process, I got approved for the part; I was officially Remington Steele," he told Associated Press television writer Jerry Buck in 1983.

Brosnan had arrived in Hollywood and it was a somewhat surreal experience. "It was so exhilarating. First of all, you're bathed in this blue light, where everything is set against the harsh blue sky and the space above you is vast. Then you're confronted with being inside a car and not being able to walk in that space, and you're driving to places that seem rather lonely. Ultimately it felt like putting on a beautiful coat, it just felt easy. It came with a lot of feelings of displacement, but I was doing something I had always dreamt of," he told *Interview* magazine in 2002.

His portrayal of the suave, sexy, wise-cracking Steele opposite Stephanie Zimbalist as the owner of the 'Remington Steele' detective agency shot him to TV stardom, not just in the U.S. but across the world. The series was a major international seller. A writer for *The Washington Post* commented in 1982 that Brosnan 'could make it as a young James Bond'. The series had been running for three seasons before NBC decided to cancel it. Brosnan's rising star seemed to be fading fast. 'Until a few months ago, Brosnan was enjoying the fruits of a steady if unspectacular TV career. He was a household word if your household tuned in to his weekly turn as the suave, flim-flamming 'detective' Remington Steele, but when NBC shelved the series after three seasons this spring, there seemed little reason to regard him as more than another leading man without a portfolio,' an article in *Playgirl* magazine in 1986 commented. The piece also points out that fans mounted a public campaign to return Brosnan to the role. Ironically at the same time he was offered the role of 007 after Roger Moore announced he was retiring from the part. The publicity was astounding; Brosnan was front page news around the world. But then, famously, NBC reversed its decision on *Remington Steele*, brought it back and held Brosnan to his contract to appear. This of course meant that he lost the Bond role. "It's just a pisser having to go back," was Brosnan's succinct comment about these events. Timothy Dalton got the Bond role in 1987's *The Living Daylights*. To add insult to injury *Remington Steele* was off the air within the year.

Brosnan bounced back with some very visible film roles including a co-starring assignment with Michael Caine in *The Fourth Protocol* in 1987. In 1992 he headlined in the sci-fi movie *The Lawnmower Man* and a year later teamed with Robin Williams in the comedy feature *Mrs Doubtfire*. The publicity that surrounded the Steele/Bond controversy had, it seemed not hurt his career in the least. 'His recent imbroglios have certainly made Brosnan better known, and attracted more sympathy than any of his successes,' commented one reporter in *Playgirl* magazine. Brosnan was stoical about the turn of events, commenting, "Talk about your luck of the Irish: if I fell into the river Thames, I'd probably come out with a new suit."

That was to prove a fateful comment. Soon after *Mrs Doubtfire* Dalton turned down an opportunity to play Bond in *GoldenEye* and Brosnan became the obvious next choice. In June 1994 he was confirmed as the new James Bond. He was signed for a three-picture contract with an option of a fourth Bond film. His portrayal of a tougher, more ruthless James Bond than his immediate predecessors drew critical kudos. It didn't hurt that the film was a big box-office hit. Brosnan reprised the role in *Tomorrow Never Dies* (1997) and again in *The World Is Not Enough* just two years later with equal success. In 2002 Brosnan made his fourth and final screen splash as Bond in *Die Another Day*.

Following the release of *Die Another Day* there was a seemingly never-ending stream of media reports and speculation as to whether he would step up for yet another Bond role. Brosnan seemed to hold all the cards as far as his career was concerned. He had wisely arranged with Bond producers to allow for work in other movies between Bond films, and so had been able to avoid being typecast as Bond forever it was reported. Brosnan denies that. "I don't remember saying this needed to be in my contract. The contract was for playing Bond, and it didn't stop my playing other characters, but I was very aware of typecasting. You have to… you have to look down the road and see where your career is going, and in one sense that was how DreamTime was born. You want to have control over your profile, your career and what you do with that. In my case I created a company, Irish DreamTime with Beau St Clair, for that very purpose. Over the passage of time the hope was that we would have something valuable. Also DreamTime (allowed) me to be an actor and a producer and if I wanted to direct, that too… it was as hard and fast as that. I'm very proud of the company and the productions – each one of the (six films) we made I am very proud of, and all are fine pieces in one way or the other."

Speculation about the Bond role would come to an abrupt halt in February 2005 when he announced that he was quitting the role. British actor Daniel Craig was signed and went on to a triumphant debut as the new 007. Brosnan was an enthusiastic supporter of his successor, praising him without reservation as "a great actor".

Brosnan's first role after the Bond years was that of Daniel Rafferty in the 2004 release *Laws of Attraction*, followed by *The Matador* (2005) in which he brilliantly portrays a world-weary hitman. He was nominated for a Golden Globe award for the role. He triumphed in the title role of the 1999 re-make of *The Thomas Crown Affair*. More recently he co-starred with fellow Irish actor Liam Neeson in *Seraphim Falls* (2007). Critics gave both actors enthusiastic reviews for their performances in the film, which went out on limited release, but were generally underwhelmed by the movie itself. Brosnan, at the time of writing this book is in rehearsal in London for a film adaptation of the ABBA musical *Mamma Mia!* Brosnan became a naturalised citizen of the United States, but he has retained his Irish citizenship saying, "My Irishness is in everything I do. It's the spirit of who I am, as a man, an actor, a father. It's where I come from." He has homes in Malibu, California, Hawaii and Dublin.

Colm Meaney

Brosnan has also spoken recently of making a Western film with fellow Irishmen Gabriel Byrne and Colm Meaney. Dublin-born Meaney once appeared with Brosnan in an episode of *Remington Steele*, and with Fionnula Flanagan in an episode of *The Father Dowling Mysteries*. Meaney shot to international renown as Miles O'Brien in the CBS-Paramount TV series *Star Trek: The Next Generation*. Meaney's film credits on both sides of the Atlantic are formidable and include the memorably bemused Dublin dad in the film adaptations of Irish author Roddy Doyle's Barrytown Trilogy *The Commitments, The Snapper* and *The Van*. His performance in *Snapper* earned him a Golden Globe nomination. Known as one of the most versatile character actors on the screen today, Meaney aced a Welsh accent as 'Morgan the Goat' in the romantic comedy *The Englishman Who Went Up a Hill But Came Down a Mountain*. He co-starred with Irish-American actor James Cromwell in the family film *Owd Bob* about the trials and tribulations of a rural English farming community and its sheepdogs. Other major credits include *Die Hard 2, Dick Tracy, Into The West,* the Ron Howard-directed *Far and Away, The Last of the Mohicans, Under Siege* and John Huston's classic adaptation of the James Joyce short story *The Dead*. He also had a major role in the highly acclaimed *This Is My Father* (1998), written and directed by Irish-American director and cinematographer Paul Quinn, whose brother Aidan Quinn starred in the film.

Aidan Quinn

Quinn, who was born in Chicago to Irish immigrant parents, spent much of his boyhood growing up in Birr, County Offaly where his mother's family came from. He lived for much of his youth in Dublin and attended St Joseph's school in Blackrock. After leaving school he took numerous odd jobs in Dublin before heading back to America where he enrolled in acting classes at the Piven Theatre Workshop in Chicago.

The Dead (1987) directed by the legendary John Huston. Shown second and fourth from left: Helena Carroll and Colm Meaney.

His first film role was in *Reckless* (1984) playing a leather-clad rebellious teen opposite Daryl Hannah. His breakthrough role as Dez, Rosanna Arquette's love interest in *Desperately Seeking Susan* drew critical acclaim for the relatively unknown Quinn. His first starring role came with the 1985 NBC telefilm *An Early Frost* about a young attorney dying of AIDS. He was nominated for an Emmy for his performance. His first 'Irish' role was in *The Playboys*, about a travelling troupe of actors in Ireland. His most visible and notable film role was as Harry Boland in Neil Jordan's magnificent *Michael Collins* with Liam Neeson in the title role. He was memorable as the upstanding good citizen brother of wayward Brad Pitt in *Legends of the Fall* in 1994. Quinn's list of screen credits is lengthy and includes Pierce Brosnan's *Evelyn* and Aisling Walsh's *Song for a Raggy Boy* (1993) in which he plays a teacher and Spanish Civil War veteran, horrified at the sadistic activities taking place in an Irish reform school. His most recent outing was HBO's *Bury My Heart At Wounded Knee* (2007), which deals with the annihilation of the Native Americans. He plays Henry Dawes, one of the architects of the government policy on Indian affairs. Notably, Belfast-born Kenneth Branagh directed Quinn in the Robert De Niro starrer *Mary Shelley's Frankenstein* (1994).

Kenneth Branagh

Born in a working class area of Belfast in 1960 Branagh moved to London with his family when he was nine. His interest in a stage career came when he saw Derek Jacobi perform *Hamlet*, and he made the first step to fulfilling his dream when he was accepted at the age of eighteen into the Royal Academy of Dramatic Arts in London. He went on to win RADA's Bancroft Award for his work as a student. After graduation, he was awarded a membership in the Royal Shakespeare Company. Following enormous acclaim for his work with the company he eventually quit to form the Renaissance Theatre Company with David Parfitt. Legendary British actors such as Judi Dench, Richard Briers, and

Derek Jacobi joined the cast list of the fledgling company. Branagh's cinematic directorial debut came with his acclaimed *Henry V* (1989), a realistic, often bloody film that contrasted starkly to Lawrence Olivier's regal 1944 version. Branagh was hailed for his direction and for his performance in the title role, and was dubbed by some critics as 'the next Olivier'. He was nominated for Oscars as both Best Director and Best Actor.

Aidan Quinn (seated) in a scene from *Bury My Heart at Wounded Knee*.

His Hollywood debut came in 1991 when he directed and starred opposite Emma Thompson in *Dead Again*, a romantic thriller. The film was both a critical and box office success and brought more industry kudos for Branagh who appeared next in the ensemble comedy *Peter's Friends* (1992), in which he plays a neurotic Hollywood-based British screenwriter married to a hyper Hollywood screen actress played by Rita Rudner. Stephen Fry and Hugh Laurie co-starred. The film played to some enthusiastic reviews but was hardly a smash hit. Branagh put his faith once again in the Bard for his next outing, an acclaimed screen version of *Much Ado About Nothing*. In 1994 he took the role of director and actor in *Mary Shelley's Frankenstein*, with bleak results when critics generally panned the film. Branagh's reputation as the world's finest interpreter of Shakespeare for the screen today continued with the 1996 adaptation of *Hamlet*, a four-hour marathon with an all-star cast supporting Branagh's title character. Kate Winslet, Julie Christie, Robin Williams, Charlton Heston, Jack Lemmon and Derek Jacobi were among the star cast list. The film earned Branagh a Best Adapted Screenplay Oscar nomination.

Subsequent films however failed to show Branagh in the same 'boy genius' light, in particular his villain in the generally panned *Wild Wild West*. Branagh's achievements in British theatre and on film however are testimony to a brilliant talent that has consistently wooed audiences around the world. He has been praised in more recent years for his screen work, in particular for his role as Gilderoy Lockhart in *Harry Potter and the Chamber of Secrets*.

Belfast-born Kenneth Branagh came from the heart of British theatre to Hollywood acclaim. This is a scene from *Celebrity* (1998), directed by Woody Allen

Award-winning actor and former school teacher Brendan Gleeson goes back to school as 'Mad-Eye' Moody in *Harry Potter and the Goblet of Fire*.

Brendan Gleeson

Another Irish alumnus of Harry Potter's school is internationally acclaimed Dublin-born actor Brendan Gleeson, who plays battle worn Alastor Mad-Eye Moody in the *Potter* series. A former teacher, Gleeson left the profession to pursue a career in his first love, acting, and joined Irish theatre company The Passion Machine. Gleeson landed his first starring role in *I Went Down* (1997), which was followed by his much-acclaimed role in John Boorman's *The General* (1998). His performance gained him awards for not only Best Actor at the 1998 Boston Society of Film Critics Awards, but further awards by the London Film Critics and the Best Actor award at the 1999 Irish Film & Television Awards.

Over the past few years, Gleeson has appeared in numerous successful films, most recently John Boorman's *The Tiger's Tail* (2007). Other recent credits include August Nicholson in M. Night Shyamalan's *The Village; Cold Mountain* directed by Anthony Mingella; Ridley Scott's *Kingdom of Heaven; Breakfast on Pluto* directed by Neil Jordan; Wolfgang Peterson's *Troy; Black Irish* directed by Brad Gann; *Studs* directed by Paul Mercier and *Beowulf* directed by Robert Zemeckis.

Gleeson's rise to fame began when he appeared in Jim Sheridan's *The Field* (1990), followed by a number of small roles in such films as *Far and Away* and *Into The West*. Gleeson attracted the attention of Hollywood, when he starred as Hamish in the film *Braveheart*, alongside Mel Gibson. Other notable screen credits include John Woo's *Mission: Impossible 2*, Steven Spielberg's *AI*, John Boorman's *The Tailor of Panama* (with Pierce Brosnan in the lead), *Country of My Skull*, Danny Boyle's *28 Days Later*, and Martin Scorsese's *Gangs of New York*, which starred Daniel Day-Lewis and featured Liam Neeson in a cameo.

CHAPTER 27

BELOW THE RADAR — GABRIEL BYRNE

"I've never been able to track your career; you're always flying below radar," Steven Spielberg once said to Gabriel Byrne. At the time Byrne thought this a bit offensive. But he later told a writer for *Detour* magazine, "Then I thought, no, actually that's a very complimentary thing to say, because that's what I do, in a weird way. I don't plan it out. I'm always attracted to things that I feel are a bit different."

That approach to his work has been one of the great hallmarks of the actor-writer-director-producer's career. From his very early work at Dublin's avant-garde Project and Focus Theatres to such diverse film roles as Irish-produced *Frankie Starlight* (directed by Geraldine Fitzgerald's son, Michael Lindsay-Hogg) and *Into The West* or his enormously acclaimed work in *Miller's Crossing* and *The Usual Suspects*, to playing opposite an animated – literally *animated* – lead actress in *Cool World*, Byrne has been unceasing in his quest for roles and films that stand out from the usual. 'In the six years it took to bring *Into the West* into being, Byrne rejected roles in *Die Hard*, *Alien³*, and *Patriot Games*. He even said 'no' to $1 million to play the heavy in *Lethal Weapon 3*: all this so that Byrne along with Mike Newell (*Enchanted April*) and screenwriter Jim Sheridan could bring off *Into the West* for $6 million, which in Hollywood isn't considered a movie budget,' an article about Byrne in the Knight-Ridder newspaper syndicate noted. Byrne himself once said of his films, "Most of the choices that I've made have had interesting and offbeat directors. They make the kind of movies I like to see myself."

Byrne is not only a gifted and highly acclaimed actor but an Academy Award-nominated producer as well – honours that came his way through his desire to bring home to Ireland some of the benefits of his influence in the international film industry. He was the executive producer on the film *In the Name of the Father*, made with Hollywood money in Ireland. It was directed by Jim Sheridan and was based on the story of the Guildford Four, the Irishmen unjustly convicted – later overturned – of a bombing near London. The film earned several Oscar nominations, including Best Picture.

Gabriel Byrne and other Irish cinema luminaries such as Sheridan, Neil Jordan, Pat O'Connor, Pierce Brosnan and Fionnula Flanagan are widely praised for dedicating major portions of their career, energy, time and finances to ensuring that the once elusive dream of an indigenous Irish film industry can be a reality. Irish cinema talent, both established and emerging, can today find a place to flourish without having to move lock stock and barrel to Hollywood, as did so many in previous generations. Shortly before the release of *Into the West* in 1993, which he executive-produced and

co-starred in with Ellen Barkin and a great cast of contemporary Irish actors, a journalist asked Byrne if he would be 'single-handedly responsible for the resurgence of Irish cinema.' He responded wryly, "When you say 'resurgence,' that suggests there was ever a 'surgence.' For many years, we have been the victim of the Hollywood and the British film industries – typically [with] movies like *The Quiet Man* – which fostered a false and romantic view of the country. But some years ago film-makers like Pat O'Connor (*Cal*) came along and saw the link between the Irish storytelling tradition and the way movies were told, and we moved from literature to movies like *My Left Foot* and *Hear My Song*."

'All things considered, he has had an astonishing career for a man who didn't find his way into professional acting until his thirtieth year,' commented journalist Helen Dudar in the *New York Times* back in 1990 – when Byrne still had a way to go before reaching the global reputation that he enjoys today.

Byrne was born in 1950 near Crumlin, County Dublin. In many interviews over the years he has recalled those days fondly, and referred to the neighbourhood that nestles below the Dublin mountains, as a "great place to grow up". Crumlin was an old village about seven miles west of Dublin city around which various new housing estates had sprung up in the late 1940s and Fifties built by Dublin Corporation and Dublin County Council. It was a meld of old farmlands and new houses and new schools. He attended the local Christian Brothers where young Byrne was recruited to the Catholic missionary services. "One day, a guy came in with a slide projector and he showed us photographs of [missionaries at work in the Third World]. 'How many of you boys feel that you would have a vocation to save souls?' About fifteen of us put up our hands. I went away to England to this seminary in the heart of the countryside," he recounted in a *New York Magazine* article. He was eventually expelled for smoking cigarettes. Home again in Dublin Byrne worked various odd jobs before deciding it was time to get himself back to school and finish his Leaving Cert. He was so successful in this regard that he won a scholarship to UCD where he studied phonetics, languages, and archaeology. He would confess in later years that his dream had been to use his language and archaeology skills to find a "lost city" somewhere. He never did find the lost city, but he uncovered a child's shoe dating back to the tenth century on one dig in which he became involved. Later he moved to Spain where he gave private English lessons. He eventually washed up back in Dublin again, a city all a-glow with brilliant new talents emerging in the theatre scene, thanks in large part to the work of Deirdre O'Connell at a small back-lane theatre called The Focus, and through the artistic leadership of brothers Jim and Peter Sheridan at the Project. Young writers and actors such as Liam Neeson, Mannix Flynn, Peter Caffrey, Chris O'Neill, Colm Meaney, Johnny Murphy, Ronan Wilmot and Sean Lawlor, among many others, were finding their feet outside of the more traditional theatre venues of The Abbey and The Gate. Byrne was immediately attracted to this creative milieu and began to work and train under O'Connell at The Focus. Later he would be invited by the Sheridans to work with them at the Project. This was a theatre staging world-class productions of new and exciting plays not just out of Ireland (Mannix Flynn and Peter Sheridan's *The Liberty Suit* included) but also from abroad, including the U.S. – David Mamet's *Sexual Perversity in Chicago* was one. His work developed to the point where he gained a place at the Abbey Theatre for a time.

Then came the break that would set in motion a chain of professional experiences that ultimately launched him onto the world stage. A casting director from RTÉ was chatting with him in a pub one day and thought he'd be right for a character that was being written into a famous TV serial of the day, *The Riordans*. This long-running and much-loved series about the everyday lives of a rural Irish family was appointment viewing for most families back then, even those city folk who viewed the Irish country way of life as a foreign enterprise. Byrne described his character on the series as a "wandering Heathcliffian kind of rebel guy… a roguish character." It made Byrne a household name. Later an entirely new series, *Bracken*, was based around his character and Byrne was a fully fledged TV star in Ireland. It was this role that brought Byrne to the attention of director John Boorman, who cast him in the part of 'Uther, father of Arthur' in his film success *Excalibur*. Byrne played much of the role weighted down by clunky armour – he even played a love scene in full armour, much to the delight of his Dublin pals who teased him ceaselessly upon such prowess. But the part earned him excellent reviews in a major film and prompted a move to London. He won more good notices in various important theatre productions, including a National Theatre staging of Brian Friel's *Translations*. More film and TV parts ensued, including the acclaimed *Defence of the Realm* and *Hannah K*. During this time he worked for several noteworthy European directors including Costa-Gavras, Ken Russell and Ken Loach. He also won the title role in the 1985 CBS six-part mini-series *Christopher Columbus*.

In 1990, he made his American debut in the Coen brothers' film *Miller's Crossing*. This was the role that would place him on the top rung of his profession. Many critics consider it to be one of the best roles of his career. He plays Tom Reagan, chief sidekick to a Thirties crime boss played by Albert Finney. Reagan, played by Byrne as a native Dubliner, is up to his neck in gambling debts and sleeping with the boss's girlfriend. It's a full-time occupation for him to stay healthy and alive. 'Byrne carries the film with a steadily measured performance, defined almost as much by what he doesn't say as by what he does. Even when he's getting punched out – which seems to happen every ten minutes – he wears his

sangfroid like an inscrutable mask,' commented Juan Morales in *Detour* magazine following the film's release.

Since then he has starred in *Cool World, A Dangerous Woman, Trial by Jury, Point of No Return, Deadman* and *Frankie Starlight*. In 1995, he starred as Dean Keaton in *The Usual Suspects*, which was nominated for two Academy Awards. That same year he co-wrote and co-produced Miramax's *The Last of the High Kings*, and worked with Richard Harris and John Lynch in *This Is The Sea*, which was also shot on location in Ireland. He also wrote a screenplay in Irish, *Draíocht*, which premiered on the Irish language television station, Teilifís na Gaelige (TG4).

In early 1997 he appeared in the film adaptation of Danish writer Peter Høeg's acclaimed novel *Smilla's Sense of Snow* with Julia Ormond and also starred on the small screen in *Weapons of Mass Destruction*, a satire on media monopoly and press barons with Ben Kingsley. Following that he worked with Wim Wenders in *The End of Violence, Polish Wedding* with Lena Olin and Claire Danes, and *The Man in the Iron Mask* with Gerard Depardieu, John Malkovich, Leonardo DiCaprio and Jeremy Irons. His more recent film work includes *Wah-Wah* directed by Richard E. Grant, and *Jindabyne* with Laura Linney directed by Ray Lawrence, for which he has been nominated for best actor at the Australian Film Institute Awards.

Byrne also starred in the Broadway production of *A Touch of a Poet* over the 2005 Christmas period to rave reviews, and has since completed production on *Emotional Arithmetic*, star-

Seen here on location for his masterpiece *Deliverance*, John Boorman (centre) was responsible for the career launches of numerous Irish actors, including Gabriel Byrne and Liam Neeson.

Once written and
directed by John
Carney has become a
new poster child for
the Irish film sector.
He shot the film
reportedly for just
$160,000 using hand-
held digital camera,
natural light and live
sound. The film did
enormously well in
the U.S. and was made
with funding from the
Irish Film Board.

ring alongside Susan Sarandon and directed by Paolo Barzman. Additionally, he was nominated for Broadway's 2000 Tony Award as Best Actor for a revival of Eugene O'Neill's
A Moon for the Misbegotten. Today Byrne divides his time between writing and producing.
His first book, *Pictures in My Head* was published in Ireland in 1995 where it became a
critically acclaimed bestseller.

Byrne told the authors in a wide ranging interview for an accompanying documentary to
this book that back in the 1950s and 1960s the acting opportunities in Dublin had been
limited to a few mainstream theatres, the Abbey and the Gate included. Films usually
starred British or American actors, while "the finest Abbey actors" stood in the background
playing bit parts.

Some great names of Irish theatre such as Milo O'Shea and Paddy Bedford made their way
to New York, but the majority remained at home to live with the reality "that to make a
full-time living in Ireland as an actor was a fantasy." Referring to his years at the Project,
Byrne recalled how "in some weird coincidence" much of the talent of today's Irish screen
came together in a period of just one and a half years in that "little theatre off Essex Street"
including Neeson, Meaney, Sheridan and others. Of his elevation to TV stardom in RTÉ's
Bracken he said he was fortunate in that series to have been associated with some of the

finest screen actors he had ever encountered, including John Cowley and Moira Deedy (from *The Riordans* which preceded *Bracken*). "But they were never really appreciated," Byrne lamented. He also praised the writing on that series as "some of the best stuff ever written for television". He believed that *Bracken* represented a breakthrough in that it was not condescending to the Irish characters but told true-to-life dramas about the changing Irish society and landscape.

Of his landmark role in *Miller's Crossing* he faced a challenge in deciding whether to play the leading character as "a man from Dublin" (which he did). "I think it was the first time an Irish story was told without any reason for it existing," he noted.

Of the dream of an Irish film industry he observed, "I have seen a lot of American hits in Dublin but not an Irish hit in America." Though he did reference the great success of the low-budget Irish film *Once*, which at the time had just opened in the U.S. to great acclaim. He noted that while he also cheered the concept of an indigenous Irish film industry, there needed to be a move towards a greater control and understanding of the global distribution business before that fully becomes a reality. The film *Once* was a step in the right direction.

CHAPTER 28

THE NEW GUNS – RHYS-MEYERS, FARRELL AND MURPHY

In rounding out the story of a century of Hollywood 'greenery', it's safe to say that not since the earliest days of the American cinema has so much Irish screen talent overwhelmed the film town. Liam Neeson, Gabriel Byrne, Pierce Brosnan, Fionnula Flanagan, Jim Sheridan, Neil Jordan, *et al* have been in the limelight for a number of years. But there is a new generation of Irish screen star storming Hollywood's battlements with a combination of masterful talent, business savvy and confidence that seems to reflect Ireland's twenty-first century thrust into the forefront of the world's most affluent and successful societies. Jonathan Rhys-Meyers, Colin Farrell and Cillian Murphy are the latest youthful and worthy ambassadors in the ranks of the Emeralds in Tinseltown.

Rhys-Meyers, fatally handsome, buffed like a champion athlete and not yet thirty, talks about his career, present and future with a third-party attachment that is both entertaining and strikingly pragmatic. Speaking from the set at Ardmore Studios Ireland of the hugely successful Showtime period series *The Tudors*, Rhys-Meyers shrugs off formalities while asking to be called simply "Johnny". His critically acclaimed outing as a surprisingly trim and handsome Henry VIII in *The Tudors* has caused a sensation among cable TV viewers in the U.S., and brought him to the attention of an audience far more extensive than even his previous star-billed Irish, English and Hollywood film outings exposed him to. *The Tudors*, together with his inspired portrayal of Elvis Presley in a CBS biopic in 2005, has cemented Rhys-Meyers' stature in the top ranks of Hollywood's star system. He maintains a rock steady attitude to the entire affair and seems focused as much on today's roles as he is on the great scripts that might be awaiting. And he is not forgetful of the fateful beginnings that got him here. "The short-thrust version of what happened is, yes, I was found in a pool hall in Cork," he confirms. This in response to a query about his true beginnings on the road to fame. The popular story has it that Cork-born Rhys-Meyers, having left school at the age of sixteen, was knocking around a pool hall when casting agents who were looking for Irish boys to appear in the film *War of the Buttons* spotted him and asked him to audition. "And then I did audition (for *Buttons*). I did loads of auditions in fact, but I didn't get the part." There followed many more trips from Cork to Dublin for auditions. "There was all that travelling up and down from Cork to Dublin, all the hack work, I did it all: I auditioned for far more movies than I ever got." Though the situation has clearly come full circle for Rhys-Meyers he observes candidly, "These days you have to fight for the really good stuff, the really good projects. The trouble is you don't know what they are. If you could pick up a script and see that a certain director, a certain actor and a certain (director of photography) and a certain writer is attached you could say all that's fantastic but it doesn't necessarily make it a great picture. You might have all the right ingredients but you have to cook it properly and it has to have the right taste and it's only a few movies that hit that right sort of temperature."

Rhys-Meyers clearly has an eye for the 'right ingredient'. His first film role came with the 1994 production of the Albert Finney and Brenda Fricker-starring *A Man of No Importance*. It was a small role, but his screen presence was obvious to critics even at that embryonic stage of his career. The film is the tender story of a Dublin bus driver in 1960s Dublin who has a passion for Oscar Wilde and sets out to produce *Salome* at the local church hall. His work in that first film was without the benefit of any formal acting lessons, he says. "I went for one day to the Gaiety School of acting because I was considering getting some acting lessons. But I abandoned it for the course of the journeyman… I decided to do something much more difficult, that is knocking on doors and annoying people. For every job that I got there were seventeen or twenty that I didn't. I was prepared to take anything because I said to myself that I wanted as much experience as possible. Experience is very advantageous, not from the point of view of talent, which you grow or you don't, but from what you get by just operating on the set. I believe that part of what makes me appealing to work with from a director's perspective is that I know what I'm doing on the set because I have done it so much. For me going off and doing the journeyman work and being away from home in crummy hotel rooms in parts of the world you can't spell and in insignificant parts was (the best training)."

The knocking on doors and the journeyman way of life finally paid dividends when he was called in by Neil Jordan for a role in the epic *Michael Collins* starring Liam Neeson. "Well the fact is, yes, I was asked to do the film with Neil Jordan and the part was the smallest on the page and I thought insignificant. And so I went to see Neil and told him that I wanted to play Vinnie Murphy because the character had a name. I sat down and said (doing a Cork accent) 'Hello, I'm Johnny from Cork,' and he said 'right. And have you been given a bit of a script,' and I said 'yes, but I'd really like to do Vinnie Murphy' and he said 'right' and then I can't remember the exact line now, but it was basically that I was reading the part that was written which was called the 'Smiling Youth'. I said 'Oh jaesus' to myself because it wasn't that good to be 'The Smiling Youth'. But I did it anyway (the reading) and I left the room and thought 'well at least it was a good chance to meet Neil Jordan even if I don't get the part. Then my agent rang me up and said that I had the part of 'The Smiling Youth' and he said 'you can't turn it down, you have to play 'The Smiling Youth'. But I was thinking 'I can't say to people that (I'm in *Michael Collins*) and when they ask me what part I'll have to say 'The Smiling Youth'. You'd sound like a fool. So I used to say I was playing a gunman."

That 'Smiling Youth' role turned out in the end to be the gunman who shoots and kills Michael Collins. Rhys-Meyers' icy, calculated, calm portrayal of the gunman created a riveting character and a chilling scene when he aims and calmly pulls the trigger of his rifle… and changes the course of modern Irish history. But it was touch and go on the day of the first call when shooting was in progress. Rhys-Meyers had been back-packing in Vietnam and had been "stuck in Thailand for four days" on the return journey. On his arrival back in the farmhouse in Cork where he was staying he "arrived in the door and took my back pack off and then the phone rang and it was Robin, the second AD (assistant director) on *Collins* saying 'I'm just ringing to say that your pick up in the morning is at seven thirty, not six. And I went 'great, for what?' And the reply was 'ha ha, now you're joking aren't you?' They had brought the part up a week." Rhys-Meyers headed straight for the train to Dublin and checked in the same night to the Davenport hotel where he was picked up the next morning right on schedule.

Jonathan Rhys-Meyers as Henry VIII in the hit series *The Tudors*.

He points to that early role working with Jordan as a perfect example of learning as you go in the film business. "What I said about getting experience really came into play in that film. There was this one shot where Neil wanted me to run down behind a wall and look out so I could see all these Free State soldiers outside the pub. So I kept doing it and Neil would say 'cut… Johnny, you have to come out (from behind the wall), you have to come out further.' But I felt that if I came out they (the soldiers) would see me. What I didn't real-ise was that from the camera's point of view it didn't look so strange because (the soldiers) were so distant. It wasn't until I saw it (on screen) that I realised this."

As he continued to learn and to blossom in his chosen profession over the following years the parts became bigger and far more visible, from the rock star role (in which he did his own singing) in *Velvet Goldmine* (1998) to the coach in the 2002 soccer hit *Bend It Like Beckham* or the ambitious, ruthless tennis coach climbing his way through the social ranks in Woody Allen's *Match Point* – for which he won a Chopard award at the Cannes Film Festival. More industry honours would follow with a Golden Globe Award and an Emmy nomination for his portrayal of *Elvis* in the CBS production in 2005. A year later he was playing opposite Tom Cruise in *Mission Impossible III*. And, of course, he is the driving force behind the hit series *The Tudors* on Showtime which was filmed in Ireland. "I have a huge attitude of gratitude and I think that I've really been lucky, and hopefully now the wheels won't buckle," he says. "It's difficult in your early twenties to garner any really worthwhile roles because they don't write them. Now that I'm almost thirty I believe the best parts for me to play are still to be written. You are more expansive in your thirties and the roles open up to you… you have different life experiences and it shows through. You just get a bigger understanding of human nature and character… and that comes through."

Rhys-Meyers had recently bought a home in Los Angeles at the time of writing. "I view Hollywood as an extraordinary place because incredibly gifted people from all over the world end up there. The movie stars over the years have all come from somewhere else, they descended into this hubbub because of the weather and the fact that you could be guaranteed (ideal filming conditions). Being Irish in Hollywood is therefore not so extraordinary. It's more extraordinary to have a Hollywood career back here (in Ireland) where somehow it seems so out of place." But he adds that there is today in Ireland a much more vibrant environment for film talent to grow than in years past. "The support structure was a help for my generation. *Braveheart* and *Michael Collins* helped open it up even further as an industry (which began) with *My Left Foot, The Company of Wolves, The Crying Game*, in the Eighties and Nineties. It has been a very interesting period for Irish film that began with Jim and Neil. Before that you had John Huston and of course John Boorman making films in Ireland and you had David Lean come with *Ryan's Daughter* and so you always had a few films being made in Ireland, but it was always Hollywood films. Then Jim and Neil started making Irish films with the help of Noel (Pearson) and Stephen Wooley. And then there were the four lads from Santry (U2) and Paul McGuinness. All this opened up to the world not only a friendly country but a society with great artistic integrity."

Colin Farrell

Colin Farrell's climb to the top slot on Hollywood's star totem pole began as inauspiciously as Rhys-Meyers' but has been equally as dramatic in terms of the circumstances and the speed at which it all happened. Born in Castleknock, Dublin, Farrell had been knocking around different jobs, including a stint as a professional line dancer, in Ireland before his brother Eamonn, who now runs a prestigious performing arts school in Dublin, persuaded him to take acting lessons. Farrell joined the well-regarded Gaiety School of Acting for a year before leaving to pursue a freelance acting career. He landed a part on the BBC miniseries *Falling for a Dancer* and that was followed almost immediately with a plum role on the BBC series *Ballykissangel* about the everyday, often bizarre events in a small Irish village. Farrell's rugged good looks and youthful exuberance combined with a worldly wise Dublin attitude and accent to make him a household name almost overnight.

In 1998 Farrell landed a role in London in a play called *A Little World of Our Own* which was attended one night by Kevin Spacey, who would recall being bowled over by Farrell's performance and presence. 'About four minutes into the play my friends and I began looking at each other and saying, "Who the f*** is this kid,"' Spacey told Deborah Schacht

Colin Farrell pictured
with director Oliver
Stone on the movie
Alexander.

in an interview for *Vanity Fair* in 2002. Spacey invited Farrell for drinks afterwards. He noted,
'Sometimes when you reach a certain stage you meet people with a certain dangerous ambition. Colin never struck me that way. He talked about his family.' Spacey helped Farrell land
a role in the Irish-made film *Ordinary Decent Criminals* (starring Spacey) while also introducing him to the powerful Hollywood organization Creative Artists Agency. Farrell's strong
outing in the film was noticed by leading Hollywood director Joel Schumacher who was casting
for his Vietnam war-era movie *Tigerland* (2000) at the time. He was summoned by Schumacher,
who was in London, for 'a chat,' as Farrell would recount in the *Los Angeles Times* in October 2000.
'We had a little laugh. He was on his way out shopping. He had more important things to do. I
thought it was a waste of time. And then he called and said he'd like me for the part of Bozz.' The
role saw Farrell play an anti-war "troublemaker" who is drafted into the Army at the tail end of
the Vietnam war. The character's dynamic force of personality gradually brings his fellow recruits
around to his way of thinking. 'The film is down and dirty, and Farrell, exuding confidence,
toughness and vulnerability, delivers the kind of performance that leaves everyone asking,
"Who is that guy?" as John Clark commented in the *Los Angeles Times* upon the film's
release.

Schumacher in fact had not made an instant decision in London to cast Farrell as Bozz. He sat
on the flight back to Los Angeles mulling over the prospect of a relative unknown (certainly in
Hollywood) taking on such a critical American part. He called Farrell in Dublin and asked to
read for the part and to put it on tape. Schumacher would later tell the *Times'* Clark, 'He did
the audition in his living room in Dublin with his sister holding the video camera and doing
all of the off-screen dialogue in this thick Dublin accent saying, "Oh, Jesus, I don't want to go
to Vietnam…" Colin was great.' When the film's producer Arnon Milchan was told that "a kid
from Dublin" was to play the lead "there was a moment of hysteria." Farrell was stunningly
brilliant in the part, mastering an authentic Texan accent without the benefit of a voice coach

(the film's budget did not extend to that, though Farrell did spend some time in a small Texas town before filming). But Farrell didn't just impress the critics and Schumacher. He proved himself an outstanding colleague with his fellow cast members when, as it was reported, a very famous (unnamed) celebrity visited the set and invited Farrell and Schumacher to dinner. After initially accepting, Farrell decided not to take up the offer after discovering that none of the other cast members were invited. 'Judging by the ecstatic reaction his *Tigerland* performance is getting him in America, he's obviously got what it takes to make it big. The son of a former professional footballer for Shamrock Rovers, he originally intended to follow in his father's footsteps,' wrote Ben Falk in the (London) *Observer* shortly after the film's release. (Eamon Farrell was indeed a famous Irish professional soccer player).

Not long after *Tigerland* Edward Norton dropped out of a major new upcoming movie *Hart's War* to star Bruce Willis. The plot centres on a young army officer who defends a fellow P.O.W. in a prison camp court-martial. The film's director Gregory Hoblit screened *Tigerland* for MGM executives and then for Bruce Willis. Neither Willis nor Hoblit had the slightest notion that Farrell was not an American-born actor. Willis recounted in *Vanity Fair*, "When I first talked to him he said 'This's Cawln Furl,' or something like that, and I thought, I get it. He was pretending to be American." Farrell of course clinched the part and was again triumphant in the role, drawing yet more positive critical nods from the American press as the young U.S. army officer defending a fellow prisoner against trumped up charges. Four days after *Hart's War* completed filming Farrell was on the set of Steven Spielberg's *Minority Report* in Los Angeles starring Tom Cruise. The futuristic cop movie released in 2002 saw Farrell playing an ambitious detective hunting down a cop played by Cruise, who has been framed for a crime that has to yet to be committed. Farrell was rocketing to the top. Farrell once said of himself in a *Sunday Times* interview, 'I sneaked in through the back door. That's one of the luckiest things that's happened to me, because I don't have to live in LA. I can just go in for meetings and then get the hell out of there.'

After that, it was top billing all the way. Schumacher cast him in the lead role of the thriller *Phone Booth* after Jim Carrey dropped out of the part. The film centred on a not-so-ethical New York publicist who picks up a ringing payphone only to hear a voice commanding him not to hang up or he'll be shot on the spot. The 2003 release was not a box office hit, but Farrell, who commanded the screen for almost the entire movie, proved himself yet again to be a major new force in Hollywood. Later came the high-profile Hollywood release *S.W.A.T.* and then the historical blockbuster *Alexander* with Farrell in the title role and directed by Oliver Stone. The film, and Farrell's performance, received mixed reviews. His next film the 2005 Oscar-nominated *The New World* was another historical epic – this time about the early English settlement of Jamestown in Virginia in the New World. The Terrence Malick film met with mixed reviews, though Farrell was generally praised for a powerful, physically demanding performance. Later came the big-budget Hollywood actioner *Miami Vice* co-starring Jamie Foxx. The movie was hardly a critical success, but it did enormously well at the U.S. and worldwide box office. More recently, Farrell, who resides in Dublin, established a new independent production company with the aim of financing important new Irish films. His stated passion about making movies in Ireland was illustrated with the 2003 movie *Intermission*, the Dublin-set film directed by John Crowley. The plot centres on the struggles of a young couple to make their way in life and their various offbeat friends. Farrell plays a no-holds-barred bad boy of the streets.

Cillian Murphy

Intermission also starred another Irish actor on the rise, Cillian Murphy, a close friend of both Farrell and Rhys-Meyers. Born in Cork, Murphy's father was a school inspector and his mother was a teacher. He studied law at University College Cork, where he became more interested in the stage than in the legal profession. His first professional stage role was as Pig in Enda Walsh's *Disco Pigs*, a role that he reprised for the 2001 independent feature of the same title directed by Kirsten Sheridan, daughter of Jim (*see Chapter 23*).

Murphy gained much critical attention over a number of years playing in a wide selection of stage, television and film roles in Ireland and England, including the mini-series *The Way We Live Now*. Hollywood began to sit up and take notice of Murphy when the Danny Boyle movie *28 Days Later* took off in America with him in the lead role. In 2003 came *Intermission* and then later strong parts in such Hollywood films as *Cold Mountain* and *Girl with a Pearl Earring*. His big breakthrough came with the 2005 Hollywood blockbuster and box office hit *Batman Begins* in which he played the terrifyingly evil Scarecrow a.k.a. Dr Jonathan Crane.

His next role confirmed him as one of the most valued leading Hollywood actors when he scared the pants off audiences worldwide as the maniac killer Jackson Rippner opposite Rachel McAdams in the thriller *Red Eye* (2005). Then came the role that had critics and audiences raving about his seemingly bottomless talent – Patrick 'Kitten' Braden in Neil Jordan's *Breakfast on Pluto* in which he plays an Irish transvestite fighting social stigma and desperately seeking an identity. The following year he co-starred with Liam Cunningham in Ken Loach's tragic tale of the Irish War of Independence, *The Wind That Shakes the Barley* which won the Palme d'Or at the 2006 Cannes Film Festival.

CHAPTER 29

OTHER MEMBERS OF THE IRISH CAST LIST

Over many meetings and interviews we have been asked how it would be possible to include the stories of each and every Irish artist who has made a mark in Hollywood? Time and again we heard the phrase "and who can forget (so and so)?" and in each case the questioner referred to screen talents of various disciplines. So it is with great privilege that we present this tapestry of work by the Irish that has been weaved through a century of cinematic celluloid. Here is an ethnic group that helped hone a new avenue of entertainment, the moving picture. The enormous reservoir of talent includes Irish writers George Bernard Shaw, Sean O'Casey, and Jonathan Swift whose stories Hollywood harvested for its movies. (Shaw even won an Oscar for *Pygmalion* in the Best Adapted Screenplay category). The great musical talents of Ireland also have been plucked by Hollywood from Dublin-born Victor Herbert for many a 1930s era musical to Van Morrison and U2 today. Following is an honour roll of lives that would in each case have been illuminating chapters in their own right in the preceding book, had space allowed.

Max Adrian: He was born Max Bor in Enniskillen in 1903. He had a steady career as a journeyman character actor and had a modicum of success with his high camp screen persona. Films include *The Primrose Path* (1934), *Henry V* (1945), *The Pickwick Papers* (1952) and later in the 1970s such films as *The Boyfriend* (1972) and *Uncle Vanya* (1972).

Patrick Bergin: Born 1951 in Dublin, Bergin began his career as a stage actor and went on to acclaimed screen performances in numerous films including *Mountains of the Moon* (1990), *Sleeping with the Enemy* (1991), *Patriot Games* (1991) co-starring Harrison Ford and *Suspicious Minds* (1997).

Ann Blythe: Born to Irish immigrant parents in the U.S., her porcelain skin and angelic voice featured in many musicals such as *The Great Caruso* (1951) and *The Student Prince* (1954), and as a dramatic actress in such notables as *Mildred Pierce* (1945) and *The Helen Morgan Story* (1957) for which she received an Oscar nomination.

J.P. Burns: Born in County Meath, Ireland, he was a prolific television and film actor in Hollywood, having previously enjoyed a highly successful stage career (with many Shakespearean roles) in London and Canada. A trained baritone, his screen credits include *The Molly Maguires* and a host of major TV series in the 1960s and 1970s including *The Big Valley*, *Mission Impossible*, *The Velvet Trap* and *The Magician*. He died in Hollywood in 2006 and is buried in his hometown of Oldcastle.

Madeleine Carroll: The daughter of a Limerick-born father, this cool, ladylike blonde actress of the 1930s appeared in John Ford's *The World Moves*, Alfred Hitchcock classic *The 39 Steps* and David O. Selznick's *The Prisoner of Zenda*. She left Hollywood during

World War II to serve as a nurse in France. She resumed her film career in the late 1940s in such movies as *An Innocent Affair* (1948) and *The Fan* (1949).

Brian Donlevy: Born in 1901 in Portadown, County Armagh, he came to Hollywood via Broadway (having served as pilot in World War I) and endeared himself to audiences as a tough-talking guy with a heart of gold. His characterisations were strong and distinctive. Credits include *Jesse James* (1939); *Destry Rides Again* (1939) and *The Glass Key* (1942). He worked in Hollywood up until his death in 1972.

Roma Downey: Best known to TV audiences for her starring role as Monica in the hit U.S. series *Touched by an Angel* which ran from 1994 until 2003. The series was sold to broadcasters around the world. Born in Derry in 1960 Downey received one of her earlier breaks when cast for a major Broadway role by Rex Harrison. She later went on to give a memorable performance as Jacqueline Bouvier Kennedy Onassis in the 1991 U.S. mini-series *A Woman Named Jackie*. She is married to reality television super entrepreneur Mark Burnett. Although she downplays the fact, Downey is noted for her active role in numerous charities.

Creighton Hale: Born in Cork as Patrick Fitzgerald in 1882, he came to the U.S. in the early 1900s as part of a travelling theatre group. He had a stellar career in the Hollywood movies from the silent era to the 1950s and appeared in some 200 films including *The George White Scandals* (1934), *The Fighting 69th* (1940), *Sergeant York* (1941), *The Maltese Falcon* (1941) and *Casablanca*. He died in 1965 *(See also page 102)*.

Lumsden Hare: Born in Ireland in 1875, Hare was a character actor in Hollywood movies whose credits include *Clive of India* (1935), *Gunga Din* (1939), *Rebecca* (1940); *Julius Caesar* (1953) and many more. He died in Beverly Hills in 1964.

Valerie Hobson: Born in Larne, County Antrim in 1917. A luminous actress who played uppercrust types in Hollywood and English movies, she appeared in *The Bride of Frankenstein* (1935), *Great Expectations* (1946), *Kind Hearts and Coronets* (1949) and *Knave of Hearts* (1954). She died in 1998.

Victor Herbert: Dublin-born composer whose work so influenced the great musicals of 1930s Hollywood that a musical was made of his life entitled *The Great Victor Herbert* (1939).

Sean McClory: Born in 1923 in Ireland this imposing character actor, formerly of the Abbey Theatre, spent most of his career in Hollywood. Screen credits include *Beyond Glory* (1949); *Rommel: Desert Fox* (1951); *The Quiet Man* (1952); *Dianne* (1957); *Bandolero* (1968). He died in Hollywood in 2003.

Keith McConnell: Born into a well-known Dublin business family in 1923, McConnell lived much of his adult life in Hollywood working constantly in television and film, often playing gentlemanly, uppercrust British types. His many film credits include *Mutiny on the Bounty* (1962); *The Fighting Prince of Donegal* (1966); *4 for Texas* (1963) *Time After Time* (1979). TV credits include *The Treasure of Alpheus T. Winterborn* (as Sherlock Holmes) (1980); *Ironside* (1974); *Mission Impossible* (1968) and *Rawhide* (1965). He died at his home in the Hollywood Hills in 1987.

F.J. McCormick: (Real name Peter Judge, 1890–1947) A member of the Abbey Theatre and garnered some Hollywood credits including John Ford's *The Plough and the Stars* (1936).

Niall MacGinnis: Born in Ireland in 1913 his credits include *Helen of Troy* (1956); *Alexander The Great* (1956), *Lust for Life* (1959), *Shake Hands with the Devil* (1959) and *The Shoes of the Fisherman* (1968). He died in 1977.

North from Hollywood Club around 1929.

Siobhan McKenna: Belfast-born McKenna was a consummate stage actor who appeared occasionally in films. She was a luminous and spirited performer whose movie credits include *Playboy of the Western World* (1962) and *Dr Zhivago* (1965).

Noel Purcell: Dublin-born in 1900, Purcell was a stalwart star whose career in movies spanned the latter part of his life from Huston's *Moby Dick* (1956), *Lust for Life* (1956) and *Mutiny on the Bounty* (with Richard Harris and Brando) (1962) and filmed in Ireland *The List of Adrian Messenger* (1963). Noted for his grey beard and striking features, Purcell had an impressive presence on screen.

Milo O'Shea: Born in 1926, this former Abbey actor had a high-profile film and stage career. Film credits include *Never Put it in Writing* (1964); *Ulysses* (1967) where he played Bloom; *Romeo and Juliet* (1968); *Barbarella* (1968); *Loot* (1970) and *The Verdict* (1982).

Robert Shaw: Though raised in Scotland, this Hollywood star made his home in Ireland. With a career that spanned twenty-five years, he played major roles in such noted films as *The Dam Busters* (1955); *From Russia With Love* (1963); *The Caretaker* (1963); *A Man For All Seasons* (1966); *The Battle of Britain* (1969); *The Sting* (1973) and *Jaws* (1975).

Martin Sheen: Actor Martin Sheen is proud of his Irish roots. His mother Mary Anne Phelan was from Tipperary. His father was Francisco Estevez from Spain. Sheen is no stranger to Ireland either. He starred in the film version of Hugh Leonard's acclaimed *Da*, shot in Ireland and more recently took time off from his film and TV career to read English Literature and Philosophy at NUI Galway. Sheen's eldest son Emilio Estevez is also a highly regarded film and TV actor in Hollywood. Sheen's screen career has been prodigious from Terrence Malick's early classic *Badlands* (1973), in which he portrayed a murderer in a chilling performance that was reminiscent of James Dean, to his pivotal role in Francis Ford Coppola's *Apocalypse Now* (1979), to playing the U.S. president in the hit television series, *The West Wing*.

Constance Smith: Born in Limerick in 1928, she starred with Jack Palance in the cult movie *Man in the Attic* (1955) and presented the 1952 Academy Awards. Her screen credits include *The 13th Letter* (1951); *Red Skies of Montana* (1952); *Treasure of the Golden Condor* (1953), *Taxi* (1953) and *The Big Tip-Off* (1958). She died in 2003.

Richard Todd: Born in Dublin in 1919, he became the darling of post-war movies in such classics as *The Hasty Heart* for which he was nominated for an Oscar in the role of a terminally ill Scottish soldier. Other credits include *The Virgin Queen* (1955), *The Longest Day* (1962) and *The Dam Busters* (1955).

Stuart Townsend: Born in Howth, County Dublin, he made his first stage appearance in a production of the Gaiety School of Acting, where he was studying. His professional stage bow came with the John Crowley (*Intermission*) directed *True Lines*, which was produced in Dublin and London. Early film roles came in the Irish independent shorts *Godsuit* and *Summertime*. His first feature film was *Trojan Eddie*, a 1996 UK/Irish co-production. In 1997 he landed a lead role in the British romantic comedy *Shooting Fish*. Townsend played a suave con artist in the film, which brought him to international attention. He has appeared in a number of big budget films including *Queen of the Damned* and *The League of Extraordinary Gentlemen* as Dorian Gray.

And Finally: Our apologies to those and to the families of those who may have been inadvertently overlooked in the foregoing cast list.

Jewell Pathe's Bathing Beauty Pirates capture Vitagraph Ships in a publicity shot for *Captain Blood* on Balboa Beach, California in 1924. The film was re-made with Errol Flynn in 1935 by Warner Bros.

ACKNOWLEDGEMENTS

The publisher wishes to thank the following organisations and people who gave permission to reproduce work in copyright.

© Andrew Parnell (Chapter 21 icon) © Ardmore Studios (p. 180) © BFI (p. 45) © Bord Scannán na hÉireann / Irish Film Board (p. 183 and Chapter 28 icon, 208 and back cover, 220 and back cover, 224, 228) © Brian Drew (Chapter 7 icon) © Carol Highsmith/Library of Congress. Additional information from source (pp. 11; 12; 13; 21) © Clinton Steeds (p.19) © Columbia Pictures (p.162 and Chapter 19 icon) © Continental Distributing (p.175) © Davida De La Harpe (Chapter 22 icon) © Dimension Films (p. 200) © Mike (p.33 *below*) © G.A. Duncan from the cover of *The Complete Guide to 'The Quiet Man'* published by Appletree Press (p.138) © Gaumont British (p. 35) © Granada Television (p.177) © HBO (p. 213) © Hexodus (Chapter 1 icon) © International Classics (p.169) © istockphoto.com/ijoe (Contents Page) © John Murphy (Chapter 18 icon) © Julie Kertesz (Chapter 20 icon) © Panoramic Photographs, Prints and Photographs Division, Library of Congress (p.20 additional information from source; p 230 (Ref: pan6a18052) © Library of Congress. Prints and Photographs Division (Chapter 2 icon (LC-DIG-pplot-13725-01420); p.28 (Ref: LC-USZ62 – 92412); p. 34 (Ref: LC – USZ62 –123761); p. 78 and Chapter 8 icon (Ref: LC – USZ62 – 103843); Chapter 17 icon (Ref: pga 00454); p.231 and Chapter 29 icon (Ref: pan6a24591) New York World-Telegram and the Sun Newspaper Photographic Collection (Chapter 4 icon (Ref: LC-USZ62 – 57943); Chapter 6 icon (Ref: LC – USZ62 –123257) George Grantham Bain Collection (pp. 38 (Ref: LC – DIG – ggbain – 22360); p.42 (Ref: LC – DIG – ggbain – 22325); Chapter 5 icon (Ref: LC – DIG – ggbain – 32981); p.48 (Ref: LC – DIG – ggbain – 38783); p.51 (Ref: LC – DIG – ggbain – 37545); p.72 (Ref: LC – DIG – ggbain – 29882) © Los Angeles Dept. of Water and Power (p.16) © MGM (left-hand page icon and front cover (Gene Kelly); pp.64; 100; 107; 118; 124 and Chapter 13 icon; p.132, Chapter 11 and Chapter 15 icons; pp.134; 142 and cover (Grace Kelly image); pp.149; 208 and Chapter 26 icon and back cover) © MGM / UA (p.164) © Miramax Films (p. 191) © Miramax (pp.196; 217 and Chapter 27 icon) © Miramax Pictures (p. 214 *top*) © Orion Pictures (p.182) © Paramount Pictures (pp. 24; 41; 81 and Chapter 9 icon; 145; 193) © Photofest (pp. 8; Introduction icon; 39; 54; 57; 59; 62; 111; Chapter 16 icon and title page, front cover case; 219) © RKO Pathe (p.22) © Republic Pictures (p. 140) © Showtime. Photograph by Mikki Ansin (p. 198) © Treasure Entertainment Ltd (Chapter 24 icon) © Trustees of Muckross House (Killarney) Ltd., Muckross Research Library (pp. 31; 33 *top*; Chapter 3 icon) © Twentieth Century Fox (pp. 69; 84; 88; 121; 188) © Twentieth Century Fox Film Corporation (p.151) © United Artists (pp.76; 105; 116; 155; 202 and spine; 128) © Universal Pictures (pp. 90; 205) © Vestron Pictures (p. 212) © Walt Disney Pictures (p.158) © Warner Bros. Pictures (p. 74) © Warner Bros. (pp. 95 and Chapter 14 icon; 96 and Chapter 10 icon, 109 and Chapter 12 icon; 195 and Chapters 23 and 25 icon; 214 *below*, 226 and back cover) © Worlds 2000 / Ardmore Studios (p.186)